B·U·I·L·D·I·N·G
FENCES
OF WOOD, STONE, METAL, & PLANTS

B·U·I·L·D·I·N·G
FENCES

OF WOOD, STONE, METAL, & PLANTS

JOHN VIVIAN

Illustrated by Liz Buell

WILLIAMSON PUBLISHING
CHARLOTTE, VERMONT 05445

Library of Congress Cataloging-in-Publication Data

Vivian, John.
    Building fences of wood, stone, metal, and plants.

    Includes index.
    1. Fences – Design and construction.   I. Title.
TH4965.V58   1986   690'.89   86-32489
ISBN 0-913589-27-6

Cover and interior design: Trezzo-Braren Studio
Cover photos: Jack Williamson
Typography: Villanti & Sons, Printers, Inc.
Printing: Capital City Press

Williamson Publishing Co.
Charlotte, Vermont 05445

Manufactured in the United States of America

16   15   14   13   12   11

CONTENTS

FOREWORD

At work in the study, I heard an unaccustomed thud above my head, then a small rumble down the back stairs, and before I knew it I could see through the window a little blond head bobbing up the garden hill with both dogs wagging alongside.

At just eighteen months, our first-born had decided to climb out of the crib all by himself – landing, as always, at a dead run.

Sam and accomplices were through the broccoli plantings and halfway to the pasture in pursuit of a cabbage butterfly before we caught up with them, Louise still coated to the elbows in pottery clay, and me breathing hard from a sprint around the barn. There was no hope that the little guy would forget how he had managed his brief escape. Clearly, we needed a fence – and fast. I had lost forever the chance to cut locust poles and split withes from white cedar with a froe and drawknife for the quaint wattle-hurdle fence I'd read about in the old country-living books. That afternoon we drove to town looking for more down-to-earth fencing supplies.

FUNCTION BEFORE APPEARANCE

That first backyard fence was a strictly functional baby containment – certainly no candidate for a *Better Homes & Gardens* cover. Funds were too short to pay a professional, or even to buy prefabricated panels to be home installed. The only do-it-yourself fence-building book in print at the time was Sears, Roebuck's chain-link brochure, so I extemporized a 4-foot high, lightweight picket fence from the cheapest materials I could find.

For fence posts I used 2 × 4 × 10 PT studs – that is, 10-foot lengths of two-by-fours pressure-treated with a toxic mold- and bug-proofing. It's that green-tinted wood, used for patios and decks that they stack off in an uncovered corner of the lumberyard. Fence posts needn't be perfectly true except between horizontals, and I dickered the price down 20 percent for taking the warp-twisted boards.

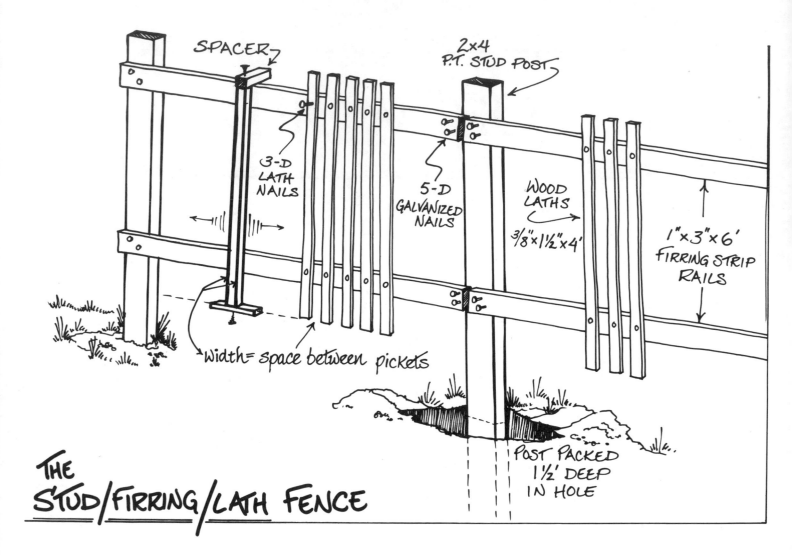

SPACER

3-D LATH NAILS

Width = space between pickets

2x4 P.T. STUD POST

5-D GALVANIZED NAILS

WOOD LATHS

3/8" x 1 1/2" x 4'

1" x 3" x 6' FIRRING STRIP RAILS

POST PACKED 1 1/2' DEEP IN HOLE

THE STUD/FIRRING/LATH FENCE

I sawed the studs in half and sunk the 5-foot lengths about 6 feet apart in holes as near to 1½ feet deep as I could hack with a garden spade in our stony New England soil. I set each post on a flat rock at the bottom of its hole and tamped rock and soil around the posts in successive 3- to 4-inch layers with the head of a wood-splitting maul.

For horizontal fence members, or *rails*, I trimmed to length 8-foot, 1- × 3-inch clear spruce furring strips. These are boards milled to ¾-inch by 2¾ inches, cut 8 feet long, and called "furrin'" around our parts. I fastened them to the posts with 5d galvanized nails. I hammered on one rail 6 inches above the ground and the other an even 2½ feet above it. That gave neat-appearing parallel rails, even though the ground was rolling, and the posts had been set at slightly different depths leaving the alignment of their tops a little ragged.

For the pickets I used common wood lath: pine strips ⅜-inch thick by 1½ inches wide that are rough cut to a convenient 4-foot length and sold in bundles of sixty or

so. As anyone who has refurbished an old house knows only too well, lath is the thin wood stripping old-time carpenters used to support wall plaster. Lath was nailed onto firring that had been nailed to wall studs, floor joists, or rafters. It's rough and splintery till painted, so it warps easily. But it goes up fast; I didn't even cut the tops to a traditional picket-point or saw-tooth half-point, but put them on square-ended. I fastened the laths 1 inch apart on the rails with 1¼-inch 3d lath nails – a large-headed, skinny, 1/16-inch-thick box nail made to slip into thin wood – so I wouldn't split the bone-dry lath.

A straight piece of inch-wide hardwood with a lug glued and screwed on to hook over the top rail served as a spacer to set the lath pickets an even 1 inch apart. This jig also had a cross member fastened at its bottom, just 4 inches below the lower edge of the bottom fence rail, so it arrayed the pickets at an even 2 inches above ground. I'd set a picket with the spacer, put in the top nail, check plumb with a carpenter's level to be sure the picket was perfectly vertical, then nail up the bottom.

I couldn't get any galvanized 3d nails, and I knew that unplated steel would rust and streak painted or naturally weathered wood. So I spritzed the head of each lath nail and the wood around it with a shot of silver paint from an aerosol can as a sealer. Sam and Louise soaked the thirsty new wood with leftover white latex house paint that washes out of anything with soap and warm water – even little kids' hair, if you get at it quickly enough. I discovered that the silver aerosol paint made little shiny circles under the cover coat at each nail head. A primer coat would have masked them, but we weren't that concerned with appearance.

Finally we all dug up a 2-foot-wide strip garden along the outer perimeter of the new fence. I spaded the sod, Louise loosened the clods, and Sam lectured each newly-exposed earthworm in turn.

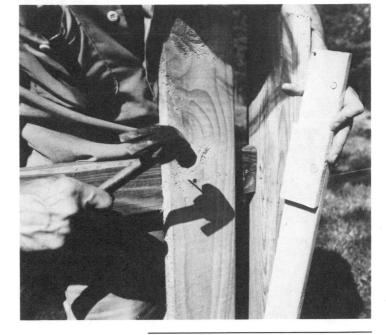

Using a spacer to set the first picket in from a post.

COST BREAKDOWN

In late-'80s dollars, the cost of my quick-picket fence per 6-foot bay (the assemblage of horizontal rails and vertical pickets between two vertical posts, *but including only a single post*) would be:

One 5-foot length of PT 2 × 4 @ 0.30/linear foot =	$1.50
Two lengths of spruce furring (standard 8-foot lengths trimmed to 6 feet with 2 feet of scrap for kindling) @ 0.11/linear foot =	1.76
Twenty-eight laths (half a $6.00 bundle of sixty, less rejects) =	3.00
¼ **lb. nails** =	0.20
Latex exterior house paint @ $10.00/gallon =	1.50
Total:	$7.96
COST PER RUNNING FOOT:	$1.33

CHEAP, QUICK, EASY . . .

The fence was comparatively inexpensive, quick, and easy to put up. It was not intended to last forever – though it's now well into its second decade. It corraled Sam and his younger sister, Martha, till they were old enough not to wander off after butterflies. It kept the chickens and occasional got-loose larger stock out of the dooryard and prevented skunks from raiding the trash, too. And since twist-ties pushed so easily through the slats and plant tendrils grabbed so readily to the rough lath, the outer face of the sunny east end of the fence served as a support for an annual succession of half-high sweet peas (both flowering and eating kinds), tomato and cucumber vines, gladioluses and delphiniums.

. . . AND USEFUL

There's nothing like a backyard fence for hanging things on and draping things over: we poked strawflowers and broomcorn to cure in the spaces between the top pickets, tacked newly tie-dyed T-shirts and wet poster-paint masterpieces on the slats to dry, and laid blankets and tents and sleeping bags, sails from our little boat, and winter clothes just out of mothballs over the fence for sun-sweetening. In time the fence served as a trellis for climbing roses and a Thompson white seedless grape vine. And fence posts proved the best place ever to nail up-facing orange halves each spring so the Baltimore orioles, newly arrived from their tropical wintering grounds, would feel at home and hang their nests high in our maples.

Once that fence went up, we couldn't imagine how we'd gotten along without it.

There have been a lot of fences since the first one; Sam is old enough now that he'll be chasing toddlers of his own soon. We've built privacy fence from flat wood planks to screen a porch till a barrier of living plants grew up, have put up wire-fabric and chain-link fences for pets and made farm fence of all kinds. For twenty springs between snow melt and May (when both the trout and blackflies begin biting) I've built and repaired stone fence around our fields and pastures for no better reason than to harden winter-softened back muscles and lighten the severe look of the wire-fabric or electric fence that discourages Martha's horse from wandering off more often than he needs to and keeps varmints from lunching off the ducks. And I've built fences of cement block, with and without a gentling brick veneer, to contain and screen a hog yard and other even less lovely vistas.

FENCE HAS MANY PURPOSES

An old-fashioned rose bush complements a picket fence with a z-gate.

I'll not attempt to guess your reason for wanting a fence. Perhaps it is aesthetics: a wood fence, whether painted or let weather to rustic gray, a stone wall graced with an iron gate or rambling roses, or a living hedgerow of primly trimmed evergreens or half-wild brambles – each frames your home, your lawn and gardens. A fence truly sets your place apart.

When you build a fence you are drawing firm lines around the portion of this lovely green-and-blue planet that you choose to call your own for a time, establishing boundaries between what belongs to you and what belongs to others. Plainly put, fences are intended to keep in what you want kept in and keep out what you want kept out. And they can do it with an architectural statement ranging from a gentle request to a stern command. A wide-eyed, open-faced post-and-rail fence with roses growing inside says to a passerby: "We hope you enjoy looking at our flowers and our cool and shaded and well-trimmed lawn every bit as much as we do." A waist-high brick wall garlanded with ivy and morning glories says: "This is our place. Nice isn't it? If you've been invited in, welcome . . . but please latch the gate behind you."

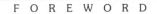

Even sterner fences that say "Keep out!" – no apology needed – can be polite about it. There is no more pleasant and less penetrable fence than a stout hedgerow of brightly blooming rosa rugosa or dusty gray Russian olive; brick pilasters framing each side of the drive punctuate the hedge and discourage casual entry, even if there's no gate. A black-painted Victorian iron fence smiles with agreeable scrollwork, the medieval palings at the top relieved with hand-wrought fleur de lis or filigree. A tall, flat, opaque privacy screen – even if right on the street, in California in-town style – can present an agreeable variety of shape, color, or texture. Grim and institutional chain-link fence with barbed wire at the top can be softened with strips of bright vinyl or earthy bark woven through the steel mesh. I'm told they are even trying to meliorate the hostility of the Berlin Wall – preeminent in recent history among fences built for the wrong reasons – with strips of grass and shrubs.

A thick, mixed evergreen barrier.

WHAT'S TO COME

Do you like the idea of setting your place apart with crisp, white, all-American pickets? Perhaps you prefer a high, sturdy, flat-panel privacy fence. I'll show how to make these and other wood fences from scratch. You may not consider splitting rails with an ax, Abe Lincoln-like, or shaping pickets with a saw the fun that I do, but I'll show how to do those things – and also how to purchase components ready made for quick installation. Want to keep poultry or sheep or horses around the place? This book will present all of today's options in livestock fence, and I'll describe in detail our own horse fences, Martha's in-town poultry pen, the run we made for Max, our little attack-Yorkie, our quadruple-threat vegetable-garden fence, and a universal version of the recent arrival from Down Under: high-tensile electrified livestock/deer fence. I'll discuss my love affair with dry-laid stone walls and a more business-like relationship with mortared block or brick fences – all from the viewpoint of easy do-it-yourself construction using the most economical and easily obtained materials. And living fence: I'll cover hedges and windbreaks and bramble barricades and show how you can help maintain the ancient art of establishing and maintaining a European-style hedgerow.

Well planned and carefully done, it all builds into good fence.

Testing the electric wire on our triple-threat garden fence after harvesting some fresh produce.

1

PLANNING YOUR FENCE

Don't raise any fence on an impulse. An excess of enthusiasm can result in a visit to a cut-rate fencing installer who by sundown can have your place surrounded by a great raw expanse of stapled stockade, rickety pickets, or shoddy split rails.

You won't like the result, but you'll be stuck with it. A front-yard fence not only sets your place apart, it surrounds and presents it to public view, much as a frame sets off (or ruins) a fine painting. A garden or pasture fence will permanently segment your living space, restrict your movement, and change the flow of your outdoor work. And any fence can make a psychological, physical, and legal imposition on neighbors and your community. So, please think before you fence. Secondhand fencing isn't worth much, and taking down a mistake can be more expensive than installing it in the first place. A fence that doesn't do what you want, or that alienates neighbors or gets you a lawsuit or an injunction from the local zoning authority can create costs of another order.

It's best to plan ahead, and to do so you must first decide what you really want a fence for.

ANALYZE YOUR REASONS

The function, timing, location, size, and extent of my first fencing effort were decided for us by an energetic toddler. The appearance, design, and construction methods were secondary, dictated by a need to keep costs at a minimum. Your decisions may not be so easy and clear cut. None of our own subsequent fences have gone up as fast as the first, and the increased time spent on later fences has mostly been due to planning.

Decide what you want your fence to do for you. If it must serve more than one purpose, weigh each carefully and balance one against the others: inexpensive poultry netting along the side-yard line will keep the rabbits from mowing down the bean seedlings, but the net gets floppy and rusts, and your neighbors might not appreciate looking at it every day. Best to choose a slightly more costly but also more attractive wooden fence, or screen the netting with a line of shrubs, or brace the top and plant vines as a screen. Below are the usual reasons that people put up a fence, along with some of the inter-related variables you should consider before sinking your first post hole.

A Physical Barrier

If all you really need a fence for is to keep a small child or pet in the yard, to isolate a swimming pool, keep the sheep from wandering, or prevent uninviteds from trespassing on your property, you want a barrier fence, one that will keep in what you want kept in and keep out what you want kept out – and that's that.

But any effective barrier fence works both ways; the fence will also restrict your movement. You may decide after hard consideration that the interference in your life would be so great that you don't really want a fence at all.

A newly retired neighbor of ours found that he couldn't trim the grass right up to the elegant picket fence he built around his meticulously tended acre-and-a-half lawn without spending hours with a pair of scissors or resorting to a flexible-line power trimmer that nicked off the fence paint. He ended up cutting out sod on the walk side of the fence and planting a low yew hedge. On the inside he replaced sod with a ribbon of wood chips and planted roses in it. The result is gorgeous, but the digging cut into his first summer of full-time fishing and golfing, and more than once he wished he hadn't built the fence in the first place.

And I kick myself for the fence I rigged around the vegetable garden on our country place to keep out our free-ranging poultry. It's no fun to finagle the tiller through the single, narrow, and inconveniently-placed gate. In that case the alternatives to fencing that I considered were to pen and wing-clip the birds as I do in town, or try to choke down store-bought eggs and wake up without a rooster's morning call. The alternative I *failed* to consider was to plan the fence better.

So, with any fence – but particularly with a barrier or protective fence – live with it in your imagination for a while. Be sure you aren't making more work for yourself than you bargained for.

A Boundary

Some homeowners need a fence to define their turf: to let the world know that what lies within is well loved and that unbidden incursions aren't welcome. People are loath to cross any barrier unless it's posed as a taunt or a dare or an arrogant command. Even a line of low wickets is more effective than a stern *Keep Out* or *Keep Off The New Grass* sign. There are some deep psychological mechanics lurking there somewhere, I suppose. Defining our domain is a natural human instinct, and fencing is, after all, the most obvious way to do it. Don't feel you need to explain if the idea of a fence surrounding your place makes you feel a little warmer in winter. Go ahead and build it.

Privacy

Don't want the neighbors inviting themselves into your croquet games? Don't like the idea of bending over in the garden in positions that would look undignified (to say the least) from the street? Get tired of having to wave and smile cheerily at every neighbor going past even though the lawn mower still won't start after the hundredth pull? You either need to move to the country or build a privacy fence.

A privacy screen must almost always be person-high or taller to be effective. Any tall board fence will do; just increase the height of the picket fence covered in chapter 2 and butt the verticals together. Thin plywood panels set into a wood frame make an inexpensive screen – and any high stone or brick wall makes your home a fortress. But plan ahead: solid fence can block air and light flow – turning your yard or patio into a dark, airless prison. Consider slatted screens or jalousies, or latticework brick or cement block, or fences of translucent plastic sheeting.

This nicely graduated stockade fence divides two small backyards.

A louvered fence admits plenty of air and light while permitting the sight of only a very narrow strip of your yard or patio. Horizontal louvers can be arranged so that no one can see in unless he's standing right on top of the fence (even then he can't see anything but the sky or the row of begonias you've planted along the fence's base). Vertical louvers permit views of only a narrow strip inside and close to the fence. My favorite privacy screen is one I saw on the street side of a garden in San Diego. Made of narrow, 8-foot-tall naturally finished redwood slats hung vertically from pins at top and bottom so they'd swivel freely, the fence could be opened or closed or set at any angle to catch the sun or ocean breeze like a giant sideways venetian blind. Stout metal rods were attached by interlocking eyehooks to the top, middle, and bottom of each slat and run through slots drilled into vertical posts placed every 5 feet along the fence. By moving the rods, the owners could adjust the opening between slats, and they could dog the rods down tight with big thumb-screws threaded into the posts to keep the slats from rattling in the wind and to close the fence up tight for the night.

For the Good Looks of It

All pastures and some houses look better with a fence around them. Fences can change the apparent size of areas of property. If your home is located in a great expanse of open range, a fence part way between road and house can foreshorten the distance and make the place look more welcoming from the road. But if the house is right on the street, a low fence between curb and foundation can create an artificial sense of distance, providing a buffer between the bustle of street activity and the peace and quiet we all associate with home.

A low stone wall with plantings in front of it can transform an ordinary house into a standout in a neighborhood of ordinary lawns. Houses in new developments can look – well, new – till the lawn is established and trees have a few years to grow. A fence of rustic or weathered-looking wood can make your place look like it had been there all along while surrounding homes continue to stick out like so many newcomers. On the other hand, a shiny new chain-link, or a raw and unstained wood fence, or one that is newly painted or stained a uniform dark brown, can make a house look even *more* newly built than it is. Choose your fence with an eye to its aging qualities if your house is a new one. Any of the semitransparent wood stains that let wood grain show through would be a good choice. A boundary of hedge, annual flowers, and quick-growing vines can give a new fence stature. For a new steel-mesh fence, plant ornamentals or consider interweaving thin, unfinished strips of wood veneer into the wire and letting them weather.

A well-designed and -installed fence, one that is tasteful and in keeping with its area but that makes the property stand out, will increase the property's value by many times the investment in fence materials and labor. A fenced home just *looks* more cared-for, desirable, and valuable.

Weathered white cedar posts and rails. Cape Cod, MA.

Protection from Wind, Sun, or Noise

Much as we may love the outdoors, we want it to stay where it is, and a fence can help. In the south a sun screen is a blessing, in the north a fence can keep windchill from your plantings. In any urban area a fence can create a haven of surprising peace and quiet while the traffic rages just outside. I'll never forget a lawn party at a house right on Mt. Auburn Street in Cambridge, Massachusetts, after a Harvard-Yale game some years ago. The chill fall winds were blowing leaves, football programs, and street dust around outside, wood smoke was in the air, and the traffic was fierce. Harvard had won the day, and few at the party, which was held in a yard enclosed by a tall wood stockade fence, would have minded any intrusion from the outside. But, except for a low traffic rumble, the garden was a haven of quiet and good cheer.

Slats, plywood, fiberglass panels, cement block, or bricks make effective sun, sound, and wind barriers. A thick living fence, in conjunction with a screen, can go far to mute noise and alone can block some wind. I know of a beach-rose hedge on the coast of Maine that will break all but the most fierce sea breezes. If you place a lawn chair close beside it, you can get an early start on a summer tan in April – when just on the other side of the thick prickly fence the ocean-chilled air can frost your breath.

Segregating Space

Fence objectives considered so far most often assume a boundary fence. But fence can also cut in and through your property, to good or ill effect. Pools, gardens, and tennis courts are obvious places for fences to subdivide larger properties. In planning fences that subdivide a larger area, be especially alert to disruption of traffic flow, a problem I'll address in detail below. Even on small properties, judicious use of fence can make areas appear larger and more interesting. A rear wall or fence can be made to look like more than a screen for the back alley if you give it life and texture. Break the monotony and create depth by varying a single plane with niches and alcoves filled with plantings. One old friend of ours places his trash containers behind a tall, bleached-cypress screen with a huge clematis vine covering it; the vine is lavishly covered with purple flowers the summer through and with exotic seed pods in fall and winter, and the trash area has become the focal point of the yard.

If you study the landscaping books recommended below you'll see dozens of color photographs showing imaginative ways fences and walls can be used to mold interior space.

LEGALITIES

Fences are in great part a North American creation. Our continent's European settlers came from lands that contained walls a plenty – whole walled cities, in fact. But beyond the towns and active farms, open land was largely unfenced commons. Such laws as there were required livestock owners to herd or "fold" their livestock in small pens to keep them from harming property or crops. Not till the land-enclosure acts of the seventeenth and eighteenth centuries was much open land walled or fenced.

But in the wild and heavily forested New World, pioneers learned to fence the wilderness out and their livestock in. Even in the grassy plains of the West, the era of open range was short-lived – destroyed forever by the advent of barbed wire in the latter part of the 1800s. Along with the fence came fence law, and that can affect your planning.

In the countryside or small towns, so long as the fence is on your own freehold property and well inside your property line, it should cause no problems. But placing a fence too close alongside roads, or through easements, or even across commonly traveled "ways" inside your property can cause difficulties. Check with the local authorities to find just how far beyond a road's center line and onto the berm (which you most likely consider your property) the municipality's jurisdiction extends. If you live in snow country, find how far back from the road a fence must be if it is not to interfere with and sustain damage from the road crew's plow and the mountains of snow and slush they pile up each year.

Sinking a post hole into buried power lines, telephone cables, water or gas mains can cause costly problems that you don't need. Check on utility easements and attendant regulations; there will be a map and regulation book in the nearest local-government offices. If you need written permission to dig near a utility easement, you'd best obtain it even if the line is buried beneath property that you feel is yours free and clear.

If a cart- or hiking path crosses your land, find out exactly what easements, or rights of access (formal or informal) may apply to it. You can imagine the ill feeling you'll incur if you fence off a popular hiking or riding trail – even if justified and within your legal rights. I closed a trail at our country place to motorized traffic after a raucous moonlight snowmobile party awoke my daughter the night she got home from having her tonsils out. I must have been more forceful than necessary; now even horse riders and hikers avoid the place.

In cities and larger towns constraints on putting up fences can be more formal and more restrictive than they are in the country. Glass and barbed wire are usually prohibited near walkways or streets. Setbacks from roads, sidewalks, and abutting property lines may be strictly defined and enforced by zoning ordinances. Many history-conscious towns limit the size, materials, and design of fences, and all auto-safety-conscious municipalities limit fence height. Fence is commonly restricted to 6 feet in height along roadways, since a tall fence at a busy intersection can limit drivers' vision and cause accidents. The height of living fences, too, can be restricted; if you plant a tall hedge, the town fathers may force you to remove or trim it to size in the interest of public safety. Four feet is a common maximum hedge height.

Impinging on neighbors' property can cause permanent ill will, and perhaps a lawsuit. If the surveyor's stakes at the corners of your property are not apparent, you should obtain a copy of the city, town, or county survey or *plat* of your property to be sure of your boundaries. The most recent survey of your own property will be on file in the registry of deeds and can be dug up most readily and copied for a small fee by a real-estate agent, lawyer, or title-insurance company employee who knows the archives. Your mortgage banker may have a copy, as may the lawyer who passed title. If you plan to do major construction – of a brick garden wall along a boundary, for example – a new survey may be required before you are given a building permit. Such a survey is a good idea even if no permits are required: moving tons of well-laid stone or well-mortared brick isn't easy.

It is also a good idea to obtain a copy of the local zoning bylaws and building codes and regulations before building a fence of any substance. Study and follow the law, and if you have any questions at all, consult a lawyer or a building or fencing contractor.

COURTESIES

Preliminary legalities assured, do your best to obtain abutting neighbors' agreement before going ahead with a fence, even if it only shades a strip of their lawn and they only see it when passing in the car. You may decide that a twin-face fence – with both sides equally attractive – is a good investment in neighborhood harmony. Or you may find that the family next door has been thinking as you have and is willing to split the expense of a shared boundary fence. Perhaps your fence or wall could butt up to and continue one on their property.

Even if you and the neighbors are best of friends today, the relationship can change, and you may find your properties divided by a "spite fence" that becomes a subject of hateful argument. In any shared-boundary decisions, you should obtain the services of a good lawyer. Each party should retain its own lawyer to work out all the small details if the property values at stake are high. Have the fence line surveyed, and draw up an agreement that specifies rights and obligations of both parties, including shared upkeep and terms for eventual termination of the agreement and removal of the fence by yourselves or successors to the properties.

Agreements with abutters satisfied, be sure that none of your more distant neighbors are offended at either your wish to fence your property or your choice of materials. A fence makes a considerable change in a neighborhood. Make it plain that you are fencing your land, garden, kids or animals in – and not fencing the neighbors out (even if you are). If you encounter resistance, stress the fence's ornamental advantages and its enhancement of all neighborhood property values. Few people will object to your raising a tasteful and architecturally appropriate fence once they've had a chance to voice their concerns; after all it is your property you are fencing. But the sudden and unannounced appearance of a new fence – especially one built by new arrivals or in a neighborhood where fences are uncommon – can be seen as an exclusionary and even hostile act by sensitive individuals. Tell the neighbors of your plans, invite their comments and suggestions, and any ruffled feelings will be mollified.

REVIEW YOUR DESIGN OPTIONS

If you are like me, the picture that came to mind when you first hit on the idea of building a fence was a purely conventional design. I think "fence," and I automatically see a row of pickets about a yard high and pointed at the top, painted white, with a single, low gate and either a Tom Sawyerish kid painting it or rambling roses growing on it. It's a Norman Rockwell picture of Main Street, i know, and I make no apology for either the picture or the fence. But architects and landscape designers have been dreaming up more innovative fence designs for centuries, and you should take advantage of their creativity.

Before you draw up a plan for your fence, take a weekend afternoon to go to the local library and look through the books in the Architecture, Building, and Gardening sections. Then go to the nearest bookstore or garden-supply outlet and look over the *Sunset* magazine-style fence books. In racks of magazine-shaped books on a variety of home-and-garden topics you'll find 90- to 160-page books covering fences and gates. They include dozens of color photos and illustrations of marvelous fence designs – and some excellent construction plans and building directions for ornamental wood fences, as well. The best known publishers are the *Sunset* editors themselves (Lane Publishing of Menlo Park, California); HP Books, Tucson, Arizona; and Ortho, (a division of Chevron Chemical Company, San Francisco). The ideas you'll get from any of the books are well worth the time spent – and the price of any you decide to purchase.

Also you should send for the (free) book list of the Brooklyn Botanic Garden. There are enough ideas for fences, gates, walkways, walls, and drives in the Botanic Garden's Handbook Number 45, *Garden Structures*, to base a full-sized book on. Price of any of the handbooks is $2.50 plus 80 cents postage and handling for the first title.

STONE FENCE
ORNAMENTAL, WOOD
LIVING FENCE
HORSE FENCE
LOW, WIRE MESH
ELECTRIC FENCE
CHAIN LINK
POULTRY WIRE

MATERIALS

When you have determined what your fence is to do and removed any legal or social obstacles in the way of doing it, the next step in your planning is a trip to the nearest fencing contractor to check out styles and prices and to see what the raw materials look and lift like if you plan to build your own. Look in the Yellow Pages under Fence. Most building-supply outlets also sell fence materials, and many will stock the tools you'll need as well. Check prices from the tools lists in the following chapters covering your chosen fence style. Post-hole diggers and fence stretchers and concrete mixers are expensive, and you may want to rent the gear. Some contractors, Sears, Roebuck, and most equipment-rental stores have the larger items for rent.

Steel fence comes in bundles of steel stakes and rolls of fence fabric that can get very heavy: erecting a wire-fabric fence of anything but lightweight mesh needs a crew of strong backs, or power equipment, or both. Bricks and concrete blocks aren't too heavy individually, but before undertaking a wall, be sure you want to keep lifting them all day for a week or more.

By contrast, wood fence and some hollow-metal fencing is easy to put up yourself. It comes as raw stock, in precut pieces, or in ready-nailed *bays:* complete sets of two or three horizontal rails, with already nailed-on vertical members called *siding* or *infill*, attached to one vertical member to be sunk in the ground – the *post.* Get an idea of prices: prefabricated fence bays can be cheaper than loose parts at some contractors' yards. Also seeing fence firsthand gives you a better idea of its texture and proportions than any photograph. The wood looks terribly pale and raw out there in the yard and may set you to thinking about stains and paints, too.

Inspect the differences between the cheap and more expensive grades of fence. The lightweight grade of steel fence post or chain-link fabric will look positively flimsy beside the premium grade. Quick and cheap grapestake or stockade fencing (half-rounds on thin rails that nail to rough, 3-inch round posts) will pale beside a fence with nicely squared 4-inch posts with finials milled into the tops, mortised rails, and scroll-cut siding. If you are in the market for a living fence, visit a nursery and compare the visual impact and price of the larger specimens against the economy of smaller plants. Don't forget to divide the considerable cost difference by the number of years you will have to look at the little stuff before it reaches the height of the larger. What is most economical can be a hard question: half-round stockade fence or seedling hedge both have a place. But purchasing bargain-basement fence may prove to be no saving in the long run. You'll be looking at that fence for decades.

DRAW A PLAN

When you have decided on your fence material, make a scale drawing of your property to use as a fence plan. If your place was professionally designed or landscaped, the architect's drawings are ready made for your fence plan. I make my own using engineering paper with little blue squares on it, assigning so many linear feet to each square. Graph paper, or simple lined paper with ruled lines drawn in to make squares will do fine, too.

Pace off the boundary lines and distances on your property and sketch outlines of buildings and plantings and lawn-and-garden features to scale. Do a draft in pencil, double check the distances, then ink in the final lines of everything that will stay put: buildings and large trees. Leave small plantings and movable items such as swing sets and the garden in pencil; fencing often makes you re-think the entire layout and want to move everything around. Make photocopies of your plan; you'll be doodling over it longer than you think.

Now sketch in the established traffic patterns through the property. Foot and paw traffic will be different at different times of day and different seasons of the year. Try to predict how it will change over the years, too, as the family matures. In sketching traffic patterns, don't forget that young children and their bikes need easy and repeated access to the street, pets must get free for their usual patrols, refuse collectors and delivery men mustn't be inconvenienced, and wildlife needs in-and-out access if you value their visits.

When you have the property and traffic patterns mapped, sketch in your planned fence and gates. Involve the whole family in the project, and be prepared to do some stern analysis of your way of life. The backyard that you'd as soon turn into a fenced garden may serve the kids as a ball park and the dog as an exercise yard, and you may discover that a spouse has been thinking privately of putting a swimming pool there. You'll discover that every family member has a different route getting from the street to the front door, and each will want the gate located appropriately.

Kids with bikes are a particular problem if you want a gated yard fence. Latches are hard to reach for someone under 5 feet high who is balancing an armful of school books, a hockey stick or baseball bat, and a two-wheeler – and you can be sure the gate will never get closed behind *any* young biker. If the gate has an automatic closer, it will bang into the bike's rear wheel as the rider tries to scoot through. And if kids on bikes are a problem, parents with both arms full of grocery bags are worse.

Have fun in your fence planning. Just remember, you want to find the simplest solution to the problem: a fence that keeps in what you want fenced in and keeps out what you want kept out – while effecting minimal interference with your family's way of life. If a fence becomes a serious barrier to any individual's travel pattern, it can become a family problem. Best to solve the difficulties on paper or in conversation before the fence goes in.

THE ART OF FENCE PLANNING

Now you have drawn out and argued over your layout and have consulted the picture books to get a good idea of the variety of fence designs you might consider. Next comes the creative part. What type, material, size, color, and texture do you and yours want in a fence? What style of fence matches your pocketbook, your home, and your style of living? Many answers will be suggested through the balance of this book. You'll have to make your own decisions, though – and you should have some idea of the principles of design that are considered by landscaping professionals in creating a fence. Here are the most basic.

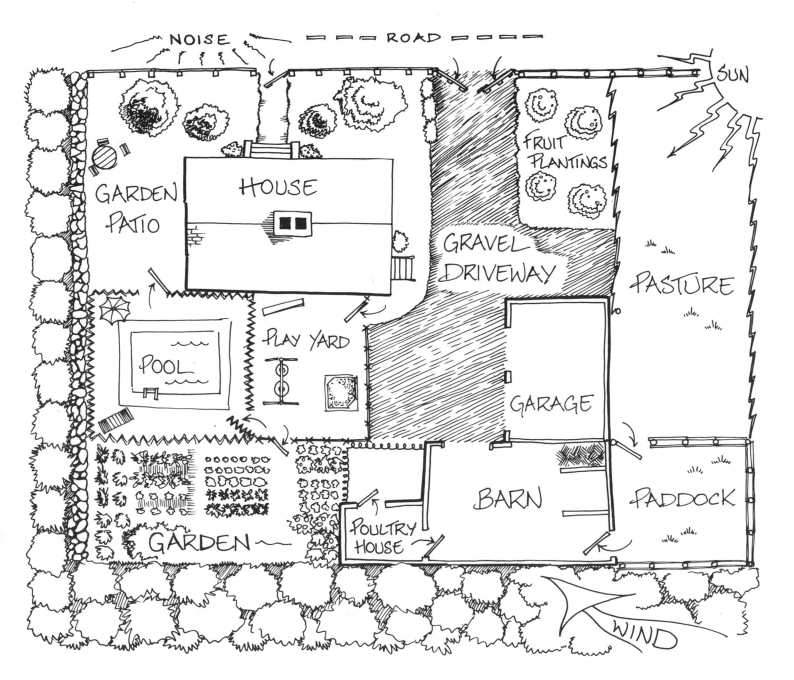

FRONT ELEVATIONS   CHOOSING HEIGHTS & DESIGNS

DESIGN ELEMENTS

Balance. That a fence or other structure should fit visually in its surroundings is the single most important element of design. A residential fence usually commands the foreground or background of its setting; it should compliment rather than magnify or overpower other major design features; house, plantings, walks, gardens, and lawn accessories. A tall, ornate black-iron fence goes well with a four-story Victorian town house but would frown down disapprovingly on a sprawling suburban ranch, which for its part, would look good with rugged split rails – a casual fence that would poke fun at the straight-laced Victorian. On the other hand a brick or stone fence would go well with either house. The ranch could handle a rough stone wall, while the Victorian design should be of dressed stone or evenly-laid brick, at once more ornate and more regular than the fence appropriate for the ranch.

Structural Unity versus Variety. The lines of a residential fence can pull the elements of a property together as they restate the lines of the home and grounds. But the fence should also provide a relieving contrast. The few horizontal rails and many vertical posts and slats of a picket fence complement the horizontal lines of a clapboard house, for example. Repeating a house's design and ornamentation pattern board-for-board in a fence, however, would be monotonous or even outrageous in the hands of any but a trained designer – and a talented one at that.

Proportion. The relationship between the dimensions of a fence affects its appearance. In particular, the height of a fence's bays should bear an appropriate proportion to the bays' length; that is, the fence shouldn't be too tall or too squat. As I'll suggest in the next chapter, a pleasing shape for a fence is one in which bays are *about* half again as long as they are tall. A square bay is more severe and formal, but acceptable. Oddly, in-between shapes are often unsettling. Look at the fences around you for confirmation of this observation.

Definition. A fence should make the house, plantings, and other elements in its setting stand out; it should never dominate (well, almost never). A too-tall board fence can ruin the effect of a low flowering tree, whereas a low stone fence can accent the tree's rounded, upright stance. A fence that is close to a house and of an improper height, proportion, and scale (see below) can make the house look squeezed, leaving the viewer with a vaguely unsettled feeling.

Scale. Scale refers to the size relationships of part to whole. Don't install a great massive brick wall around a little cottage – or if you must, lighten it up with open latticework along the top.

Simplicity. Design elements look best when surrounded by open space – typically at least half as much open space on all sides as the element itself occupies. A fence contains space, segmenting your property from the open space beyond. It will make the design elements within it appear larger and closer together, and a pleasant yard can suddenly appear to be crowded and busy when it is fenced. Don't be surprised if you have to remove plantings or other elements after the fence goes in; better to plan for doing so beforehand.

Rhythm. The line of the fence should be consistent with other lines in the landscape – curved walks or plantings, for instance, which narrow in perspective to guide the eye from feature to feature. Fences and buildings intrude flat, square shapes into a natural world of curved lines and surfaces. They can complement or fight with one another. You need a natural or trained artistic sense to evaluate rhythm.

Contrast. Large should match against small, dark against light, bright against dull. Use contrast in color or shape sparingly in fencing; always let a fence provide an understated effect. Have buildings or plantings stand out in contrast to the uniformity or low-keyed effect of the fence, not vice versa.

Background. Every landscape needs a neutral background against which to display its key elements, much as a plain mat sets off a small picture within a large frame. A fence can make a perfect contrasting backdrop for bright flowers or a lovely house.

Focal Point. A lawn-and-garden layout should muster its design forces to stress its major element. The long mall and reflecting pool before the Washington Monument in Washington, D.C., the gardens of the Versailles Palace, and the path leading to the front door in your own yard are examples. Have your fence reinforce the effect of the dominant feature, not muddy it. An ornate gate belongs right in front of the front door. A curved path that looked good without a fence might place the gate off to one side. You would then want to straighten the path so the gate and focal point coincide.

Perspective. Any object placed between a viewer and a distant object can seem to increase or decrease distance. The illusion of distance can be created by a low wall or fence placed in the middle distance. It masks the immediate foreground behind it, making the background appear to recede.

Formality versus Informality. The more regularity, the more repetition you include in a design, the more formal and imposing it will appear. Nicely milled planks and dressed stone are more formal than rough-textured materials. A central gate between two matched junipers is more formal than one offset to one side with a large lilac bush on one flank only. Decide how formal you want your place to appear. A rugged stone wall can add instant dignity to a small and unpretentious cottage, while a whimsical, iron-filigree fence can put a smile on a glowering, four-square brownstone.

Balance, definition, and those other artist's concepts are pretty vague, I know, and you can surely think up at least one exception to every rule listed. Nevertheless, how you arrange these intangibles is crucial to the look of your fence; you can't ignore them. In planning for the appearance of a fence, it is a good idea to make a drawing or take a photograph of your house/yard facade and sketch the planned fence on it to see if it looks right. You can draw again and again in a fine-tipped, nonpermanent

felt-tip pen on a cheap Polaroid print and erase the marks with a moist tissue.

If your plan just doesn't satisfy you no matter how you juggle the lines and proportions, trust your instincts and admit to having more native taste than architectural training. Ask friends for advice; often a fresh eye can come up with a solution.

Failing that (especially if your plan is unconventional), you should consider seeking the advice of a landscape architect or an experienced fencing or landscape designer-contractor, even if you plan to do the heavy work yourself. Look in the Yellow Pages under Landscape Architects and Landscape Contractors. These professionals are trained and experienced in balancing all the design elements as well as costs, zoning regulations, and other complications, to help you come up with the effect you truly want. An initial consultation won't cost a lot, and just hearing a trained mind toss off the considerations and complexities you've been inventing on your own – quickly and with conviction, skill, and ideas you never dreamed of – will be worth the fee. If you decide to leave design in part or wholly in trained hands, you'll have a fence that you can be sure looks top flight, even though you've saved half the cost by doing the cutting, sawing, digging, and hauling yourself.

2

WOOD FENCE

Wood is the most congenial of fencing mediums. Lightweight and easy to work, wood can be sawn, bent, planed, or molded to nearly any size or shape. It can be left to weather naturally or you can paint or stain it to match any color scheme. Vivid panels, airy pickets, rustic post-and-rail, resolute board screens, or sturdy railroad ties – the choice is limited only by your imagination and pocketbook. Once again I refer you to the picture books and suggest a fence-viewing drive through town – with a stop-over at a nearby fencing contractor – to get ideas for fences that match your environs.

Wood fence goes up quickly in the four steps I followed in putting up our first lath-and-furring-strip baby barrier:

1. **Plan and lay out the fence for the use intended under given cost and design constraints.**
2. **Sink vertical posts.**
3. **Affix horizontal rails or stringers.**
4. **Nail up the siding or infill.**

AN ELEGANT BOARD FENCE

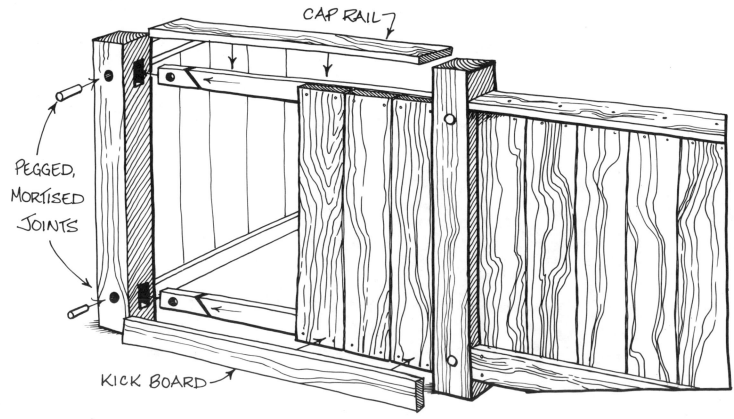

CAP RAIL

PEGGED, MORTISED JOINTS

KICK BOARD

DESIGN
(and price) A BAY

First step is to design your wood fence in detail, then find out what your several construction options will cost. On graph paper make a frontal drawing to scale of a typical fence bay (section of fence between one vertical post and another).

You can buy or build bays of any shape, height, or length you like. But remember the principles of design in proportioning height and width of bays to your materials and setting. A 1½-story house set 25 feet from the road on a narrow lot might look good with a 4-foot-high board fence in 6- or 6½-foot sections. A taller house in the same location needs a taller fence, perhaps with narrower bays. There, an open-picket or lattice design might be indicated, lest the place look like a prison. Either home set deeper on a larger lot might need a taller fence but one with wider bays, lest the fence be swallowed up by the greater expanse of lawn.

For accurate design and best economy, you must plan according to the way lumber is measured. Following are lumber measures that are standard throughout North America – along with sample prices for lumber from various sources in my own area. The cost figures are to give you an idea of price variations only; you'll have to do your own comparison shopping.

Timbers

Split posts and rails come in no standard sizes; their measurements depend on the tree and the splitter. But don't plan on using rails longer than 10 feet; longer sizes are getting hard to come by as older timber is cut and not replaced. In our part of New England, 10-foot, hand-split rails cost between $8 and $12 apiece, and a hand-split post with mortises for two or three rails costs about $12. Antique cedar rails from virgin-growth trees, if you can get them, and new white ash (a hardwood which comes closest to approximating the old white cedar) will cost about the same.

Manufactured "peeled-post-and-rail" fences are made from round rails with ends turned to 2½-inch dowels that are plugged into drilled posts or cut into lozenge-shaped paddles that fit into corresponding cut-outs or *scarfs* in the post. Those do come in standard sizes: 8 feet long usually and with two to four rails – 1 to 1½ feet between rails.

Lumber Grades

You can also build a fence from planed dimension stock from a lumberyard. Lumber is graded by independent sawyers according to specifications of several forest-products-industry associations. Most building codes specify graded lumber for structural components, but grading systems differ among areas, uses, and wood species. A tree that is sawn 2 inches thick and graded "Dimensional Select No. 3" for structural use can be given "Appearance Grade No. 2 Common" when sawn 1 inch thick for shelving. And a lumberyard may grade the same stick "Su-

NOMINAL AND ACTUAL SIZES OF COMMON FENCE BOARDS

Nominal (rough) size (thickness × width)	Actual (finished) size (thickness × width)
POSTS	
4 × 4	3½ × 3½
6 × 6	5½ × 5½
RAILS OR STRINGERS	
2 × 2	1½ × 1½
2 × 3	1½ × 2½
2 × 4	1½ × 3½
2 × 6	1½ × 5½
SIDING	
1 × 4	¾ × 3½
1 × 6	¾ × 5½
1 × 8	¾ × 7¼
1 × 10	¾ × 9¼ *
1 × 12	¾ × 11¼ *

*Note: fraction changes from ½ to ¼ for widths over 8 inches.

premo" to sell it. Lumber grades are essentially meaningless to a home fence builder. You'll have to judge your own wood.

The sizes of standard lumberyard stock are given in a three-number series: the first number gives the thickness of a board in inches, the second gives width in inches, the third gives length in feet. The typical fence rail (also termed *stringer*), or horizontal framing piece, is 2 × 4 × 8. You'd expect that to mean 2 inches thick by 4 inches wide by 8 feet long. Only lengths are true as given, however; an 8-foot board will indeed be 8 feet long. Width and thickness measurements can be misleading. By tradition, lumber measurements are given of the rough-sawn board as it comes off the saw – before it is air dried or planed smooth – and those *nominal* measurements are larger than the *actual* size of the board you buy.

If you buy rough lumber, you will get an accurate measure – or, if not accurate, at least close to the nominal size. To finish lumber, however, about ¼-inch is removed from all four sides of a board to make it smooth, so the nominal 2 × 4 (× 8) ends up being an actual 1¾ × 3½ (× 8). See "Board Feet Demystified," below, for more details.

Measuring center-to-center to locate holes for the gate posts.

Posts

Good posts come round or square, 4 or 6 inches through or larger, and of any length in even increments from 6 feet up to the size of a telephone pole. The length you buy depends on how much post is below ground (24 inches to 4 feet) plus the above-ground height, which will be the distance from ground level to the fence's top rail, or to the top of the siding . . . or higher if the post is to extend above the siding and be ornamented. Eight-foot posts will serve for most fences. A 4 × 4 × 8 *PT* post – pine that has been *pressure treated* against rot and bug damage – costs about $5. Round posts of white cedar in the same size but from a stronger wood that is naturally rot-resistant, cost half again as much or more.

Two-inch-thick stock for rails or stringers can be ordered in 2-, 3-, 4-, 6-, or even 8-inch widths and up to 16 feet or longer, but 2 × 4 by 8s, -10s and -12s are the most common and economical rails. Most buildings are framed with 2 × 4 × 8s, and you'll find the best values in that length. An 8-foot air-dried 2 × 4 in lumberyard pine or hemlock from a local sawmill will cost $1.25. Pine 2 × 3 × 8s cost 75 cents and can make economical stringers for lightweight fencing.

One-inch boards for siding also come in true 8-, 10-, and 12-foot lengths, and in widths as given in the table. Number-2 kiln-dried pine from a lumberyard in 1 × 4 × 8 boards costs $3 and up: 38 to 50 cents per running foot. Native air-dried pine from a local mill costs a third as much.

Precut pine pickets (1 × 3 × 4) will cost about 60 cents apiece; 6-footers will run $1. Fence-grade white cedar pickets run at least $1.50 apiece. I can get red oak planks that have enough blemishes to eliminate them for furniture use in true 1 × 6 × 8s for $1.20. The wood has a sour smell but makes good horse fence.

Plywood (for inset panels) comes in 4- × 8-foot sheets. Be sure to get *exterior* grade, with at least the side to view veneered with clear-grain wood: *Sanded AC* is the designation. Cheapest plywood, at about $7.50 per sheet, is Philippine Mahogany or Luan-finished AC in ¼-inch thickness. Both must be framed with reinforcing boards every 1½ to 2 feet lest they warp. Half-inch Luan ply, which won't warp so easily goes for about double the ¼-inch price.

Most hardware outlets stock glass, plastic, and fiberglass sheets in yard-square or smaller panels for window glazing that can also be used for fence infill; you may have to special order larger sheets for a fence screen.

BAY MEASUREMENTS

A fence bay is conventionally measured from the center of one post to the center of the next: so many feet "on center." A bay that is 8 feet long (8 feet on center) is most common in prefabricated fence. You can build your own bays any width you like, but since most building materials are sold in 8-foot lengths, material prices will be lower if you stay close to the standard.

Important: don't plan to nail up fences using lumber as it comes from the yard. Ends are not always evenly cut and are often scarred from transport or dyed to denote grade. Good carpenters always trim boards – flat 1-inch-thick ones, at least.

Measuring Stringers

Here's how to measure rails or stringers for an 8-foot bay using a 4-inch-square post butted up with rails to each side of the post and "toenailed" on.

A stringer of:	
8 feet × 12 inches/foot =	96 inches
less actual width of one 4 × 4 post =	3½ inches
equals trim length of stringer:	92½ inches

So, trim about 2 inches from one end, measure 92½ inches, and trim off the excess – about 1½ inches.

A carpentry tip: trim one end of the board and measure carefully from the cut to the other end. Never measure in from each end to trim a board; you'll cut it short every time. Once having made the calculation correctly, you can use the first cut board as a template to trim every stringer to the same length without thinking about it – but don't use each new cut board to measure for the next. That will introduce errors too, much as a rumor changes as it is passed from one person to the next.

Measuring Siding

Infill boards must be end-trimmed, too. (One-inch stock has ragged edges more often than framing members such as 2 × 4s, which good carpenters *do* use straight from the lumber pile.) Let's say your plan calls for 4-foot-high vertical siding. If you cut a 12-foot board in three 4-foot-pieces, only the center one would have two clean, true edges. Better to trim the board a bit at each end – say, 1½ inches and have a fence with siding boards that are an inch less than 4 feet high but perfectly cut:

12 foot board × 12 inches =	144 inches
less 1½ inches trimmed at each end =	3 inches
trimmed length:	141 inches
divided by 3 =	47 inches per siding board

The same tip repeated: with flat boards too, trim a bit from one end, measure off a board length from that cut, then another, and then any others. Don't cut in from both ends; the middle board of a 12-footer cut into three 4-footers will be off-size.

To sum up: design with lumber as it comes, using actual thickness and width, and planning to trim the end of each board.

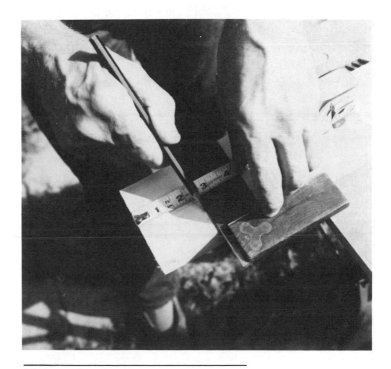

Marking a board with a try square.

DESIGN VARIABLES

Throughout this book and others, and in your fence viewing, you'll see any number of designs that you can copy or modify to your taste and needs. But all are variations on a simple theme: posts sunk firmly in the ground, rails or stringers nailed or bolted onto posts, and infill nailed on the stringers. Here are the variables to consider in designing your bay.

Bay Dimensions

Open split-rail fences can be made long and low – 4 feet high with 10- or 12-foot bays – and look fine. But fences with planked bays just naturally look best when proportioned as 8 to 5, an ideal length-to-width proportion in landscaping. A low picket or butted-board fence with long, rectangular 8-foot bays looks weak, unassertive, and lazy. A fence with square bays looks busy.

Check fences in your neighborhood. I bet you'll find that custom designs with 3- to 4-foot pickets or boards butted together are arranged in 6-foot bays. A length-to-height ratio of 6 feet to 3.75 feet fits the 8:5 proportion mentioned. Draw your bay so that length is to height as 8 is to 5, and deviate only after careful consideration (and after the stake-and-string trial that I suggest later on). To determine the best bay length from a given height, multiply height by 1.60. To get height from length, multiply length by .625. Or, use the following table:

EIGHT-TO-FIVE RATIOS	
If the fence height is:	The ideal bay width is:
3 feet	4 feet, 9½ inches
3½	5 feet, 7¼ inches
4	6 feet, 4¾ inches
4½	7 feet, 2½ inches
5	8 feet
5½	8 feet, 9½ inches
6	9 feet, 7¼ inches
6½	10 feet, 4¾ inches
7	11 feet, 2½ inches

Posts

You don't have much choice in size and shape of posts. Anything smaller than 4-inch rounds or 4 × 4 squares makes a lightweight fence. The 2 × 4s I used in our first baby fence were strictly an economy measure. Posts 6 × 6 or larger aren't structurally necessary unless your fence has to resist large livestock or tremendous winds.

But you may choose to accent posts in the design – perhaps in a massive 6- or even 8-inch post-and-rail fence, or in a fence with carved finials on the top of square posts. A 4 × 4 post is too thin to stand out strongly against standard 3- or 4-inch vertical siding, and here you're better off using 6 × 6s or even 8 × 8s for posts. That large stock is expensive; cheaper is to vary the alignment of siding and rails to accent posts or box a 4 × 4 square post with 1-inch lumber set out on spacers of any size to make a more formal, massive post.

Rails and Rail-Post Joints

The number of rails (stringers) a fence needs depends on the size and weight of infill and on the length, thickness, and strength of these horizontals. Two rails will do for most residential fences up to 4 feet in height. Look closely at other fences using materials of similar dimension to yours and consider adding another rail *if* bay dimensions match the 8:5 ratio given elsewhere, siding is pickets or 1-inch-nominal butted boards, and:

—**2 × 4 rails are strung flat and distance between rails exceeds 2 feet;**
—**2 × 4 rails are on edge and distance between rails exceeds 2½ feet;**
—**distance between 4 × 4 rails exceeds 4 feet.**

If infill is heavy plywood or boards that are thicker than 1 inch, use your judgment; add extra rails or sink a short support post at midpoint in the bay for the bottom rail to rest on. You don't want a sagging fence.

Stringers serve mainly to hold the infill to the posts and are a design component that is too often ignored. It's so easy just to nail stringers on the front of posts (about

4 inches from top and bottom) – stringer boards flipped up on edge and the ends of adjoining boards simply butted together. Then the infill is nailed onto the rails, making an unbroken line of boards. That is the most common type of home-built fence. It can be sturdy and visually effective, but it is inelegant carpentry. The stringers hold the infill out away from the posts disdainfully. I prefer fences that are more friendly – and more imaginative.

Nailing the stringers to the *back* of the posts and the infill to the *front* of the stringers insets infill within posts, pushing the larger dimension of the posts forward to vary the texture of the fence. If the posts are higher than the siding, they will stand out well in the design.

Nailing the top stringer flat to the top of the post, with the lower stringer(s) *toenailed* (with nails going in at an angle) on flat between posts is a still tidier design. With 4 × 4 posts and 2 × 4 rails, all framing members are the same width and feel good going together. But boards hung in the flat tend to bend, and the fence can become swaybacked. Use three stringers on any flat-railed fence but a light picket design with short bays. Or strengthen the top stringer by using 4 × 4s, or make a stringer of two 2 × 4s on edge with ½-inch plywood spacers between them. Here too, infill is nailed on in an unbroken line unless larger posts are used.

The height of rails on posts can be varied. Rails can rest atop posts or be lowered several inches. With a lower rail and the bottom of the infill 6 inches above ground level, you can nail on a kick board – an old colonial ornament that also prevents small animals from entering the yard.

Inset Rails

Inset rails are more elegant in appearance and also allow you to use the post as an independent design element: rails and siding are set back into the plane of the fence posts, creating surface contrast.

Toenailing 2 × 4s set *on edge* flush with the back edge of 4 × 4 posts insets the siding members 2 inches. That's less of an inset than if rails are butt-joined to the backs of the posts, but it will still add depth to the design.

A *dado* joint, where horizontal slots are sawed in the insides of posts to accept stringers set in the flat, makes for a stronger joint. Or, you can saw ½-inch-deep slots in front or back of the post to accept stringers arranged on edge. Notch both post and stringer, and you have a *mortised lock-joint.*

Most elegant, and strongest, are full *mortise-and-tenon* joints – a board-fence version of the housed joints of a post-and-rail fence. If you like the idea of working wood, adding this fine touch to rough fence carpentry could be the beginning of a productive hobby. Get a good set of wood chisels, a sharpening stone, (and a book on cabinet making for more details on wood joinery than I can provide here). Plan to cut 1¾- × 3¾-inch through-mortises in 4 × 4 posts to hold 2 × 4 rails set on edge and notched so tenons will overlap inside the mortises of line posts. Ends are easy: uncut stringers just plug in. Mortised corner joints get complicated – the mortises meet in a right-angle-shaped hole through the post, and when the mortise is cut out a 4-by post is nearly hollow. You are advised to use large-size end and corner posts.

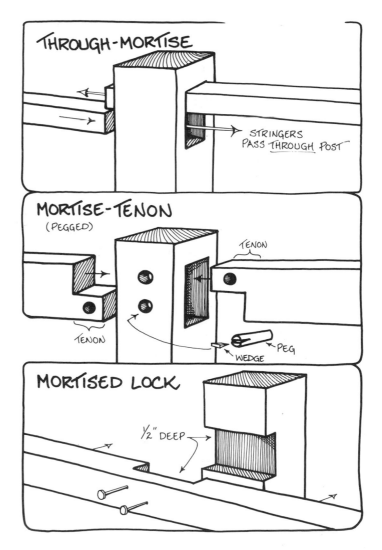

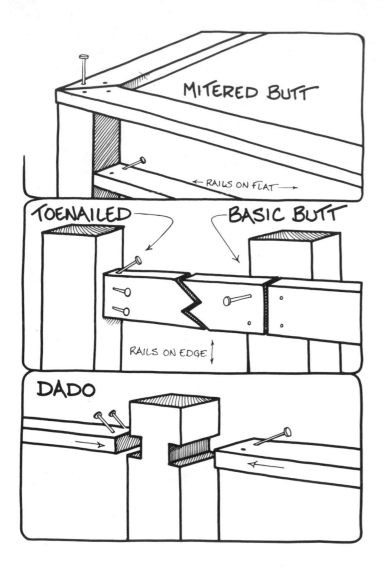

I'd peg the joints. Drill holes through the side of the post and into stringers to accept birch dowels (available in several diameters from any lumberyard). Soap the dowels to make them go in easily and hammer them home. Unless you are bashful about showing off your craftsmanship, cut the dowel ends so that ½-inch sticks out. Or cut the dowels off flush, split them in the hole with a chisel, and hammer in a thin hardwood wedge to lock them in place. I use slivers of black walnut left over from making musical instruments. With a light stain, the walnut shim and birch dowel contrast with the softwood post as subtle evidence of fine fence carpentry.

Be sure to include the length of the tenon—the length of rail that fits into the mortises—in the rough rail measurement when planning and when ordering stock.

Siding

With post and rail design set, experiment with various ideas for siding.

If you want a picket fence, your verticals needn't be whatever is conventional in the neighborhood (usually 1- × 3- or 1- × 4-inch wide stock in 36-, 42-, and 48-inch heights with pointed tops that the local mill turns out). If you have the ambition to cut your own or are willing to pay a bit extra for a custom milling job, make your pickets wider or narrower. Have the tops square, rounded, scalloped or "picketed" in a broad-leaf or arrowhead design. The distance between pickets can be varied too, although a third to a half of the picket's width looks best; too small a space looks cramped, and with too large a space the fence looks gap-toothed.

Experiment on the drawn-to-scale plan you have made of your fence bay. When you've hit on a width and spacing that appeal, calculate the number of pickets you need:

1. **Subtract one inter-picket space from the length of an installed rail—the distance between sides of successive posts.**
2. **Divide the remainder by the width of one picket plus one inter-picket space.**
3. **Ask your grade-schooler to help with the arithmetic needed to adjust rail length, picket width, and spacing to match reality.**

Example: assume we're using true 6-foot rails, nominal 1- × 4-inch finished board siding (*actual* width: 3½ inches) with 1-inch spacing.

$$6 \text{ feet} \times 12 = 72 \text{ inches/rail}$$
$$\underline{- \text{ one space} \quad\quad - 1 \text{ inch}}$$
$$71 \text{ inches}$$

71 divided by 4½ (width of a picket + width of a space) = 15.777

That's fifteen and .777 pickets. What in the name of reason to do with the .777? Well, .777 of 4½ inches is about 3½ inches – the actual width of a picket. You could increase the rail by a ½-inch inter-picket space (to 72½ inches) and add one more picket. That's what I would do (what I have done, in fact). Or you could absorb the extra space by spreading the original fifteen pickets out by 1/15th of the 3⅕ inches – that's a smidgin less than 15/64ths. But this isn't cabinet making; round the 15/64ths up to 16/64ths, which rounds down to ¼-inch. You'd separate pickets by 1¼ inches.

Try both solutions on your scale drawing.

Using a 2×2 to brace a top rail for nailing.

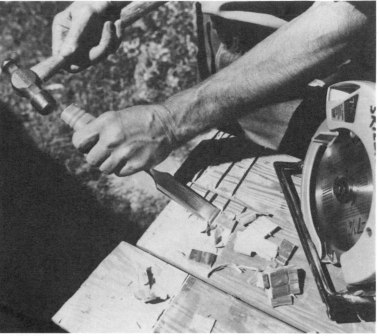

To overlap fence boards, I make shallow saw cuts, then remove excess wood with a chisel.

BILL OF MATERIALS

Without realizing it, perhaps, you've worked up the basis for your materials order.

The number of posts you need in a run of fence (between end posts) equals the number of bays in that segment of fence plus one.

The number of stringers needed equals the number of bays times the number of stringers per bay. Add in at least two for measuring mistakes and three or four extras for gate stock.

The amount of siding is the number of bays times the number of boards per bay (plus 10 percent for waste and a half-bay's worth per planned gate). See the section on gates, below, for details on gate hardware.

Calculate the number of long nails you need by multiplying stringers per post, times the number of posts, times five. The number of short nails equals number of infill boards per bay, times two, times the number of stringers, times the number of bays. Details on nail sizes follow.

You will need gravel or crushed rock to pack and drain post holes: 1 to 3 cubic feet per hole. Gravel is sold by the ton or cubic yard; add up the total number of cubic feet (posts × cubic feet per post hole) and divide by 27 to find yards needed. Look under Concrete in the Yellow Pages for the nearest gravel pit. Expect to pay about $3.50 per yard for bank-run gravel and up to $10 for crushed rock. I have a pickup truck and haul my own small loads, but I have to pay $35 per hour (both ways) if a big dump truck has to haul it for me.

You may want to set posts in concrete. See chapter 4 on working with cement for details.

LAYING OUT

With your bay designed and a preliminary lumber order made out, it's time to prove your design on the land. Put together a fencer's layout kit:

Layout materials include a spool of white mason's line. You use it in every phase of fencing, so get a good supply – at least enough to go around the fence twice. Cotton is friendlier to work with than synthetic line; it sells for 215 feet for about $2. High-quality no-stretch cotton cordage is getting hard to find in the polyester age, but it's worth looking for. You'll find it at a building-supply outlet or lumberyard. They'll have the goods that the pros use. Hardware stores cater to the consumer, and the mason's line they stock these days is liable to be nothing but nylon "parachute cord" – cheaper than the cotton at 270+ feet for about $1.50. It's stretchy, but it works all right if it's all you can get and if you can tie a knot in it that will hold. (Be sure to touch the ends and any cuts with a flame to seal the cord against ravel. And *don't* touch the black bead of melted plastic till it cools; it's hot! To tie off cotton cord, you just knot the end.)

Some experts I've read say you should get a professional mason's cord with corner blocks to hook onto the work, but neither I nor anyone I know has seen a set of cord and blocks for sale outside the trade in thirty years.

To lay out your fence you'll also need wooden stakes. If you don't have saplings handy to cut and trim to length, buy the cheapest wood you can – as long as the height of your fence plus a few inches to sink in the ground. A bundle of 8-foot furring strips or a bundle of 4-foot wood lath is about the cheapest wood available in our area.

BASIC HAND TOOLS FOR FENCE LAYOUT

Hatchet (for sharpening and hammering in stakes)
Line level
Crosscut hand saw
Steel tape measure
Right angle
Plumb bob (chalk line/plumb bob)

The Crosscut Saw

Even if you plan to purchase your fence in prefabricated sections, you will need a good hand saw. I have a whole wood-working shop full of power saws, but when fencing, I use the hand saw more than any of the others. You don't have to run an electric cord all through the yard to use it.

You'll be cutting across the grain of posts, rails, and infill material that have already been *ripped* or cut lengthwise, with the grain. Be sure you get a saw with a *crosscut* blade, having teeth that are set so they angle out in alternating directions as you look down on them. Don't get a *ripsaw*, with teeth lined up like so many little shark's fins in a straight row, and don't get a *combination* saw that will neither rip nor cut cross-grain very well. Length, number, and set of teeth will be stamped on the saw's blade. A common size – and the best for rough fence carpentry – is 26 inches in length with eight points to the inch.

You used to get what you paid for in saws, but the makers are beginning to dress consumer saws in flashy sheaths and fit them with plastic handles for a premium price – designer hand saws. A price of $25 should get

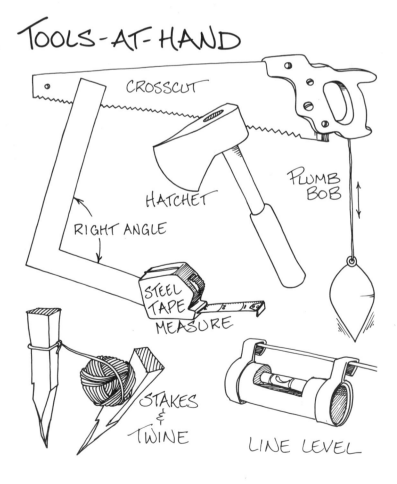

TOOLS-AT-HAND

CROSSCUT

HATCHET

RIGHT ANGLE

PLUMB BOB

STEEL TAPE MEASURE

STAKES & TWINE

LINE LEVEL

you a fine saw, but the clerk will know the best value. And don't be afraid to ask for help, even if you are a newcomer to lumberyards and intimidated by builders' jargon. It can be baffling, as in the following conversation I overheard in a local yard not long ago.

"Mornin', Billy," the weathered Yankee carpenter said to the eager young clerk behind the counter. "I need three ten-foot PT four-by-fours – no warp, no rot; a hundred-eighty-five board feet of clear one-by-sixes in eights, ten eight-foot prime two-bys, three pound 'a six-penny galvanized common, and two pounds 'a ten."

"Sounds like a fence, Mr. Perkins," said the clerk, writing up the order. "Butted siding boards, I'd guess?"

"Yep," says the builder, a man of few words.
"Forty-footer, would it be, Mr. Perkins?"
"Yep."
"Four feet high?"
"Yep."
"Eight-foot bays?"
"Yep."
"Only goin' down two feet, though?"
"Far enough."
"Prime stock – likely the new Adams house?"
"Yep."
"Like that delivered, Mr. Perkins?"
"Please."
"To the building site?"
"Yep."
"Plan to get it today, do you?"
"If I don't have to spend all day gabbin', I do."

Before I learned that those terms do indeed describe components for 40 feet of board fence, I often walked out with the wrong goods rather than ask questions that might reveal my ignorance.

Don't you do the same. These days I get good service by showing workmanlike skill in knowing precisely what I am after in terms of results but asking for expert help on secrets of the building trades. Try it yourself – tell the salesperson that you need a good saw to cut so many fence boards of this thickness and that species across the grain but don't know one saw from another. You'll get a brief lecture on choice and utility of wood saws by a sales clerk who should be flattered to show off some inside know-how. He may go so far as to tell you one saw in stock is a better value than another.

Measuring nails using the scale on the back of a Stanley steel tape.

The Steel Tape

You can get measuring tools in steel straightedge, folding wood, cloth, and steel-tape designs. The same armchair authorities who recommend cord with mason's end blocks would have you spend $30 for a 100-foot-long hand-crank reel of cloth surveyor's tape. For fencing, a 12- or 15-foot steel tape is fine. It will still set you back more than $10, but it will make all your fencing measurements, it contains a spring rewinder for easy retrieval, and it's stiff, so you can maneuver it when it is fully extended. The tip has a hook with a notch and a hole in it. It will hook over a corner of wood or brick for quick measurements (staying put only so long as you maintain tension on the hook), and if snagged over a small nail will stay in place to let you make precise measurements at your leisure.

New steel tapes can tell you more than lengths and widths. The last time I asked for help with nails (I can never remember the "penny" sizes from one project to another), the clerk told me to get a new steel tape from Stanley because it gave nail sizes on the back. My twenty-year-old Stanley steel tape worked like new and still does, but I bought the new model. In addition to nail sizes, it has decimal conversions to ease us into the Metric Age, number of nails per pound, wood-screw sizes, chisel-sharpening angles, surveyors' conversion tables, and sandpaper grits. It also gives nominal versus actual lumber sizes and the formula for board feet used to compute lumber costs. The tape tells, for example, that nomi-

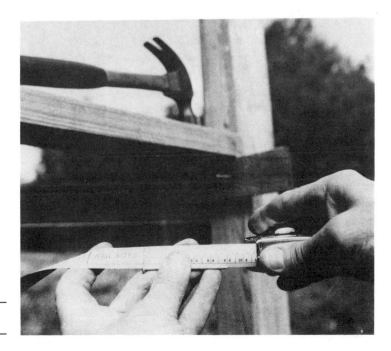

nal 2 × 4s actually measure 1½ × 3½ inches, and you pay for .667 board feet per linear foot. I don't own any stock in The Stanley Works, but I recommend their informative tape measures: making a few trade secrets easily available to us outsiders is a good practice that is long overdue.

Levels and Squares

You need tools to build your fence to be plumb (straight and vertical in all dimensions), level, and square (so angles are all a perfect 90 degrees) to property lines, buildings, and other wood members in the fence – unless your fence is consciously made to deviate.

The little *line level* is a plastic or metal tube containing a vial of liquid with a bubble in it. If you hook it over a line and adjust the line till the bubble is dead center in the eye of the vial, that line is level.

The line level can serve to true up posts, rails, and siding if fastened to a long, true board. But better would be a 6- or 8-inch *torpedo level* or a long metal, wood, or plastic *tradesman's spirit level* that has two or three leveling eyes to define level for two dimensions at once.

You'll also need a tool to define the 90-degree angle, or square. A simple *try square* is a carpenter's constant companion: with a 6-inch steel blade protruding at 90 degrees from a wood or plastic handle, it is used to prove every joint. Mine is an heirloom with a well-worn rosewood handle and a brass bolster, and I value it highly.

A *carpenter's square* is a steel 90-degree angle that measures 24 inches on one leg, 18 on the other. In addition to showing the inch- and foot rules, it is stamped with scales that a trained carpenter can use to lay out rafter and stair angles without using math.

A *combination square* is a try square with a handle that slides along the blade. It also contains a leveling bubble.

I use all those tools but would recommend a 2-foot spirit level and a carpenter's square if you only want to invest in one of each. At about $15 apiece, they will prove the most useful choice for fencing and will serve for other carpentry and masonry projects in years to come.

The Plumb Bob

A weight with an eye at one end and a point at the other, the plumb bob is suspended on a string to determine that a board or other member is straight down and vertical. Get a combination plumb bob and chalk line. Encased in a hollow plumb-bob-shaped canister is a length of line that can be pulled out and reeled in. Hang the bob from a string or nail, and the end of the canister will point toward the center of the earth to indicate straight down from the point of attachment.

You'll also need a squeeze bottle of powdered blue chalk. Puff the chalk into the canister. Then, when you unreel the line, it will be covered with chalk. Pull the line tight along a board, pull the line out a fraction of an inch and let it snap back, and you've made a straight chalk line to mark saw lines or locations for fence stringers.

Trial Layout

You've already drawn a plan of your fence, determining post locations, bay lengths, gates, and all. I'm sure that seeing the layout on paper changed some early preconceptions. Now, please take the time to make another trial that I guarantee will give you even more insights. Lay out the fence in three dimensions with stakes and twine – at least where it is open to public view along the front of the house, where it runs through currently undivided living space, and where any gates will be located. Hammer in full-length stakes where each bay will start, and string a length of twine around the stakes at both the top and bottom levels of the siding boards. Build in twine gates – a single string with a loop in it will do. The neighbors may think it a little peculiar, but live with the string-fence layout for a week or more – or until you are absolutely sure you like it.

Negotiating Slopes

The trial layout is where you can picture how to run the fence up and down grade – a problem you may have faced in theory on paper but now can see in three dimensions.

Recall, there are four ways to negotiate slopes:

1. Both frame and infill rise in steps.
2. Frame is stepped, but infill is sloped.
3. Both are sloped.
4. Frame is sloped, but infill is stepped.

Building wood fence on a grade goes faster if rails are sloped, even though sawing the angled joints takes concentration. A post should go in at each break in elevation on a varying grade. The nailing positions of all rails on all posts are kept an equal height above ground, and

rails are inset into notches in the posts or simply toenailed on – with nails going in at an angle through top, bottom, or sides of the rails and into the post. Sloped rails work best with simple fences, and a fence that follows grade in a sloping line is more casual and natural and goes best in thin, pointed pickets or *grapestakes*, half-round redwood slats, that are common in West Coast wine country. Some people find an unbroken line of stakes unimaginative or even unpleasant – almost serpentine – when the fence undulates downhill. Relieve the effect by insetting rails so the posts stand out to break the monotony.

Stepping the rails – so that all are horizontal – requires more careful measuring and is just about essential for fence designs incorporating inset panels or finely mortised joints. Stepped bays are more formal and go best with broad fence members – wide planks or panels. A stepped fence looks best if bays are of equal width. If the grade varies greatly, however, that will make the height of steps between bays vary also; you may wish to vary bay width and change step height. If you do step bays or square off tops of boards on a sloping frame, you are imposing order on nature – leveling what isn't. Plan very carefully. Visually, a stepped fence is a series of blocks marching up a hill in what should appear military precision. The height and length of the bays must be proportioned tastefully, or the fence can look like a file of rag-tag volunteers rather than a well-disciplined column of regulars. See how the mockup looks, and change it till you are satisfied.

Set up your stakes and lines and try out different slope-negotiating schemes till you find one that you like.

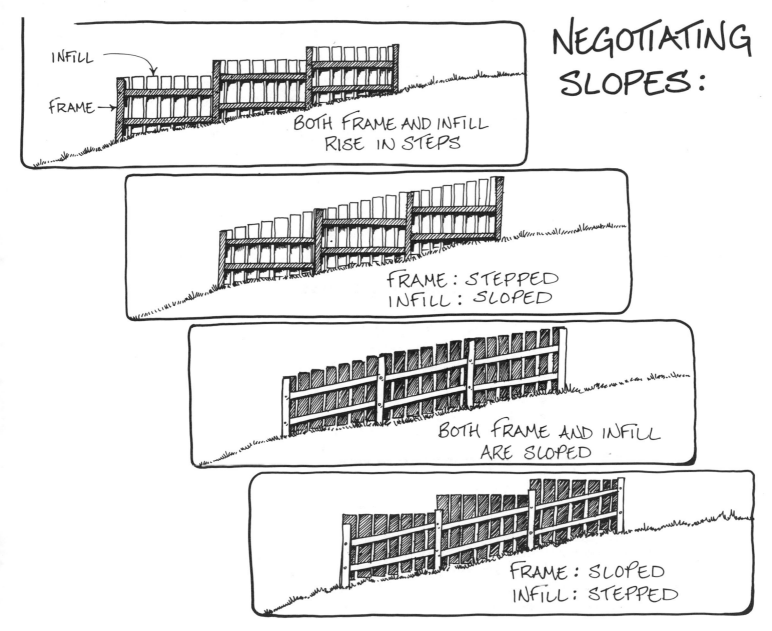

NEGOTIATING SLOPES:

INFILL

FRAME

BOTH FRAME AND INFILL RISE IN STEPS

FRAME: STEPPED
INFILL: SLOPED

BOTH FRAME AND INFILL ARE SLOPED

FRAME: SLOPED
INFILL: STEPPED

ADJUST THE DESIGN

Don't be surprised if the string-and-stake prototype interrupts traffic patterns in unanticipated ways, that gate locations prove to be inconvenient, or a gate's planned direction of swing must be reversed. The fence may make the house look too big or too small, too crowded by prefence plantings or too estranged from the walk or roadway. If so, make the mockup more realistic still; add a third or fourth string to the twine and stakes. If that doesn't settle the matter, staple newspaper or plastic sheeting over the strings to approximate the fence's final look. Then experiment with different heights, different bay lengths, different gates, and different layouts altogether. Make your mistakes in prototype, not in boards and nails. We toyed with a string-and-stake layout for one fence over an entire spring and half the summer before settling on a layout that was entirely different from any of the plans we'd drawn up on paper.

Only when you are happy with the layout, take it down and live *without* it for a while just to see if you really want the fence. If you decide you don't want a fence after all, let me know, will you? This book will have served an unintended purpose if it has saved you several hundred dollars and a lot of unhappiness. If you still want a fence, though, it's time to get on with it.

Arranging layout line on a pair of batter boards.

VISIT A CONTRACTOR – Again

Take your plan to a fencing contractor and see what a professional job would cost, installed. You will find that price for the same frontal design will vary as much as 200 percent by thickness, grade, and species of wood, from $25 to $75 a bay in our area. Custom fence is expensive, comprising materials plus labor costs that run about $50 an hour for a two-man crew with an earth-auger-equipped small tractor. They can put up a prefabricated yard-sized fence in a half-day and from 100 to 500 feet of custom-built fence a day, depending on fence style and ease of drilling post holes. That's an awfully broad range, I know – labor alone varying from 50 cents to $4 per running foot of fence, or $4 to $24 per 8-foot bay. That's

why it pays to compare prices. Some contractors charge by the hour, others by the amount of fence installed. I'm told on good authority that still others charge by the size of your house and the brand of automobile in the drive.

See what prefab panels or ready-to-nail-up bays will cost installed and what it will cost you to buy them and put them up yourself.

Important: few prefab fences will cant over so as to go up or down slopes. You may have to use prefab on the flat and custom-built on hills.

Price ready-cut but separate parts of prefab fences for a complete assemble-it-yourself job. The fencing pros would rather do the whole job, but most of them will sell you fence any way you want it.

Finally, go to a mill or lumberyard and price raw stock. The last time I checked, I could save money buying rough-cut native lumber or finished softwoods for a home-built fence. But it was almost cheaper to buy a prime white cedar fence *installed* than to special-order cedar stock from a local lumberyard. An 8-foot bay of 4-foot-high picket fence with doweled rails and half-round stakes from one fencing contractor cost from $30 to $65 depending on which of ten styles you wanted and whether it came in spruce or white cedar. Posts were $5 to $10 more. No contractor would sell raw cedar stock in anything but 2 × 6 × 24s that they'd bought for resawing, and cedar lumber cost well over $1 a board foot if special ordered from a lumberyard.

Trying to give firm costs per foot – as is possible with other fences – is futile for wood fence. It ranges from $2.50 for really cheap stockade fence of ½-inch half-round stakes on 1 × 3 × 8 pine rails to $10 for top-quality versions of the same design – posts and installation extra. You'll have to price your own, I fear.

Save Money

Many fencing contractors resist selling you raw cedar, redwood, or other outdoor fence wood. They'll let you drive off with prefab fencing but may kite the price to make their installation services more attractive. Around our parts they charge more for loose rails and siding than for prefabricated bays, stating that it costs more to get the loose boards out of manufacturing stock than to go ahead and nail it up into bays. Still, their cut-stock prices may be lower than special orders of raw boards from a building-supply store or lumberyard. I'm not trying to dissuade you from building from scratch, but the fencing contractors do buy wood in carload lots, which you and I can't. They don't pass the savings on to you in cash, but in service, which is their business – literally.

There are other lumber options coming up – but if you aren't saving much money building your own fence rather than hiring a contractor, be sure you know it. Fencing is a learning experience, fun if you like it, and doing it yourself is the only way to get the fence you really want built the way you want it. Even *losing* a few pennies a board foot by building fence is probably cheaper recreation than an equivalent time spent playing golf or straining in a Nautilus room.

If you decide to hire the entire job out, though, get several estimates, and engage the contractor that appeals on product, price, and reputation. The latter is most important in my view. Ask for locations of earlier jobs and talk to the owners. Insist on a contract that specifies size, species, and lumber grade of all wood materials, and that details gate plan and hardware, depth of posts plus workman's and liability insurance coverage.

THE BOARD FOOT DEMYSTIFIED

Wood is conventionally priced by the board foot. A board foot is a linear foot of inch-thick, foot-wide lumber *before it is cut and planed to finished size*. By ancient tradition, you are charged for the raw stock as it comes rough-cut out of the sawmill before it is ripped to width and planed smooth – but you never see the sawdust and shavings that come off to make finished boards.

To side an 8-foot bay with vertical board you'd need eight true 1 × 12 planks, (48 square feet for a 6-foot-high fence). But after the boards are planed to be 11¼ inches wide and ¾-inch thick, you will need *eight and a half* of them. You will also need two 8-foot 2 × 4s for rails or stringers – and recall that the Stanley rule says that a linear foot of 2 × 4 is priced as .667 board feet of lumber.

To work up the practical cost figures for an 8-foot bay of 6-foot-high cedar fence, when the price is quoted in board feet:

For the infill: 8.53 planks ×
× 6 feet of length = 51.18 board feet
For the rails: 2 × 8 feet = 16,
× .667 board feet = 10.67 board feet
Total: 61.85 board feet

(And, at a dollar and change per board foot for raw cedar stock, the price would be almost the same as the $66 cost of a high-quality cedar bay prefabricated and professionally installed.)

OTHER LUMBER-SUPPLY OPTIONS

The chances are slim that you will be able to get split rails or specialty fence wood such as redwood or white cedar from anywhere but a specialist – a fencing contractor or a building-supply yard that furnishes goods for the do-it-yourselfer. Look in the Yellow Pages under Building Supplies. Display ads will say if a firm specializes in split rails, post-and-board, or other fences.

Local Mills and Native Woods

If you want to save some cash, seek out a rough-cut lumber mill. These little moving-bed buzz saws are found howling away near the woods anywhere on the continent that trees grow in abundance. The native wood is typically not graded to a timber-products-association standard, so is not code-acceptable for building construction in many jurisdictions. Our local wood goes to barn builders, to pallet- and furniture makers – and to fence builders.

If you have a country place, you can save the most money by hauling in logs from your own woodlot. It may even pay to have the trees logged out for you. Or you can buy someone else's wood of any local tree species as it comes off the saw. It is cheapest "green" – just cut, and so wet that it sprays as sawed. Green wood can't be cut thin and put up in a board fence. As they dry unsupported in the sun and wind, the boards will warp, crack, and split all out of shape. Green wood must be stacked flat to dry for months – a year or more is best. Some mills will have air-dried boards for sale at a nickel or dime a foot premium over green.

Often, local mills are the only place to get anything much but fence contractor's spruce or cedar or lumberyards' pine, spruce, or fir stock that may have been hauled all the way across the continent and is priced accordingly. In our part of New England, hemlock is a good buy. It is a rough wood but makes fine if splintery rails. Our native white pine makes lovely siding. For the best posts, the mills truck down whole white cedar logs from Canada.

In other areas small mills will cut you posts from the naturally rot-resistant heartwood that all fencers used in

the old days. The same stock would cost a small fortune in lumberyards today. Characteristics of the major fence-wood species are listed separately. Use a straight-grained framing wood for rails, but most any local lumber except truly soft softwoods such as the poplars will serve as infill. Furniture-grade hardwoods such as oak, maple, and the nutwoods bring a premium wherever they grow.

Green wood planks and rails make good rough fence once they dry out, but you'll need a truck to haul the wood from the mill, a place to stack it to air-dry for a summer or more, and a commercial ripsaw to cut the log-width planks to size. Then if you want a finished-appearing fence, you'll need access to a planer. Turning out a fence from green lumber is time-consuming and, if the lumber comes from your own trees, it is a labor of love. The money saved is secondary.

Multiple Sources

Buying finished fence components from several sources should also be considered. A discount building-supply outlet near me has redwood fence posts on half-price sale late each spring. I can get leftover pickets from another yard at a promotional price in the fall, and a third dealer has pine 2 × 4s for rails in nonstud grade (not house-building quality, but okay for fences) at 99 cents apiece now and again.

Shadow box.

WOOD CHARACTERISTICS FOR FENCE

Heartwood from large specimens of the following common trees is compacted dead wood from the inner core of the tree. It contains natural aromatic oils which will repel ground rot and insects for from five to ten or more years. Some of these species exist today largely as second-growth timber, and few such individual trees are old enough to have developed much heartwood.

Sapwood of the following species is widely sold for use in outdoor fence rails and siding.

Eastern White Cedar: naturally water-, rot-, and fungal-decay resistant, but not bug-proof, so must be treated for below-ground use. Saws easily, resists splitting, shrinking, and warping. A common lumber tree and widely shipped from its Northeastern range for fencing and outdoor furniture. Takes finishes well or weathers naturally to a soft gray.

Cypress: resistant to both insects and decay. A twisty-grained wood that can be a little hard to nail through but finishes beautifully and weathers naturally to a silver gray. A lovely fence wood, but expensive outside of the Gulf and riverine South where it is indigenous.

Species of fir, spruce, and pine not cited above. The common lumberyard stock, with low bug- and rot-resistance, but having even-grained boards that are strong and easily worked. These woods finish well but weather poorly unless bleached or sealed. Best for planed boards in sealed, primed, and painted fence. Air-dried lumber is best for fence; expensive kiln-dried is for houses.

Hemlock: poor insect- and decay resistance. The western species has light, uniform grain and finishes well. Eastern hemlock is a coarse-grained wood that gets hairy in the weather. Fine for rough fencing, though; horses love to scratch their chins on it.

Redwood: the giants of the Pacific Northwest coast, with wood that is naturally decay- and termite-resistant, weathers nicely, and finishes well. Perhaps the best of woods for outdoor use, and a natural for fences in the West.

DECAY RESISTANCE OF COMMON TREES

SPECIES	RANGE	RESISTANCE
Catalpa	Southeast	good
Bald Cypress	Coastal South	very good (scarce)
Red Cedar (eastern and western)	East and West	very good
Black Cherry	East and East-central	good (costly)
Douglas Fir	West	good
Black Locust	Applachians and North	the best
Larch (eastern and western)	East and West	very good
Honey Locust	East	very good
Red Mulberry	East	the best
Oak (post and white)	East	good
Osage Orange	Midwest, Southern Plains	the best
Eastern White Pine	East	good (scarce)
Longleaf Pine	Southeast	good (scarce)

PICKING YOUR LUMBER

Select board lengths that will divide into the required sizes most economically.

An 8-, 12- or even 16-foot 1 × 4 or 1 × 6 would be a good infill choice for a fence with 4-foot siding, though the 8-footer will usually be cheaper. For a 5-foot fence, a 10-footer would be better unless the 8-foot board is so cheap that 3 feet of waste don't matter. Do your homework and figure out what combination of board lengths will get you the lowest cost.

Choosing the Boards

Take a pair of gloves and a helper to choose your boards. Unless you know the lumberyard workers, pick your own – and don't think that you have to take boards as they crop up in the pile. Any yard worth patronizing will let you pick what you want so long as you keep the pile neat.

Ungraded, "mill-run" boards are stacked as they come off the saw; some are fine, others good only for kindling (though you may find a good 8 feet in a 12-foot board). The lumberyard has half of a board's price to negotiate with; be ready to dicker on substandard wood. Every pile of posts or strapped bundle of graded boards contains some that are warped, others with loose knots, cracks, or segments of rot that got by the graders at the mill. You'll usually find a layer of other builders' rejects on top of the pile. Set them aside, and leaf through the stack till you find what you need. Have the yard open another bundle if need be. If they object, find another yard.

Posts

Most wood decays or falls prey to termites or wood ants within months when sunk below ground; after all, it is no longer a vital, living thing, and nature wants to recycle it. Even the most rot-resistant heartwood red cedar or cypress won't last ten years, although good white cedar should last twenty-five. The longest-lasting fence posts are treated against insects and decay.

Once you could buy creosote and "penta" – pentachlorophenol – for treating your own wood, but they have been designated by the federal Environmental Protection Agency as too toxic for consumer use and have been withdrawn from the market. Besides, you had to cook posts in the stuff the way the telephone company does, or soak them for months in plastic-lined trenches or 55-gallon steel drums of preservative – all right if you are fencing acres of pasture or cattle range but uneconomical for a front-yard fence. If you *are* fencing large areas and need to treat your own posts, you can obtain restricted preservatives by permit; consult your extension agent, ask at the local feed store, or obtain the name of the paint distributor from your building-supply dealer. They will also know proper application and safety techniques.

Commercially pressure-treated (PT) posts have a greenish tinge. It will bleach to gray in time, or you can paint or stain over it. If treated to standards established by the wood-processors' associations, the posts have been infused to the core with CCA (chromated copper arsenate) or ACA (ammoniacal copper arsenate). These rot- and insect-deterrents will keep the wood sound for fifty years, while the same wood left untreated would fall over in three. If you've a choice, pick posts rated as "LP-22," the designation of The American Wood Preservers' Bureau for wood for below-ground use. Round fence posts are naturally rot-proof northern white cedar and lack the green tinge.

In our area PT posts are southern yellow pine. Posts made of that wood were sawed from logs rejected for cutting into more profitable boards. Posts needn't be flawless – just sound. Check each one carefully.

Posts of any type must be straight and unwarped in all dimensions. Look for ends with narrow, tight, straight grain. Posts with circular or wide grain will crack readily. Check all four sides for any obvious rot or insect damage, for deep splits or checks, and for knots that are loose or have a margin of sticky gum or wet, corky decay around them. A little *wane*, absence of a sharp corner because the sawyer got too close to the outside of the trunk, makes no structural difference, though wane on adjacent corners can reduce nailing area for your siding.

Rails and Stringers

Check the faces of each board for flaws and reject any with knots larger than a dime, especially small, hard, dark knots that look as though they want to pop out. Grain should flow evenly down the board; reject any with dark streaks in the grain.

Pick up one end of each length of 2 × 4 or other rail stock, pull it up close to your cheek, revolve the board, and sight down all four sides. They should be straight: the edges sharp and true, and the surface on a side in the same plane. Irregularities and warps go by names such as "cupping," "crooking" and "bowing," but they all make for difficult nailing and a potentially wavy fence.

Siding

Be especially picky with board infill. The thinner the wood, the easier it will warp. Choose clear wood with even, straight grain, true margins, and flat sides. Exposed to the weather, experiencing continual expansion and contraction, under alternating hot-cold and wet-dry conditions, knots are sure to work out in time, and big swirly grain patterns can crack and either bow or break.

A CAUTION

Fair Warning: Much of what passes as grade-1 lumber today wouldn't have passed as grade-2 years ago when older trees were being cut by firms under less economic pressure than today's timber-products industry endures. Some fencing contractors sell spruce or balsam fir as cedar, and much true cedar being sold (especially in cheap stockade fence shipped already stapled together on slim rails from the Great White North) is young and almost green; these fences won't last half as long as fences made of good wood. Some yards will pass off landscape timbers dipped briefly in green stuff (providing surface bug-proofing that won't last five years) as pressure-treated. *Caveat fencer!*

Some pressure-treated stock is put through such a quick fix that it comes out brittle, so brittle that it is stressed and potentially weakened to the point that a horse can knock over a 6-×-6 post inside of a few months. I've had one apparently perfect PT 4 × 4 × 12 warp 45 degrees in two years' time. Your best guarantee (aside from years of experience in the timber-products business) is the reputation of the firm you buy from. The old rule holds true in fencing: you get what you pay for.

I know from experience that it's easy to be tempted by cheap lumber; after all, the fence sits out in the weather and doesn't support anything. Seeking bargains is one thing; buying poor lumber is another. I have some El Cheapo fence boards that looked good when they were new, but over only four years some of them have bowed and split along knots that looked sound to me when purchased. Two boards broke clean in half.

You will be living with your fence for a long time and may regret saving a few pennies per board foot. I recommend buying the best lumber you can find.

STORAGE

If you must hold wood outdoors before using it, stack posts on level ground where they won't warp. Stack flat board on *battens* – thin boards, obtained from the yard, your own scrap, furring, or lath, laid between wood and ground and between each layer of stacked boards. If you are using wood that was stored inside, keep it covered – or better – prime or stain it immediately (and then keep it covered) till the fence goes up. See the section on finishes for wood fences, below.

LAYOUT AND BUILDING TOOLS	
Stakes	Wheelbarrow
Mason's cord	for gravel
Angles	for concrete
Carpenter's angle	Boards for tampers
Try square	Hammer
Plumb bob/chalk line	Nails
Post-hole digger	Nail puller
Prybar/rock pry	Hand saw
Shovel	Circular power saw

BUILDING YOUR WOOD FENCE

First step in construction is to lay out the fence line – a more precise repeat of the trial string-and-stake fence. Be sure you are inside your property lines, and get neighbors' permission if your layout stakes impinge on their property.

Very carefully determine the correct location of each corner of your fence line from known reference points on your plat and fence plan – from survey markers, buildings, or roadways. Measure, don't pace off distances – and always measure once for the rough estimate and again for the final before you sink a stake or dig a post hole. Measuring twice applies to lumber as well. A local carpenter's saying goes: "There's no board-stretcher in the tool box." You can't tack on either lumber or land if you've measured short.

If your measuring is easy – say the fence lines run right along a sidewalk or other established boundary, just hammer in 2-foot-long stakes a foot or two beyond each corner post, so that cord extended along the fence lines from each stake will cross over the post hole. Put a nail in the middle of each stake, and string line tight between the nails along each fence line. If paving prevents sinking stakes, string from foot-high piers of brick, concrete block, or anything else that will stay put.

WOOD FENCE

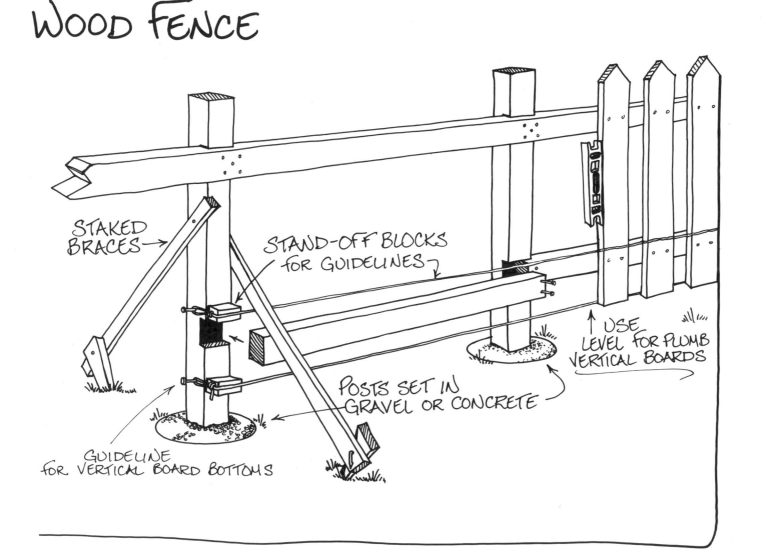

STAKED BRACES →

STAND-OFF BLOCKS FOR GUIDELINES

USE LEVEL FOR PLUMB VERTICAL BOARDS

POSTS SET IN GRAVEL OR CONCRETE

GUIDELINE FOR VERTICAL BOARD BOTTOMS

start to finish of the arc. For a fatter, lens-like curve, shorten the radius. For a flatter curve, lengthen it.

Adjusting batter boards.

Fence corners don't have to describe perfect right angles, but to assure those 90-degree turns if you need them, you can use any right angle: a carpenter's square or an unfolded sheet of newspaper laid on the ground.

Or, use the builder's 3/4/5 trick to find a right angle by measuring the triangle made by cutting off a corner. If one leg of the right angle made by the corner of a fence measures three units, and the other leg measures four units, the angle they describe will be a perfect 90 degrees *if* the diagonal between the legs measures five units. (Units can be feet or yards or multiples thereof; the longer the units, the more accurate the measurement.) If your triangle doesn't measure up, have a helper go down to a far stake and move the line till the 3-, 4-, and 5-unit legs make a perfect, tight triangle.

To describe a smooth arc – a portion of a circle – where the fence line curves:

1. **Run a straight line from where the arc begins to where it ends; you'll recall from junior-high-school math that this is a** *chord.*
2. **Find the midpoint of the chord and use a square or the 3/4/5 system to drop a perpendicular from the midpoint back away from the arc.**
3. **Now try to gauge where you'll find the center of the circle that the arc is a part of. Run a line from the perpendicular to the arc and adjust the length of the line (a** *radius)* **till it describes a fair curve from**

Batter Boards

If you are building anything but a rough-and-ready post-and-rail fence, put straight sections of line on "batter boards" to ensure that corners are square and lines level. Batter boards are 2-foot horizontal boards affixed to a pair of 1- to 1½-foot-high vertical posts, making an H shape. The verticals are hammered into the ground a foot or more beyond the end of the fence line. Sharpen the ground ends of the stakes well so they'll penetrate sod easily. You'll need a pair of batter boards to support intersecting layout lines at each corner or turn in the fence line.

Cross members of your batter boards should be high enough above the ground that the layout line will clear any rises along the fence line. But keep the line as low to the ground as possible for easiest post-hole spotting. Fix the layout cord to cross members of batter boards with large loops so the line can be adjusted easily; tie the loop with a double-overhand square knot so it won't slip, and tighten up. Each time you move the loop, be sure it is centered on the horizontal so the line will not be skewed up or down.

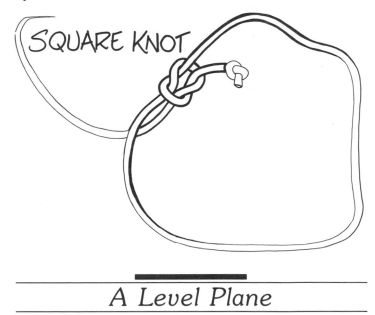

SQUARE KNOT

A Level Plane

For portions of the fence on even ground, batter-board cross members – thus, the cords attached to them – should be in the same level plane, giving you a uniform plane of reference all along the fence line. Even if you don't plan on installing perfectly level rails as in a stepped-bay fence, a level building platform, even if it's only an imaginary plane, provides a sense of certitude and professionalism.

First level the cross member of the batter board that is on the highest elevation along the fence line.

Lay a true board with a spirit level on it between that batter board's cross member and the horizontal of the adjacent batter board (that will support the crossing fence line). Sink the second batter board till the connector board is level. Then level the horizontal of the second batter board.

Run a line between one leveled batter board and another batter board at the end of that segment of fence line. Unless you know your knots well enough to tie a running bowline, fasten the cord to the batter board with a square knot – but leave a yard of twine at the end so you can tighten it later if need be by wrapping the loose end several times around the batter board. Stretch the cord drum tight and tap the new batter board in till the line level indicates that the cord is level.

Level the horizontal on that batter board. Then lay a connector board between adjacent batter boards and repeat the leveling process.

A snapline plumb bob suspended from the level line indicates location for a post.

Now repeat the line-leveling sequence – then level the next pair of batter boards, lay another level line – and continue on till the fence lines are all laid out. It will take some adjusting, but once all lines and all batter boards are level, your level plane is established.

If the line runs so far that it begins to sag (is level only at the center) install a "good soldier" – a support stake – at midline.

If the ground drops enough that the layout line is more than 2 feet above the soil, I step it down by sinking a tall post in the dip, tying off the higher level line, and starting another level line a foot lower down on the post.

Post-hole Locations

Once the line is set, measure carefully along it from where lines cross at corner-post locations, marking the center of each post hole on the string with a piece of tape or colored chalk. Make marks that can be changed easily. Under each mark stick a nail through a piece of cloth or colored-plastic sheeting and into the ground. From your scale drawing and the mockup you should know approximate distances between posts, but the real world will come up different, I promise.

Final Spacing

Prefab fence bays are usually built to be 8 feet "on center" – that is from the center of one post to the center of the next. Space your post holes accordingly, precisely 8 feet apart.

With split-rail fence, where the beveled ends of two rails overlap for 6 inches within the mortise drilled through each post, you have an inch or so at each post to fudge. Rails are usually cut to be an even 8 or 10 feet plus 6 inches of overlap for each end. So long as your marks are a true 8 feet apart, you can locate the post holes fairly casually. Again, with board fences where rails are butt-nailed on the front, top, or back of posts, you have perhaps ½- or ¼-inch per bay to fudge. (You can adjust when you nail up the infill.) For these fences, mark post locations by looking directly down from the mark on the line to the ground.

But in precision fencing – with mortised joints or using insets where components are prefabricated in the shop and measurements must be precise, use a plumb bob to spot post holes. Hang the plumb bob at the mark on the line and place the post hole carefully where the bob points.

TAMPING HOLE BOTTOMS FOR LEVEL-RAILED FENCE ON ROLLING GROUND

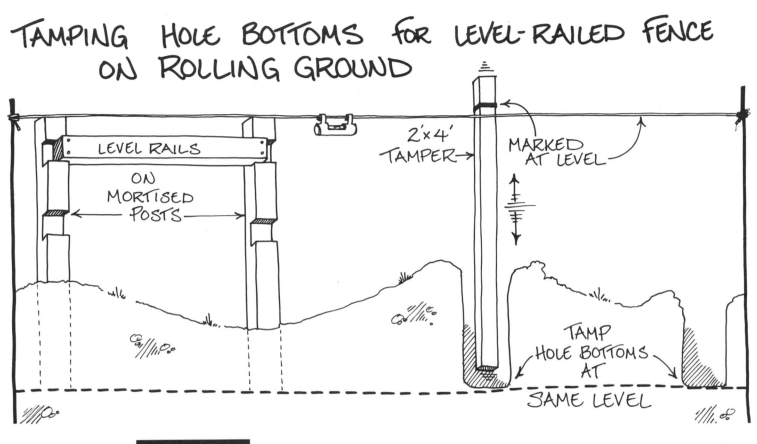

LEVEL RAILS
ON MORTISED POSTS
2'x4' TAMPER
MARKED AT LEVEL
TAMP HOLE BOTTOMS AT SAME LEVEL

Digging Post Holes

If you have laid out the fence line with simple stakes, be sure the post-hole locations are accurately lined up, pull the cord from one stake of each line, move the cord out of the way, and dig the holes. You should put in your end posts, then use the line strung from them to position each line post as it goes into its hole.

If you're using batter boards, cut a notch or make a waterproof mark where lines loop over the horizontals. Now move each line so it will be out of the way for post-hole digging – removing the line altogether if need be. *Don't remove stakes or batter boards.*

If the fence is prefabricated, trial-fit posts and rails by laying them flat on the ground along the line before you begin digging – just to be sure you've measured correctly.

DEPTH

An old rule of thumb is to dig a post hole to be half as deep as the post is high: two feet for a 4-foot fence, 3 feet for a 6-footer. In general, corner posts and gate posts should be half again as deep as line posts – the less critical supports between ends, corners, and gates. If you live in snow country, the ground will freeze and heave anything sunk too shallowly (you'll find more details on heaving in the stone-building chapter). New England fencers I've talked to go down from 2 feet to 4 feet for ornamental fence (deeper for thinner posts), and heaving *is* a problem here. I find that digging below 2 feet is unrewarding (and devilishly hard) work, but I put corners and gate posts down as near to a yard deep as my ambition permits. I suggest that you consult a contractor or fencing professional for post depths if you live in the far north, or in an area of soft ground.

The easiest way to dig post holes is to point out the locations and let somebody else do the digging with a power auger or post driver on the back of a tractor. If your post locations are well marked, a contractor can dig the holes in any diameter you want in a few minutes and for a few dollars each. They should put in at least 8-inch-wide holes for 4-inch posts in good-draining soils and increase to a 12-inch hole in clays. In adobe or hardpan that doesn't drain at all, you may need to dig a real pit and fill it with gravel to keep posts from rotting. If your soil is not a typical loam, call a fencing contractor for advice.

Old-timers used hand augers – large screw-shaped blades on a rod with a T handle at the top. The auger shaved off soil and brought it to the top of a post hole in a ribbon. Today hand augers reside quite properly in museums dedicated to the hard life lived by farmers of the premachine age. You can rent (or buy) one- or two-person augers powered by gasoline engines. These are hairy little machines that exert a great deal of torque; all that keeps the auger from lodging in the soil – to send the power head and anyone attached thereto spinning around – is your own weight and muscle. They are okay for soft soils, monsters in hard soils, and worthless in soils full of rocks much larger than your fist.

THE CLAMSHELL

To hand-dig posts for rail fence, I remove sod and soil to a depth of 2 feet or more in as small-diameter a hole as I can manage with a clamshell post-hole digger. That simple tool, which operates like a giant pair of tongs with two narrow shovels hinged together on one end, can be purchased or hired from any equipment-rental firm. Sears Roebuck will rent you a complete fence installation kit including a clamshell digger if you leave a security deposit, whether you purchase fencing materials from them or not. See the catalogue sales desk at any Sears store.

For more precision hole placement I use a sod knife – a small machete – to cut a circle around the nail-and-cloth marker (the hole double the diameter of the post) and dig as precise a hole as I can manage.

For end and gate posts for any post in problem soils, it is best to scoop out the sides of the hole near the bottom in a teardrop or flask shape to hold a concrete or tamped anchor. You can angle in with the clamshell to get that done, though a hand trowel makes a neater job.

Rocks up to the size of two clasped hands together will come out with the clamshell, though sometimes it takes some hand digging with a garden trowel to dislodge irregular ones. Still larger rocks – melon size – force you to enlarge the hole with a shovel and dig around them.

Really big rocks can pose a major problem. Under even the most nicely leveled lawns in many areas you can encounter buried boulders or solid ledge with nothing between it and China but more rock. You don't know the size of the rock you've hit till you investigate. If the stone is less than a foot down, I dig around till I find an edge and – if a prybar under the rock elicits movement indicating manageable size – I excavate the thing (and often as not find a "sister rock" just below it). If the stone proves to be immovable, and/or is well over a foot down, I use a star drill to punch a hole in it right over the post marker on the layout line.

DRILLING ROCK

An electric hand drill with a carbide bit or a rock-boring stone will wear a hole in rock, but to use it you need to get electricity to the fence line. I hand-drill holes in rock by repeatedly hammering on and twisting a ½-inch *star drill* – a steel rod with a star-shaped hardened bit end that is hit with a mallet to cut into the stone, rotated, and hit again. I drill, twist, and scoop out dust till I have a hole an inch or more deep, and use a steel pin (a ⅜-inch screw-bolt with the head sawed off once it's threaded into a ¼-inch pilot hole drilled in the end of the post) to hold the post to the rock. When the post is pinned to the rock, I fill the post hole with concrete, particularly if it's an end, corner, or gate post.

An unattractive alternative is to split the rock. That takes a hired pneumatic drill or repeated clobbering with a sledgehammer and chisels or a hardened-steel point (the prybar) over which you drop a post-driver or a length of heavy steel pipe with one end welded closed. The pipe is run down over the end of the prybar like a sleeve and repeatedly lifted and let fall. In my experience, it doesn't work on granitelike hard rock or soft rocks much over a foot thick. If I encountered more than one large rock along a fence line, I'd move the fence line or call in a backhoe (and probably ask them to bring the auger along to finish drilling post holes).

The clamshell post-hole digger in action.

Posts in Holes

With your holes in, lay out posts on the ground, ends to the post holes. If the rails are already cut, lay them out too in a trial match (if you haven't already) just to be sure the post holes are spaced properly.

Fill each post hole with 4 to 6 inches of gravel and tamp it well. I use the post itself as a tamper.

Posts to be sunk long – with tops that will be evened off after rails are affixed – can be set in casually so long as they don't go too deep. That method requires cutting off posts in the vertical position – awkward with a hand saw and dangerous with a power saw. I don't recommend it; better to buy or precut posts to length and sink precision post holes.

HOLES FOR PRECUT POSTS

Precut posts or those that are worked or inletted in any way before installation must be set to a precise depth. For precut posts in fences that will follow the ground contour, I make a hole-bottom depth-gauge/tamper from a 2 × 4 with two sturdy crosspieces nailed on and pound the gravel fill down to the desired level (2 feet below ground level, usually).

For fences with precut posts that are to be built with post tops and rails level (in level steps on sloping ground), I dig holes deeper than needed, then restring the level line. Each post must be sunk so that its base is a given distance below the level line (so the bottoms of all posts are on the same level). I mark that distance off on a 2 × 4 and tamp in gravel till the mark reaches the level line.

Do Your Inletting

If you planned for dadoed or mortised joints, now is the time to measure posts carefully and cut the joints. I would advise first-time fencers to set corner posts – with joint locations marked but not cut – in the ground and check heights and mortise locations once again with the mason's line before cutting the joints.

To make mortises, use the try square to mark rail-sized holes at opposite sides of the post, and use a power drill with a spade bit to remove as much wood as possible from the mortise holes. (Using a hand drill, have a helper sight carefully from two sides of the work to be sure you drill straight down.) Then clean out and square the mortise with chisels.

Using a 2 × 4 to firm soil around a post.

Cutting tenons at rail ends takes only two saw cuts – to remove a 1½-inch to 2-inch-deep, square notch from the end of each rail. Be sure you preplan the tenon arrangement of the whole fence so tenons will overlap. You can alternate cut-out locations on boards, or cut all boards with notches on the same side and place one rail bottom up, the next top up.

To make full dados, mark horizontal rail-end-sized cuts at opposite sides of the post, and make a series of ½-inch saw cuts (*kerfs*) in the wood, as close together as possible. Don't cut over the line you marked, and your dados won't be too wide. Knock out the waste with a hammer and smooth the interior of the dado with a chisel. After inserting the rails, toenail them to the posts.

A partial dado – a pointed notch – can be cut into posts to accept a properly beveled rail end. That is an *effective* way to set rails following contours in rolling ground; cut the notch to accept the square rail. Each notch must be custom-cut, and that takes patient measuring.

Corners in First

Put in your corner posts first unless you are using dado or mortised joints – where rails must be installed as each post goes in. An assistant is a great help in any fencing, but one is almost essential to hold up the far end of rails while you insert them into mortises or dados and then to keep the loose boards square and together while you tamp in the posts. Don't nail housed joints together till the whole fence is in, plumb, and square.

With a simple stake-and-line layout, cinch a line-up cord around the base of installed corner posts. Tack a *stand-off block* of standard-sized wood between the string and each post; I use a length of ¾- × 1½-inch furring strip.

Then, using a third stand-off block as a gauge, set line posts so they are one block's distance from the string; that way, you won't crowd the line and bow the fence.

Using batter boards, the line is reaffixed to the batter board horizontals a precise *half-post-width* plus stand-off block distance outboard of the marks denoting the original center-to-center fence line. Tack stand-off blocks on end posts and line them up so the blocks just touch the line and so the dot on the line indicating post location is at the midline of the post. Install line posts with a stand-off-block gauge. An amateur should always use stand-off blocks – and never set a whole fence directly "on the line." You are bound to crowd the line and bow the finished fence (and for the next forty or fifty years, everyone walking along the fence will form a considered judgment about your fence-making skills).

Setting Posts

To firm the post in place, I pour in enough gravel to keep the post from wobbling, level it in both vertical dimensions with the 2-foot-long spirit level, and tamp the gravel till it is fairly secure. If you find it difficult to keep the post plumb with one hand and tamp with the other, use support braces. Nail long support braces to stakes set out at a right angle to the post, start a nail in the post end of the support boards and tack them in once the board is plumb in both dimensions.

If the ground is soft or the post must stand up to wind or drifting snow, it can be anchored with a concrete collar. (See the chapter on mortared walls for details.)

For most fences, ends and corners can be anchored with alternating layers of soil and gravel – the soil to add firmness, the gravel to provide drainage and weight. I like to add in layers that compact to 3 or 4 inches when tamped down – two shovelsful per layer, distributed around the hole and tamped well. Shovel and tamp, shovel and tamp, till you reach the top. It is best to finish off with a layer of soil, tamped in a cone around the post

to shed water. Line posts needn't be so well anchored; the soil and gravel layers can be thicker, and for low fences in a good-compacting soil, firmly tamped soil alone will do.

Please think through final fence assembly before sinking all your posts. If you will be toenailing rails or butting them to post faces – assembling the fence on site – you can put in the entire post line at once. The same goes for a post-and-rail fence with generous mortises; set in all the posts, slip in the rails, and that's that. You can replace rails just as readily.

Prefab Fences

But with any fence where ends of rails are trimmed to fit into inletted posts, you must assemble each bay as you set posts. This is the way you put up the typical prefab stockade, picket, or grapestake fence where a whole bay of siding is prenailed to rails with ends rounded to dowels which fit tightly into predrilled holes in round posts. One post goes in the ground, you slip the rail ends of one end of a bay into its holes, tap a post on the other end, set that post in the ground, and on it goes.

Trimming Post Tops

Even-off random-length posts before the rails go on so you can saw them from any side and angle without interference.

For fences that will follow ground contours, you can cut a measuring board and use it to mark off the height of each post. Then, with a level or try square, carry the line from the mark all around the cut-off.

If the fence is level, determine height of one post, string a chalk line to the other end post, and use the line level to level it. Hold the chalk line tight, pull it out, and snap it several times to deposit a clear mark on each post. If the fence is on a grade, the chalk line will be slanted. String the line between down-hill faces of end posts. Mark the cut-off line by carrying a level line around the *lower* edge of the chalk mark.

While you are at it, you can snap off locations for the tops of each rail or stringer. *Always make separate measurements from the top of the post down to mark out stringer locations – not from the bottom up or from stringer location to stringer location.*

You can use a hand saw to trim posts, though sawing sideways is awkward. Faster is an electric circular saw.

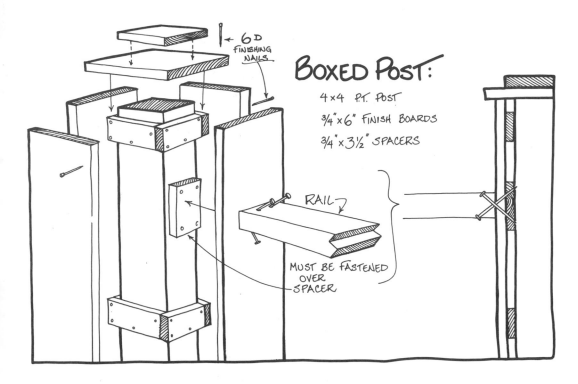

BOXED POST:

4 × 4 P.T. POST
3/4" × 6" FINISH BOARDS
3/4" × 3 1/2" SPACERS

6 D FINISHING NAILS

RAIL

MUST BE FASTENED OVER SPACER

Be sure the blade is good and sharp; you lack the help of gravity and have little leverage working at arms' length, and a dull blade can skip out of the cut. Use eye protection, and set yourself in a balanced and well-supported position with the saw at a comfortable height. Set depth of the blade to go halfway through the post, and cut from all four sides. Always hold the saw with both hands – pressing hard against the post. If the saw cut or kerf is too shallow to sever the post, finish the job with the hand saw. If the cut is messy looking (easy to do), cut square caps for your posts and resolve to precut posts and dig measured post holes next fence.

Boxed Posts

Now is the time to ornament or flesh out posts by boxing them with planks, especially for fences with rails to be butt nailed or fastened with brackets only. Mortising through a box is possible, but it's time-consuming, and the cut-outs are sure to admit rot unless you caulk them every few years. A single veneer of nominal 1-inch boards can hide the bilious tinge of a square PT post; cut four boards to post length and to post width plus a generous 3/4-inch. To broaden even further, ring the post at top, bottom, and at rail locations with spacers – any depth you like. Spacers at rail height must be at least rail-width, and an inch or two extra at top and bottom wouldn't hurt.

Cap the post with a square board. Or give it a rimmed hat – one board that is 1/2-inch or more bigger all around than the post, and atop that, a post-sized board. This thin decorative wood may want to split. It has no supporting function, so I would nail it up with box nails – skinny little nails that you won't want to use elsewhere in the fence. If boards still split, drill pilot holes for the nails. Before adding the cap, soak bottoms of cap boards, ends of boxing boards, and the post top with waterproofer.

Adding Stringers and Infill to Custom Fences

Now come the nails, screws, or bolts. Nails are cheapest and quickest to go in – and hardest to get out. I would bolt stringers to posts only when making a massive livestock fence. Screws are useful primarily to fasten gate hardware, though you may wish to screw a really elegant fence together. Drill pilot holes, countersink to bury the screw heads, and glue wooden plugs over the heads of the screws to keep the metal from corroding.

Nails come in three main types: finish, box, and common. Finish nails don't have much of a head and are good only for attaching thin wood trim. Box nails will hold light boards well enough but bend easily under an amateur-wielded hammer. Standard-thickness, flat-headed (common) steel wire nails that are *hand-dipped galvanized* (coated with zinc to resist rust for years) are best. Don't save a few cents and get ungalvanized. They will erupt in brown rust under paint or leave gray streaks down weathered fence after a few weeks of rain. Aluminum nails won't corrode noticeably, but they are expensive and fat for their length.

Nails are sized in an ancient British scale according to the one-time price for a hundred in big old copper pennies, abbreviated as so many "d." A nail that once sold at 100 for 6 pence is a 6-penny, or 6d, nail.

ALL ABOUT NAILS
(hand-dipped galvanized common)

SIZE	LENGTH	NUMBER PER POUND
2d	1 inch	870
4d	1½ inches	310
6d	2 inches	180
8d	2½ inches	100
10d	3 inches	70
12d	3¼ inches	65
16d	3½ inches	50

One glossy fencing book says to use nails that are at least three times as long as the wood being nailed on is thick. To fasten a 2 × 4 to a 4 × 4, you'd be hammering in a 4½-inch railroad spike that's longer than the post is wide. The spike would split the 2 × 4 before it got halfway through.

Use common sense (in interpreting anything you read, present company included). For 2 × 4s being nailed to 4 × 4s, I use 3-inch-long 10d nails. If they split the end of the first board, I go smaller or drill pilot holes. Those are holes just a bit smaller around than the nail and drilled only through the *nailer* – the stock being nailed on; you want the nail to have to force into the post (the *nailee?*). For ¾-inch-thick, 1-inch nominal flat boards going onto 2 × 4 stringers, I follow the rule and buy 2¼-inch 7d nails if I can get them. Seven-pennys aren't always readily available, though, and 6d will do. Eights will split the wood. (To reduce splitting by nails being put in toward the ends of boards, blunt the ends of nails with a couple of hammer taps.)

If you are sure of your measurements, you can trim your stringers and infill in the comfort of shop or garage, haul them to the job, and nail up a fence in one day. I'm never that sure of my measurements, and so I fit and cut each bay individually.

I use a pair of sawhorses made from metal sawhorse brackets and 36-inch lengths of cheap 2 × 4s and one of those portable work benches with clamps to hold the boards. I set the little bench at sawhorse height and can work boards of any length easily.

Sawing Boards

To cut boards, measure twice and mark the top and both sides with a try square. A fat black-and-red carpenter's pencil with a flat lead will make you feel like a pro. (Get soft lead that you can wear sharp; hard leads break less easily, but you practically have to gouge grooves in the wood to make a mark, and sharpening the lead takes sandpaper or a knife.)

Immobilize the board at a comfortable height – for me, that's at midthigh level so I can bend into the saw.

Place the blade of your crosscut saw to the scrap side of your mark, so you will "save the line" you marked on the board. Hold the saw perpendicular to the board, your off-hand leaning down on the work, fingers gripping the edge of the board, heel of your hand supporting the blade gently. Draw the blade backward slowly several times to make a starting notch in the wood (don't pull fast or the blade will skip and scratch you). Now draw the saw back and push it briskly forward in a natural, smooth arm motion.

Saw away like that, keeping the blade even with lines on all sides of the work to cut square. Do not push down or you'll bind the saw; a well-sharpened crosscut saw will do all the work, all you have to do is move it back and forth. It should make a sharp *zzssssssst* sound when you cut. A high squeak means you are cutting too fast or have a dull saw. A grinding sound and a blade that skips say you are sawing too slow.

With electric circular saws, the procedure is similar. Always rest the body of the saw – the *shoe* – on the long board, not the short section to be cut off, or you can get an angled cut. Siting to save the line is the same, but till you gain experience you should start each cut with a series of little notches well away from the line, working down toward the final cut. The blade makes a wide kerf; be sure you save the line.

If you are new to power saws, please read the directions that come with the machine and practice on several pieces of scrap before trying fence stock. Always have both hands firmly grasping the saw any time you pull the trigger. *Do not* try to remove or tie up the spring-loaded blade guard, even though it does get in the way a lot. I am short the ends of two fingers that show what happens when you get careless with power equipment.

Predrilling holes for a toenailed rail.

"Saving the line."

Be sure you know where the cord is before each cut; severing it and having a live electric cord binding up in the blade housing can be a shocking experience. Always hold the saw from a solid stance and firmly, with both hands. (I know I just said that, but it bears repeating.) Cutting thick stock, check blade depth before you saw to be sure you are cutting through.

Stringers

Measure your rails twice against posts in place, and cut them to size. Don't forget to use the try square to mark a cut on all sides of the board so you can guide the saw all the way through. Making angled cuts in rails negotiating a grade takes some careful thought, measuring, and sawing. If you're using a power saw, you have to adjust the shoe to cut at an angle. The blade's working depth is reduced, and you may not be able to cut through a 2 × 4. Finish these cuts with a hand saw.

Important: Holes and end cuts in wood admit water, which encourages rot. Before joining rails to posts, soak ends of rails and any inletted joints with waterproofer or primer. While you are at it, soak the cut tops of the posts also. Then nail the rails or stringers on.

Start all nails in rails being butt-joined *before* you take them to the post. If rails split even a little, drill pilot holes. Hammer the nails completely through the stringer, so the tip points out just a tiny bit to hold the board in

place on the post. Then tap the rail into the joint so the nail tips scar only wood that the joint will hide. This toehold is especially helpful with boards being toenailed on, with nails going through the board at an angle. It is hard to hold the board in place with one hand and nail it on with a hammer held in the other. (If you have trouble toenailing, tack on nailing rests – small wood strips fastened on temporarily to hold the stringers while you fasten them.)

Don't use nails at all in rails going into mortises of split-rail fences. Gravity will hold them, and you can replace a broken rail much more easily if it isn't nailed.

In dadoed and other mortised joints, the strength is in the joint, not the fastener. Use nails or pegs only to keep the boards from coming apart.

Adding the Infill

The hard part is done. Now, the siding should go up almost as fast as you can cut the boards.

For insert siding: plywood, plastic, or individual boards are set into rails and sandwiched between *keepers* – thin, sawed wood cleats or lengths of molding. I don't trust remote measurements but measure each piece of infill against its frame. (Or I measure a master board for each bay of a multiboard panel.) Once I'm sure the infill fits, I nail on the keepers, set in the infill, and snug it in place with more cleats.

If fence boards are not presawed, draw a level line along their tops and saw a level fence top.

Important: If you use plywood panels, soak edges with a top-quality exterior-grade sealer before nailing everything together.

Fastening vertical boards to butt-joined stringers, all you have to do is cut them the right length, space them correctly, be sure they are vertical (or slanted at the correct angle if you like canted infill), and that you hit stringers and not thin air when you nail the infill up.

Don't be tempted to rush to see the job completed. It's easy to botch the easy part and end up with a sloppy siding job that doesn't do justice to your framing efforts.

You can string a cord from the bottom of posts and use it to line up infill boards. If the posts are even with or higher than the infill, you can string a line from the tops of posts. Have the line level if the rails are level or arranged a precise distance above or below rails if the fence follows the land.

If the fence follows rolling country, you can use a space block; put a block as high as you want boards to run above ground under siding boards or pickets and attach each board that distance from the ground. That will give a smooth-looking fence with slightly up- and down-stepped siding-board tops. A pointed or rounded top on pickets or butted boards looks better than square. If siding is nailed on continuously without the visual relief of exposed posts, the fence may look like a giant millipede.

I like to make up a spacer – a siding-placement jig – for each fence. You can make one for any board fence. Cut a length of wood with a cleat that rests over the top and/or bottom rail. A lateral projection on top or bottom can hold the board in place for precise placement, marks on the front can show nailing levels, and a torpedo or line level affixed with elastic or a more sturdy fastener will check plumb.

Nailing

You don't want to leave hammer dents in your siding boards. Practice a little in delivering a square hammer blow – so the face of the hammer hits the nail flat, not at an angle. Woodworking hammers have a slightly rounded face so that if you hit the nail dead center, there will be no little round dimple in the wood. For sinking toe-nails home and for setting finish nails, I use a nail-set – a sharp-ended punch. (Be sure that the punch you use is tempered to be hit; don't use a mechanic's line-up punch that can shatter if struck.)

Kick Boards

An ornament that can be designed in or added to bring texture to almost any board or picket fence after it is completed is a kick board, a horizontal run of plank at ground level. These boards can frame vertical siding boards for an effect that may not appear desirable till the entire fence is up. They are easily installed.

A kick board will give the fence a solid visual base and will carry the siding down to ground level to keep small furry beasts from coming in to mow down your emerging green-bean seedlings. If it is inset, it will add depth and texture to the design, visually anchoring the fence to the ground.

Get 1-inch white cedar or softwood boards that are pressure treated to above-ground tolerances. Look for the Wood Preservers Bureau classification LP-2.

Snap a chalk line just below the lower nailing line of the siding. Set a circular-saw blade to cut only the ¾-inch infill wood, and remove the bottom few inches of the boards. Then a 1-by kick board of PT stock can be trimmed to size and nailed to the portion of rail showing. If nails are too close to the rail bottom, cut off siding at or below rail level and nail the kick board to the back of the lower rail. That will give the kick board an inset look from the front, a protruding look from the rear.

To inset the kick board, cut off siding just at the rail bottom. Frame the back of the lower surface of the lower rail and insides of posts with 1- × 1-inch wood. Then fit kick boards into the opening – wedging them in with more cleats. Nailing those cleats is a challenge. Use finishing nails, start them all in the cleat, and use a long nail-set to hammer them home.

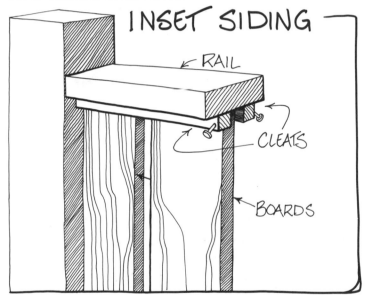

INSET SIDING

RAIL

CLEATS

BOARDS

Horizontal Siding

If you opt for clapboards or other horizontal siding, you'll have to frame the bays. Measure, cut, and toenail verticals between rails at a minimum of 16-inch intervals along each bay. If rails are inset, nail verticals alongside posts too to hold cut ends. Then measure and nail on your siding. If the wood is thin as conventional clapboarding, use shingle nails.

Speaking of shingles, a shingled fence can be a dazzler. Sheathe your bays with particle board, and shingle over it. A cap molding will be needed on top; I've seen small gabled roofs built atop shingled fences. The back of the fence will be all shingle-nail-punched particle-board and unsightly. You'll probably want to sheathe and shingle that, too.

FINISH

The fence should be finished to match its surroundings. In Hannibal, Missouri and like environs you could mix up your own whitewash of calcium carbonate (lime or whiting) and water and see if the family lad can carry off a Tom Sawyer routine. Whitewash only lasts a few months. For a more permanent finish your choices are paint, stain, bleach, or natural weathering.

Not many woods weather naturally to the lovely gray of a cypress or white cedar. Most common wood posts and all lumberyard softwood boards turn blotchy brown before aging to a blotchy gray. This can be attractive in a rustic setting if you don't realize that it is a mistake, but to look their best and last longest most fences need a finish. The fence is as much a part of the home setting as the house, and I suggest you begin your investigation of finishes for fence with a trip to a full-line house-paint store. The staff will know what primers and paints go together and will be able to suggest the proper mixtures to apply to problem woods. For example you beg for staining if you use some water-based primers with redwood and western red cedar. Open-pored woods tend to waterlog and rot when covered with some semigloss and flat finishes. In humid climates finishes should contain mold inhibiters or your fence can break out in a case of mildew. And the best long-term preservative for fence, a sealer under stain, or primer/sealer under paint, must be chosen for compatibility both with wood and the final finish. There's no aspect of fencing that calls for seasoned advice so much as finishing a wood fence. Fortunately the advice comes free with the paint.

One neat trick to take the raw look off a new fence is to paint with a gray stain/bleach the paint store can mix for you. The stain will weather off in time, leaving a nice gray color. A bleach will remove surface color from any wood. It is caustic stuff and needs to be hosed or rained on to work, so won't do the grass much good. You also have to wait a matter of months between its application and use of water repellents and stains. Here, too, I'd seek the free advice of a paint expert.

Paint for Smooth Boards

Paint is traditional for fences of pickets or planed boards – white more traditional than other colors. Be sure the wood is dry: don't paint green wood for three months, and after a rain, wait for several days of dry, hot weather to paint anything. Seal the fence with exterior-grade primer (oil-base is always recommended) that will soak into and bond to the wood. The paint bonds to the primer.

Oil-based paints are costly but last longest. If you use them, you must stock up on thinner to clean brushes, yourself, and any small helpers. Water-based latex final coats are easiest to apply and clean up. Don't expect the first coat to go far, no matter the claims on the label: 150 square feet per gallon of stain is good coverage for thirsty new siding. But primed wood will take paint well; 350 square feet per gallon of finish paint is a reasonable expectation on smooth wood. Rough-sawn planks will drink up any finish.

STAINS

Paint does need renewal every eight years or so. But a sealed and stained fence can go for decades without attention. For longest life, you should apply a sealer/water repellent and let it cure for two months. Then apply the stain. All stains accent wood's grain rather than hide it, but semitransparent stains cover less than "color" stains. Pick your shade, color, and transparency. Have all paints and stains well shaken when purchased; pigment settles and must be pried up off the can bottom and mixed through the distillates. Doing it by hand is tedious.

Brushes are traditional for putting on finishes, but they wear the unpracticed arm to a frazzle on a long fence. Rollers are quicker but only work on smooth wood and can't get between pickets. Easiest is a rented sprayer; I've used one to apply sealers and stain, primers and paint. The work goes quickly, and I recommend it. With oil coverings, get a lot of thinner to clean out containers, lines, and spray guns.

Just be sure you pick a windless day to paint. Wind blows all manner of loose stuff into the paint or stain: grass, dust, and leaves blow into the can and join the finish on the fence. The invaders must be picked out before the finish dries – or, when dry, the surface must be scraped, sanded flat, and refinished.

Do not believe the ads that tell you that if clear finishes such as polyurethane can protect bowling alleys they will cover anything. Anything indoors, maybe, but not fences. The finishes don't soak in and will peel off any wood exposed to water. I know: I painted a boat with the stuff once and spent years peeling it off. I could hide the boat in our barn, but you can't do that with the front-yard fence.

It is neatest to pull a ground cloth along with you as you paint to keep paint or stain off the grass and plantings. You may think that a few paint drops on the ivy won't be noticed, but they will look so wildly unnatural that you'll want to snip off every spotted leaf and grub out every tuft of besmirched crabgrass. I know, because I've made that mistake, too.

BUILDING AND INSTALLING WOOD GATES

The gate is centerpiece to your fence, first passage point to your home. Extend visitors a wide-armed welcome with a low, open-work gate having exposed hinges and a broad and obvious thumb latch. If you are a bit standoffish, a gate disguised as just another bay in the fence bids the passerby to mind his own affairs and keep walking. Or, if you cherish your privacy, forbid passage with a massive looking bolt on a man-high gate of 2-inch oak.

You can have a single gate or a pair – one at each end of a broad drive. You can buy metal gates to hang on wooden fence posts; they are discussed elsewhere. And you can commission architectural gates with glass windows, ornate metal scrollwork, or other striking effects from an artisan. I'll leave the building and hanging of more complex gates to professionals and advise you to do the same. Let's both stick to building wooden gates that are essentially shortened and strengthened bays hung on hinges and secured with a latch.

A plank gate on an old-time split rail fence.

A wrought iron hasp on a finely crafted double gate in a bilevel picket fence.

CONSTRUCTION OPTIONS

You've sketched the external appearance of your gate in the fence plan and elevation drawing and have already sunk facing gate posts at whatever width suits your layout. Both hinge- and latch posts are deeper than ordinary line posts and are well anchored. To make gates you have three choices:

1. **Measure carefully and make up a gate on the garage floor or other flat space, then hope it fits. Best for experienced woodworkers.**

2. **Hang and build the gate in place. This makes most sense if the gate posts are anything but perfectly plumb and square. It is easier for the novice, if more time-consuming, but it's difficult with rounded gate posts.**

3. **Hang the gate's hinge post or *spine*, measure gate rails, braces, and a master length of siding in place—but build the gate on the flat. You measure the actual wood pieces in their actual locations but build the gate on the flat, with gravity and leverage in your favor. After spending ages building gates by methods 1 and 2, the last is the way I do it.**

Using the combination square with level to check that the hole for a gate eye-hinge is square.

Frames

Options in gate-frame design are two:

1. **A Z–gate**, where (vertical) infill is attached to two horizontal rails at top and bottom that are connected by a diagonal brace board to make the Z shape. This can be a good light gate if well fastened, but it won't stand up long to heavy use.

2. **A stronger design is a box-frame gate**, built with horizontal top and bottom cross rails connected by a vertical member at each end as well as by a diagonal brace board or a cable with a turnbuckle. If screwed and glued (not just nailed together), reinforced with plywood gussets, and well hinged to a stout and well-sunk post, the children can play Hi–oh, Silver on it for a generation.

Hardware: Hinges

Gate-hardware designs are varied, but practical choices are limited. To begin with, you will need two hinges for low gates, three for gates much bigger than 4 feet or wider than 3. Hinges come in four styles.

1. *Butt hinges.* Two rectangular plates are connected by a hinge pin. One plate is fastened to the spine of the gate, the other to the hinge post of the fence. Butt hinges can be face mounted on the back of the gate or hidden in the frame; either way they allow the gate to open one way only, as do the hinges on the doors in your house. Better butt hinges come with removable hinge pins.

2. *Strap hinges.* Long hinge plates, usually permanently pinned together are screwed to both the posts and rails of gate and fence. These distribute the load of the gate's weight over a greater area of gate and fence with more angular leverage, and are dimensionally stronger than butt hinges.

3. *Combinations* have one side a rectangular plate to go on the gate post and the other a strap to fasten to the gate.

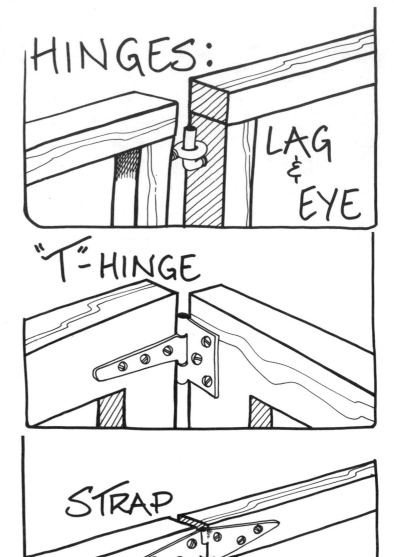

HINGES:

LAG & EYE

"T"-HINGE

STRAP

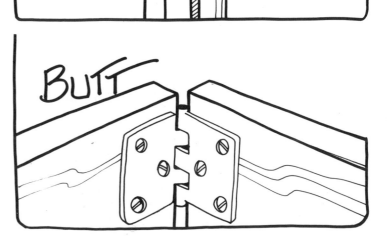

BUTT

4. *Lags* are stout L-shaped screws that thread into the gate post of the fence. The gate side of the hinge is a simple eye that slides down over the pin. This is the simplest and strongest gate hinge and the best type to use with rounded posts. Its use is limited to gates and fences made of thick wood stock; 2 × 4s are too thin to hold lags on a heavy gate.

Hardware: Latches

Gate latches come in three basic styles:

1. *External-mount.* From simple hooks to slide bolts to knob-operated lock-sets that are screwed to the outside of gate and post. Easiest to find and install.

2. *Through-latches.* With a latch string or lever-actuator on the outside of the gate and the latch inside. Installing one of these requires cutting through the gate. They range from simple string-operated pivoting wood latches to metal thumb latches to lock-sets that mortise into the gate and are similar to your front-door lock.

3. *Bails.* Wire or bentwood hoops, usually attached to the fence post, and pivot like the handle of a pail to cinch over the latch-side vertical member of the gate. They can also be fastened to gate and hoop over the fence post.

Hardware: Fasteners

Gates are subjected to constant stress from weather and normal in-and-out traffic, and from kids. The screws supplied with gate hardware are fine for cabinet woods or plastic but are seldom long or stout enough to hold in softwoods. They are often unplated common steel too, which will rust. I buy replacements right along with the gate hardware. Stainless steel is best, brass okay but soft. Get screws as long as possible: either just too short to go through the work, or longer than the work and intended to be filed or ground down. Get them as stout as possible too — but be sure that the heads are not too large to nest into the shallow cone-shaped countersink cast into the hinge plates.

Hardware: Stops

Butt and strap hinges on flat hinge posts limit the swing of a gate to 180 degrees (half a circle), but on a free-swinging eye-on-hook-type lag hinge, a gate can swing in almost a full circle. You need something to hold the gate firmly in place when it is closed and to limit swing. Also, without a stop the gate can swing beyond the working arc of a hinge, and its leverage will pull hinge fasteners from the wood. You can stop a gate with "stumble-pegs" – ground stakes – but they live up to their nickname. Most gates have stop-strips of wood fastened to the latch side of the gate or on the gate post to limit opening to one direction.

Gate stops take a continual beating, and it is best to make yours of hardwood. Two square strips of oak – one on the rear margin of the gate's latch-side vertical member and another on the latch post itself – make the neatest stop. Fix them on with long wood screws inserted through pilot holes.

If you're stopping the gate with a width of fence siding cut to extend from gate, fence (or both) into the gate opening, make it, too, of hardwood that is screwed and glued on.

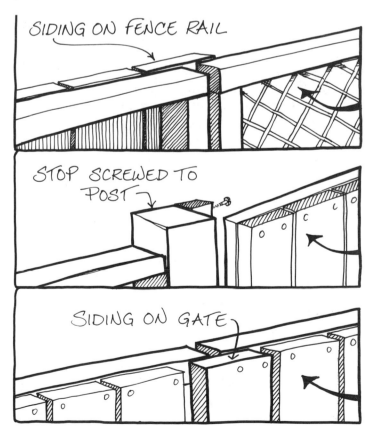

Wood

Choose your finest, hardest, clearest wood for the gate. Subjected to constant stress and vibration, a knotty gate spine will crack, and a twist-grained gate rail will split. Pick tight- and straight-grained wood that will grip fasteners securely. If you are using low-grade softwood for the fence, it is not a bad idea to purchase kiln-dried, premium structural fir, spruce, or redwood or even a hardwood for the gate frame — the spine in particular.

On a Hill

Most gates are square or rectangular and located on the level. If your gate is on a slope, you may have to angle the bottom margin of the siding; if so, be sure to hinge the gate on the *down-slope* side. If the gate is hinged on the short up-slope side, the longer down-slope dimension will hang up on the hill before the gate opens more than part way. You can also build a level sill at the bottom of the gate opening, filling in the triangle-shaped area of fence below it with gate siding. Then build a level-bottomed gate over the sill.

BUILDING THE GATE

I like to pick my hardware first. If you plan and build a gate expecting to use the hinges you saw in a friend's dooryard only to find them unavailable, you court disappointment, for a suitable replacement may be hard to locate.

Hold hinges and the latch in place on a piece of wood acting as the spine or latch post of the gate, and measure the clearances both sides of the gate need to function. Round stock will swing free with minimal clearance, but the latch sides of gates made of square stock need a 1/2- to 3/4-inch clearance if the in-side edge of the gate's latch-side vertical member is not to hang up on the gate post as the gate opens. On the hinge side too, gate and post should have a good enough clearance that pivoting hinge pins won't rub against wood. A quarter-inch is usually sufficient.

Lag-style hinges need a little more clearance than metal-plate, screw-on designs. You want to screw both the eye hinges and hinge pins in as far as you can to minimize space between gate and post — but don't screw them in so far that you can't slip the gate over the hinge pins.

Measure the gate opening carefully. Subtract clearances at sides for hardware, factor in 1 to 6 inches of ground clearance, and build your gate.

A Z-Gate

Frame this gate with your fence's rail stock. Set boards on edge or flat to match the fence, and plan toe-nailed butt joints (boards flat sides up) or (with boards on edge) stronger lapped joints with matching dados that should be screwed and glued together (see details below under box-framed gate).

Assuming a fence and gate with vertical siding (about the only way you can side a Z-gate), cut the two horizontal cross rails and the outer and inner siding boards. Set the boards square within the measured dimensions (marked on a flat floor), and nail together with one nail per joint. Take the frame to the fence, square it, and measure to be sure that the dimensions are correct and you have sufficient clearance for both sides. If your measurements are off, the single nails will pull out for easy adjustment.

Place the frame flat with the siding boards down, use a square to be sure all four corners are true, and lay the diagonal brace atop the horizontals. *It must run from the outer edge of the top rail on the latch side to outer edge of the bottom rail on the hinge side.* Mark the edges of the slanting cut where the diagonal brace meets the horizontals; scribe the lines defined by the marks and saw the brace carefully. Cut generously; you can always trim a little from the board.

Insert the brace and be sure that it does not throw the cross rails out of square. Now toenail brace and horizontals together or (better) drill angled pilot holes from brace into rail and use a long, thin brass screw to fasten the boards together.

For further strength, screw *gussets* — triangular pieces of 1/4-inch plywood — to the inside of the frame joints. Finally, turn the gate over and nail or drill pilot holes and screw the rest of the siding to your frame.

This type of gate demands strap hinges – or a combo-hinge with the strap affixed to the gate rails. To hang it, support the bottom rail on bricks or wood blocks and wedge the gate solidly in place with shims (wood shingles are best). Align the strap hinge with the top and bottom rails of gate and fence, draw an outline of the hinge and its screw holes on the wood, and drill pilot holes through siding.

Use fasteners that are long enough to go through siding and well into the rail. If the rails are on edge, you should fasten with the largest wood screws you can manage or with lags or nut-fastened bolts. With a 2 × 4 rail on edge and 1-inch siding – an actual 2¼ inches thick – I use 3-inch carriage bolts without washers. I tighten so the nut and bolt head are pressed well into the wood, then, with an electric drill and carborundum stone, I grind the end of the bolt down so that it becomes red hot and mushrooms over the nut to secure the connection like a rivet. (Be doubly sure to use eye protection if you try this!)

A Box-Framed Gate

Stronger than the Z construction is a gate built on a four-sided box frame with a wood or a tensioned-wire brace.

To build the gate in the flat, measure the gate opening. Then, calculating in needed clearances at bottom and both sides, mark out a full-sized pattern on a flat surface. Use the pattern to measure and fit pieces for top and bottom cross rails and both sides.

Joints

Square butt joints are least desirable – though they can be toenailed, then strengthened with screwed-on metal L-angle brackets from any hardware store. With careful measuring and sawing you can cut angled butts or miter joints so that ends of boards are cut to fit together at 45 degrees, like a picture frame (that joint, too, is stronger with brackets). If the frame is built on edge (with the broader dimension of the boards facing to the side), it is easier and stronger to cut lap joints using dados to remove half the thickness of each gate-frame member to overlap a correspondingly cut mate. With frame pieces flat (that is, broader faces up and down), make a notched joint. Dado the top and bottom cross rails to accept the

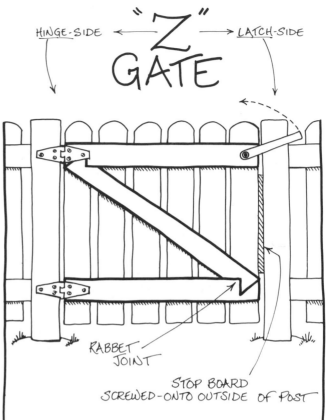

square ends of the vertical side rails; that will also exclude water from the top of the joint.

Fit the diagonal as in the Z-gate, and toenail or screw together. You may strengthen these joints with a plywood gusset on the inside of each corner.

Joints will hold a generation longer if they are glued with a waterproof cement; follow directions on the package. Be sure to clamp or weight the joints to assure a tight bond. I follow a five-step fastening procedure that eliminates clamping:

1. **Measure, cut pieces;**
2. **Trial-fit the frame, drilling all pilot holes;**
3. **Apply glue;**
4. **Screw the gate frame together with a gusset at each corner (automatically clamping glue joints);**
5. **Lay the frame down flat till glue dries and cures.**

Any kind of siding can go on a boxed frame: horizontal, vertical, or inset panels. You can nail siding to a super-strong screwed, glued, and gusseted frame. If you aren't using the extra-strength measures, screwing the siding on will add needed strength. Even with extra-strong joints, I take the few extra minutes needed to glue and screw the boards on. With waterproofing and plenty of paint or stain, the gate should last as long as the house.

Attaching Hinges

You may want butt hinges on a well-braced box-framed gate. Use hinges on a house door as your model. You can prop the gate up on blocks and just screw a set of butt hinges to the face of gate spine and hinge post on the in-swinging side of the gate. If they are hidden inside the hinge when the gate is closed the hinge plates should be inletted into shallow indentations chiseled into the spine of the gate and into the hinge post. The hinge pin itself should protrude just a bit on the in-swinging side of the gate. Again – use a properly hung door as a model.

For my money butt hinges are too weak and too picky about how they are installed for the typical gate. I prefer strap hinges or lags.

Installing the hook-and-eye hinge.

BUILDING IN PLACE

To put up a gate in place, conventional practice would have you toenail the top and bottom rails in place and nail the gate up on them. You may do that, but toenailing can split the rails and make fastening the gate frame awkward. I find it better to tack two boards across whichever side of the opening the gate won't be swinging into. Those temporaries hold the gate in place as you work. Measure and cut the four frame pieces and dado or notch the joints. Tack the frame together with one nail per joint. Place a block or bricks under the bottom rail and set the frame on it. Adjust and trim the frame members as needed to get the proper fit and clearances.

Use thin shims to wedge the frame firmly in place. Measure and cut the diagonal. Finally, nail or screw the frame together as well as you can with the sides obstructed, and affix siding. Screwing the boards on into predrilled holes is best; nailing applies a lot of pressure on the support boards. Face-mounted hinges can be attached – the latch too. Remove blocks and tacked support boards, open the gate, and insert needed fasteners through the side rails.

If using lag-type hinges, I cut and dado the gate spine to final fit. After drilling pilot holes, I insert the lag hinges in the gate post and the eyes in the spine, in effect hanging the gate before it's built. The other gate-frame members are cut to fit, tacked together, and wedged in place. Then the gate is finished as above.

Attaching verticals to the frame which has been screwed and glued.

ADDED BRACING

To strengthen a gate from the outset or to pick up a sagging gate, you can install a cable and turnbuckle. Turnbuckle kits in several lengths are available at hardware stores, or you can make up your own. Wires attach to the insides of both gate corners by eye screws, and the turnbuckle connects the wires by eye bolts threaded in opposite directions. When the turnbuckle is revolved the correct way, both bolts thread into it, pulling wire and gate corners together.

Be sure to affix a cable-turnbuckle assembly to cross over and make an X with the wooden diagonal in the gate, running from the bottom of the latch side to top of the hinge side. The diagonal brace board creates a tri-angle that suspends the gate from the top hinge but puts most weight on the lower hinge, much as an old-time pot-hook crane held a bean pot in a cooking fireplace. A wire tensioned by a turnbuckle hoists the gate up toward the top hinge, but levers off the bottom hinge.

If the weight of the gate has caused a poorly-set post to lean, affix a turnbuckle assembly between top of the gate post and bottom of the next line post. Do your best to straighten the post before putting in the wires. If the turnbuckle treatment doesn't work for long, you probably need to rebuild the gate or reset the gate post deeper and with a large concrete anchor.

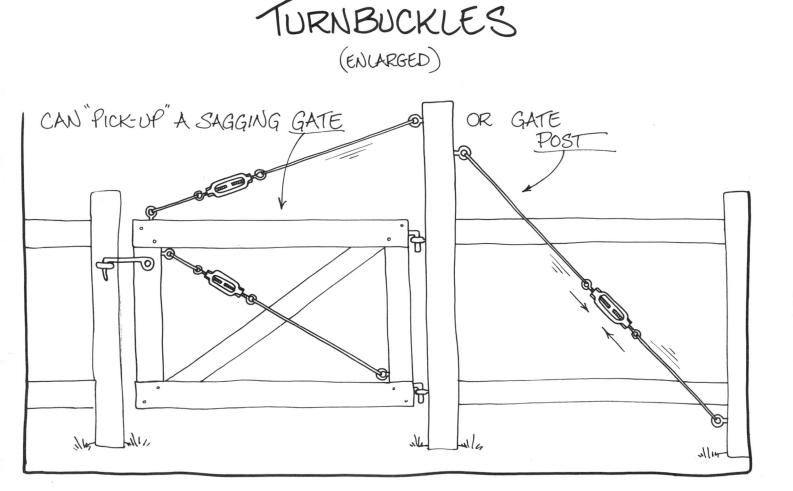

TURNBUCKLES
(ENLARGED)

CAN "PICK-UP" A SAGGING GATE   OR GATE POST

3

STONE
FENCE

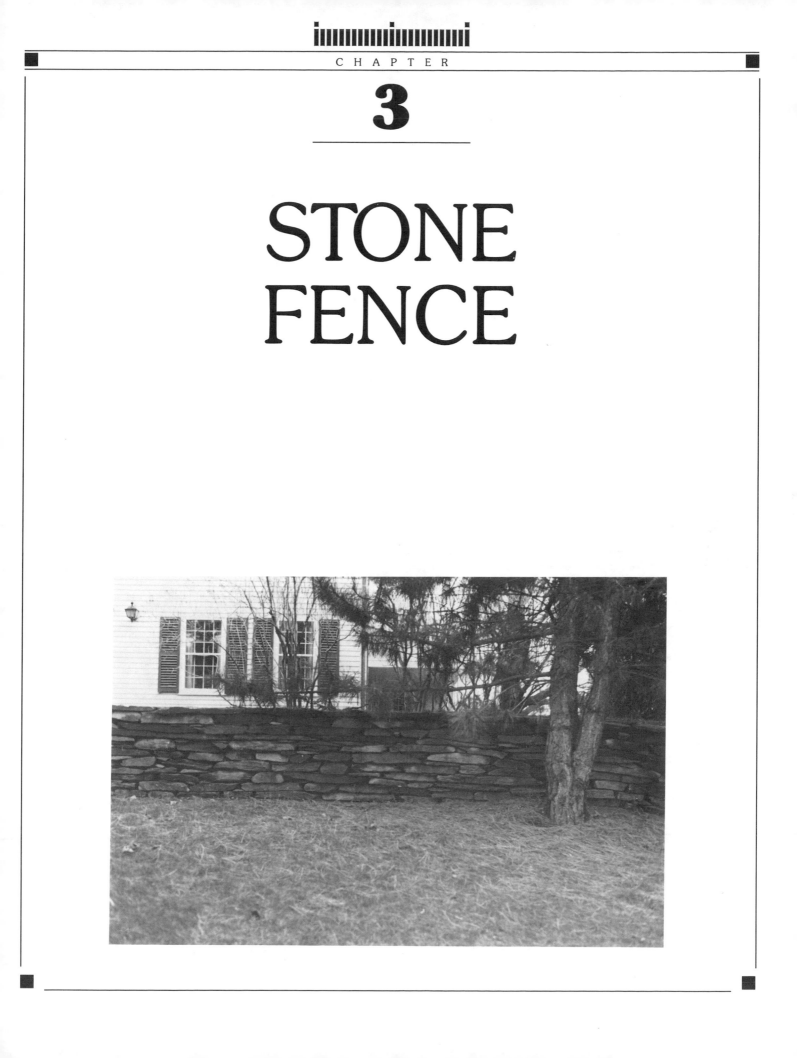

My introduction to stone work, like beginnings in so many home-owning skills, came unexpectedly, urgently, and at the wrong time. It was a rare clear morning during a rainy spring in the late '60s, and I was leaving for work from the Pennsylvania farm that provided weekend refuge from a city job.

Buildings on the place were 150+ years old, with yard-thick stone walls. The house was in fine shape, but the barn had been badly neglected. A leaky roof rested on low walls constructed as a pair of vertical rock faces laid up of rounded field stone with a mud-mortar/rubble-stone mix on the inside. Most of the *pointing* (mortar troweled into the cracks between rocks to retard weathering-out of the interior) was long gone. Winter rain and snow melt had run into the wall, frozen, and gradually worked the mortar out, and the interior mud packing gradually followed. You could see clear through the walls in places. Still, the rock had been well enough laid up to stand through generations of rain and snow.

Built-up wall.

Till that night, that is. On walking to the car I found that the night's heavy rain had washed out the southwest corner of the barn, along with half of each adjoining wall. The roof was fluttering in the wind, ready to follow the south wall downhill.

Still properly suited and tied, I shored up the roof with old framing timbers, then traded the city uniform for jeans and work shoes and ordered up a few days' vacation from work.

When the Yellow Pages failed to produce any stone masons at all, and the only general masonry contractor who'd talk to me recommended we bulldoze the stone walls and let them put up a building-code-acceptable concrete-block monolith, I set about teaching myself stone masonry the only way I could, by studying the foundation itself – walls which had been built shortly after the American Revolution by dirt farmers with no architecture degrees, no building codes, and no engines to ease the strain; just common sense and experience, simple ramps, levers, and pulleys, a team of draft animals to pull the stoneboat, and strong backs unafraid of work.

My slow-learner's repair job took the better part of a week, and most sections were built and torn down and rebuilt several times before I got them half right. But the sense of satisfaction I felt on completing that barn wall was different from anything offered by my usual labors.

FIRST LESSONS

I'd suggest that what I did for lack of any alternative – study an existing wall and copy it – is the best way for anyone to learn stone building on his own hook. Granted, a master of the trade can teach you faster and some would say better, and I've learned a lot from good masons. However, stone building is an individual skill, and once you have the basics down, you simply have to put in time working with the rock to develop your own style.

Each stone has a unique size and shape, and any rock pile will go together differently for different builders. A wood or metal or mortared-brick fence, all crisp and plumb and square, is a work of craftsmanship, to be sure. But the artistry is in the overall design; in the small details one section is pretty much identical to every other. By contrast, each running foot of each dry-laid stone wall is unique, a combination of learned craft and the individual builder's intuitive response to a complex three-dimensional puzzle having an infinite number and variety of solutions. A stone fence is a work of art in the truest sense, a creation of order out of chaos, of beauty from dross. It is as much an improvement on nature as can be accomplished by the hand of man.

And, my, it is satisfying. A hard-won satisfaction, though: rock is dead weight that goes up hard and comes down harder. Even a little yard-high garden wall with a shallow footing weighs a ton or more per linear yard. So, before you lift that first stone and drop it into place in your fence, be sure to take care that it doesn't do you damage as it moves in either direction.

SAFETY FIRST

Building with stone is a totally engrossing task that tempts one to forget safety. With proper outer wear, you can ignore the occasional dropped or rolling stone. Insteps and toes are at particular hazard, and a tough leg covering and sound boots let you put a foot anywhere that best leverage demands without worrying about injury.

Your most valuable piece of equipment is a healthy spine – and you can't buy one of those. Know the old adage, "Lift with your legs, not your back"? Well, forget it in stone work. Don't lift any rock that's bigger than you can heft easily with your arms alone, sitting down. Roll the big ones, slip them, slide them, or flip them over end to end. Use ramps or levers or sleds. When you must use brute, unleveraged force, get behind and push (back straight, using your arms or legs). Or move the stone sitting down with back straight, heaving up with your arms and shoulders.

Bending double at the waist and heaving up on a heavy rock is an invitation to serious back injury.

Please start off slowly. Anyone in average good health can work stone. But you may be employing muscles that haven't seen much recent use. So, go easy at first, particularly if (like me) you get the urge to raise a stone fence the first warm spring day following a muscle-softening winter. Chances are the rock has rested where you first find it for upwards of 20,000 years. It's in no hurry to move.

STONE BUILDING APPAREL

Here is a list of protective clothing to wear when working stone.

Gloves. Horsehide or leather-palmed canvas to withstand abrasion and knife edges on the rock.

Shoes. Steel-toed leather boots that are ankle-high at minimum to protect against rolling or falling stones.

Trousers. Canvas or heavy denim material, with reinforced knees if possible for the hours of kneeling needed to move and adjust stones in the wall.

Eyewear. Unbreakable safety goggles to protect against flying splinters any time you are drilling, dressing, or carving stone.

The tool kit

Your main tools will be your arms, hands, and back. You'll need a truck or a vehicle with a trailer to move rock any great distance, hand barrows or carts for short hauls, and stout (2-inch or thicker) planks and hardwood dowels or lengths of steel pipe to serve as rollers to get large rock up onto a wall. Helpful if you have to move, dress, or break up large rock slabs is a set of stone-working implements. Prybars for unearthing or moving large stones, as well as sledgehammers and chisels, can be found at any country hardware store or in mail-order or wholesale catalogues under Trowel Trades or Mason's Supplies. A mason's level is sometimes helpful in setting individual stones, particularly at the upper layer, or top *course* of a wall and when leveling out stone tables, benches, and such wall furniture as gates and steps. You'll also need your fence-builder's twine, line level, and stakes.

Star drills, railroad spikes, and other gear that I use for occasional quarrying and stone dressing may take a little searching. Pointed quarrier's sledgehammers and such niceties as wedge-and-shim splitting tools for hand quarrying are available to the trade, and modern quarriers use pneumatic jack hammers to drill rock and dyna-mite to split blocks out. If you want to take up quarrying and shaping stone, visit your local burial-monument works for advice and tool sources.

Don't forget to wear a long-sleeved shirt and safety goggles during any hammer-and-chisel work. Rock chips can be sharper than a surgical scalpel, and they fly off the work at considerable speed.

STONE FENCING TOOLS

Here is a list of basic rock-working tools:
Twine, stakes, and line level. Needed for setting level courses of stone in the fence.
Large prybar. Four-foot steel bar gives leverage to extract rocks from the ground and move large stones up on the wall.
Hand sledgehammer. With or without mason's toothed face, for splitting and dressing rock.
Mason's chisels. A large, broad-bladed brick mason's chisel and a narrower stone chisel for working the rock.

Transporting stone

Rock in small quantities can be hauled in a fat-tired, flat-bedded contractor's wheelbarrow, but you have to lift it in. Easier are those two-wheeled, box-bodied garden carts. You can set them up on end and roll stones in. The steel-box models sold at retail are sturdier and better for stone work than the handsome but lightweight stained plywood variety sold by mail order.

Using any garden cart, keep loads small. I let a cart full of rock bump down off a low ledge one time, and one of the pretty chrome spoked wheels collapsed. If you have a tractor (even a small lawn tractor), or a draft animal, you can build a rock sled or *stoneboat* to haul rock to the fence line. You just roll stones on and off again. The sled will make serious gouges in your lawn, but nothing worse than the digging, rolling, and scrabbling around of the building process. You'll likely have to rebuild the lawn along the fence line once your wall building is done, anyway.

A STONE-BOAT

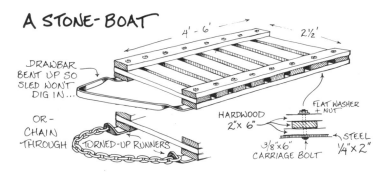

DRAWBAR BENT UP SO SLED WON'T DIG IN...

OR - CHAIN THROUGH TURNED-UP RUNNERS

HARDWOOD 2" x 6"

FLAT WASHER + NUT

STEEL ¼" x 2"

3/8"x6" CARRIAGE BOLT

4' - 6'   2½'

MOVING LARGE STONES UP ↑

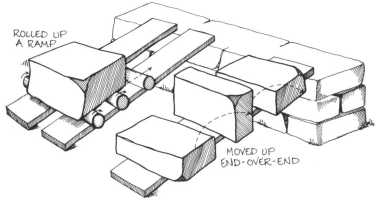

ROLLED UP A RAMP

MOVED UP END-OVER-END

READING THE ROCK

Most of what I've read about stone building presumes a good supply of "table rock": soft, fissile – easily splittable – *sedimentary* stone laid down eons ago in *strata*: successive layers of alluvial silt, sand, or tiny seashells that settled at the bottom of ancient seas. Many sedimentary formations will split along stratum lines with the tap of an ax; then the even sheets will cut as square as brick after a shallow groove is scratched in the surface. If you have access to good-building sedimentary stone, count yourself fortunate indeed. Much of it is lightweight, too (for rock).

On my own Berkshire mountain plateau, there's a mix of the other two major rock types. Interspersed all too liberally through the garden loam are field stones – locally called "cobbles" or "hard-heads." These are more-or-less round hunks of *igneous* rock – formed of minerals that melted deep in the earth, then cooled to become hard rock such as granite. They were broken out of the pre-Cambrian shield in far northern Canada eons ago and rolled down to us by the Pleistocene glaciers.

Where bedrock pokes out of our pasture as ledge, there's a soft and greasy, easy-splitting mica schist, an example of the third rock type: *metamorphic*. Marble is a familiar variety of metamorphic rock, slate another. All were originally sedimentary (or other) rocks that became buried over geologic time and were subjected to enough underground heat and pressure to change them but not enough to cause a full melt-down and reformation as igneous rock.

ROCK TYPES

At first glance most weathered rock looks alike, dull gray but for exposed surfaces covered with moss or lichen. But some rocks are better for fence building than others. Chip off a chunk to identify type. Hardness will be obvious at the first blow. Look for cleavage planes or strata within the formation to determine whether the rocks will be easily persuaded to work into fence. If you have a choice of rock, here are the major varieties, how to identify them, and their fence-building characteristics.

Sedimentary: Composed of small, distinct particles from mud-size (a shale) to sand-size (sandstone); often include larger pebbles or rocks like a natural concrete (conglomerate).

Hardness: Base matrix is usually soft, will chip or scratch easily with a rock hammer or knife.

Durability: Sandstones are easily abraded by wind-borne sand; limestones are slowly destroyed by acidic rain and other water. A fence of sedimentary stone may not last more than a few thousand years.

Texture: Evenly granular within regular strata of varying thicknesses.

Workability: When stratified into conveniently thin layers, the best. Easily split and shaped into flat, even building stones. Makes the finest stone walls, statues, bank buildings, and other monuments to someone's hard work.

Igneous: With distinct, usually multicolored crystals of quartz, feldspar, and other hard minerals tightly fused together; includes granite, gneiss.

Hardness: The hardest.

Durability: Will last as near to forever as anything.

Texture: A split face will exhibit distinct, often sharp crystals; has a grain and cleavage planes, but they are hard for anyone but a quarrier to find.

Workability: Splits, but unpredictably and only with considerable effort; best used as found.

Metamorphic: Lacking both the obvious, even grain of sedimentary rock and the distinct crystals of igneous; often has a swirling appearance like a marble cake: includes schists, marble, and slate.

Hardness: Usually soft, easily worked.

Durability: Except for marbles (metamorphosed limestones), which can be quickly eroded by acid conditions, metamorphics are remarkably tough; inscriptions in 300-year-old slate grave markers remain legible when other rock is weathered smooth.

Texture: Usually smooth to the touch but often with a variegated, multicolored appearance. Cleavage planes often less distinct and uniform than in sedimentary rocks.

Workability: Varies: usually splits and shapes readily along stratum lines but exhibits jagged edges in midstratum breaks.

FINDING STONES

Unless you can afford to have good-building flat rock hauled in from a blasting quarry (in which case you can likely afford a mason to go with it), you, like me, will be building with what you have at hand. And unless you have a lot of time and patience or a pneumatic hammer and chisel to work stones into shape, you'll likely be using your stone as you find it.

In much of New England we don't have to look far to find fence stones. Rock sprouts out of our soil each spring as glacial cobbles are pushed skyward by heaving frost; the noted Yankee stone walls weren't built to add local color but to clear land for the plow.

It is considered bad form to move stone fences and may be illegal anywhere that walls traditionally define property lines. But fallen-in files of rock within property lines are nothing but long stone piles, not walls, and you should feel free to rearrange them into a proper fence anywhere you choose.

If you are not blessed with stone on your property but live in country where old stone structures are common, a landowner may be happy to let you haul off a rock pile, an old wall, or even a rickety (and possibly dangerous) stone foundation from a long-burned barn.

Quarrying mica schist. Note how easily it splits into strata.

For native stone look along river or creek beds, where roads cut through rolling country, or wherever heavy construction is going on. Rock often crops out where someone doesn't want it and is free for the taking. Be sure to take the trouble to locate and get permission from landowners, and offer payment if necessary. I recall one rock-gathering safari where our fence-building team found a likely formation just a few hundred yards down a small but deep-cutting stream from a hay barn. When we went in to ask permission to remove some of the lovely flat, stream-split shale, we found the young farmer single-handedly unloading a huge hay wagon – and a thunderstorm was building in the west. We pitched in, saved the hay just in time, and for our trouble were offered freshly squeezed lemonade, homemade cookies, and all the rock we cared to haul off.

If you're taking rock from a waterway, though, be sure you conform to environmental common sense as well as local wetland regulations. That accessible outcropping that looks so inviting may be all that keeps spring floods from washing out the river bank and inundating nearby farmland.

Removing stones from a high embankment with a sheer face can be dangerous. Especially beware of a sloping shelf of fallen rock at a cliff base. A lot of loose stone means the formation above is weak or rotten and may release high rock if you begin prying into it. A wet, soft matrix can slough down on you, most notably in west coast mudslide areas during rainy seasons. So, use common sense and keep looking up. A hardhat might be in order if you plan much work at the base of a rock cliff. Any hardware store will have them or can order one.

Even if you have to buy stone, it is cheap. The quarrying, loading, and hauling is what costs: $50 to $100 a dump-truck load in our neighborhood. Still, time spent moving stone will put your muscles into shape better than an equal amount spent on push-ups – and it'll give you a fence to admire and to increase the value of your place, to boot.

ROCK DICTATES THE FENCE

To some degree the kind and shape of available rock will dictate the internal dimensions of your fence. Don't bother to try picking larger rocks out of a gravel pit or even from a pile of fist-sized cobble stones. Unless they are mortared into place, a lot of little rocks give a wall too much *travel*. The fence shifts readily with the slightest ground movement and falls apart in short order if small stones are laid dry. You want rocks that are a good double handful and larger; the bigger the better.

The kind and configuration of available stone needn't limit what you build, however; within an hour's drive of our place are walls, fences, buildings, and foundations of big stone, small stone, round stone, and flat stone, laid as found or dressed square. I know several local fences made of potentially unstable, almost globular, field stone that have lasted with nothing but a little annual maintenance for two hundred years.

A wall of thin shims and small flat stone. Too much run in the center of the picture.

DIGGING A GOOD FOUNDATION

Adam Smith and Karl Marx would cringe in unison at the suggestion, but the main ingredients in a stone wall is neither the rock, nor the tools used, nor your own hard work. They are friction and gravity. Make your stones as immobile as possible, and arrange them in such a way that gravity keeps pulling straight down on them, and the wall will be standing long after you and I no longer can.

The more permanent you want your fence, the more solid must be the foundation, thus the more wall you must bury forever underground in a *footing*. The base of any stone structure expected to last a few hundred years must rest on bedrock if possible, otherwise on solid subsoil; bases of medieval European cathedrals go down 25 feet. So get yourself a cutting spade to slice out sod and a long-handled shovel to dig a trench. You will find that sod cuts best in early spring before the root systems grab hold or in early winter when the plants are dormant. In any season it cuts easier when wet. During the dry months I wait for a soaking rain to dig, or I let a sprinkler run overnight on any segment of sod needing removal.

You'll have to remove all roots growing in the trench. Tree roots will swell and heave any stone fence made. The smaller the tree, the faster it grows, so you may want to build your fence well away from any tree line, and you should consider cutting out saplings and small trees growing nearby before you begin excavating. It's probably easier to plan on rebuilding a wall every generation than removing a really large tree, however.

If you live in the Snow Belt, the deeper your footing, the better. A footing base below frost line would be ideal, though it's impractical if frost goes down 4 feet and your fence will only be a yard high. But freezing soil heaves stone. Simply put, winter temperatures freeze soil moisture, which expands and pushes everything above it up, like those boulders that grow in my garden each winter. Then when soil warms in spring, the water thaws and shrinks, and the wet earth sags away and down around solid objects, preparing to freeze and thrust them up again next winter. A dry-stone fence, laid without a good foundation, can absorb some of the up and down and interior motion such alternate freeze/thaw imparts each season, while a similar, but cemented wall will crack open the second winter. Still, the more of your fence you bury forever, the longer it will stand. At minimum, be ready to dig out sod and topsoil.

DIMENSIONS

The more width you build into your wall per unit of height, the bigger its footprint, and the more stable it will be. I plan the underground footing base of my own walls to be about 1½ times their width at ground level, with a gradual upward slope from *base* to *grade* (from the bottom of the trench to ground level.) I try to build each face sloping inward at about a 15-degree angle (called *batter*) from base to top. The illustration says it better; the inward slope of each face – the batter – lets gravity pull the wall down and in on itself.

No stone builder sticks to a single, strict height/width ratio, of course. The Great Pyramids slope at the angle that dunes form naturally in the wind-blown desert sand, while most old stone fences in my neighborhood are as severely upright as the men who built them.

Often as not, the availability of rock and the use to be made of the fence will determine your dimensions. Few rocks and need for a high screen make for a thin, well-thought-out wall; lots of rock and no need for screen will imply a long, low rock pile – a "thrown-up" wall, in Yankee talk. Most of the stone fence that surrounds our place was raised as somewhere to pile an oversupply of glacial cobbles jutting out of the hay field and just waiting to chip a scythe blade at mowing time – although the fences also served as some discouragement to fence-jumping cattle and still define property lines. Many real-estate deeds contain such language as ". . . 20⅓ chains running NNW along a stone wall from a large Chestnut, thence right 62 feet to a blighted Elm, thence 115 yards due North along a loose stone fence. . . ." Today, only the stone fence remains.

A "thrown-up" wall of irregular filled stones.

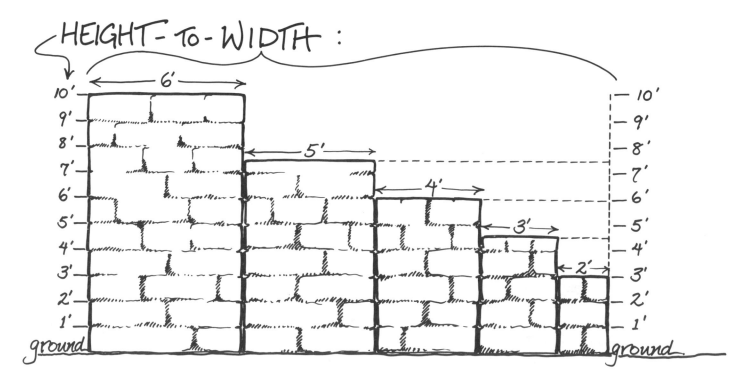

LAYING OUT

The first building step is to find a length of twine and some stakes and lay out your fence as described in earlier chapters. Unlike board and wire fences, stone fences aren't strengthened by perfect straightness of straight sections or fair curves of curved sections. But good lines are important to the look of your work. A few minutes spent double checking the layout will avoid hours of rebuilding – or a lifetime of muttering self-recrimination: "If only I'd taken the time to lay that #% ☆ ☆&@ fence out right the first time. . . ."

As in laying out any fence, string out your twine and line your stakes eyeball-straight along the fence line. Don't skimp on stakes. Too few, and a steady wind can bow the line. Then you'll have an unexpected curve in the wall. Trim stakes to be as high as the wall from base to top plus a foot or so to sink in the ground. You'll be using the stakes and line to build the entire wall – not just to lay it out for fence posts – so pound the stakes in to stay a while. If you're building along a tree line, hedge, or other barrier, put the stakes on the obstructed side of the fence line so you'll have the open side to work in. Lay out the entire wall line if you can, corners included, to anticipate tree-root, ledge, or water-course problems. Perhaps you can avoid them by moving the entire fence a few feet before the first rock is laid.

Now, dig out sod and topsoil in a strip along the line. It need be no wider than the base of the wall. I haul sod to the compost pile and scatter topsoil in the garden; where I live it takes nature a hundred years to make an inch of the stuff, and I don't like to waste it by throwing it into the woods.

Dig the trench so the bottom is perfectly flat and level. If your fence is on a slope, carry it up and down grade in shallow steps, so all base rocks will rest level.

Don't let any step rise higher than the thickness of your typical rock, which will be the thickness of the courses of rock you build into the wall.

Use the line level to adjust the guide line to be level above each stair-step. Keep it a consistent distance (1 foot is good) above grade at each step. More stakes will be needed, as you'll want one at each up- or down-step in grade. You can drop a plumb line or a measuring stick from the level line to determine depth of each step of footing floor as you dig.

This layout string will be your guide line throughout the fence building – you will need it to visually align each course of rock as it goes on, raising the line as the wall goes up.

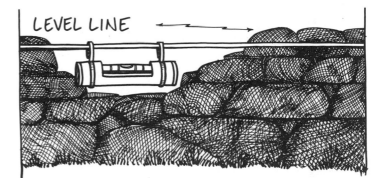

LEVEL LINE

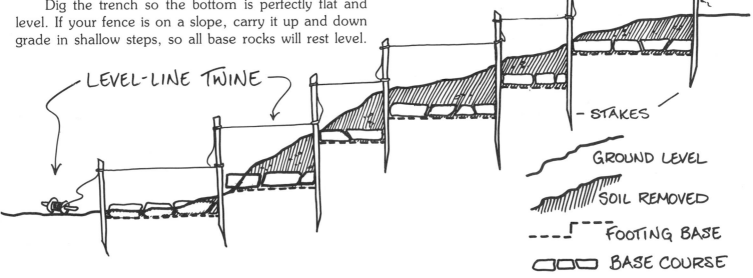

STAIR-STEP FOOTING

LEVEL-LINE TWINE

STAKES

GROUND LEVEL

SOIL REMOVED

FOOTING BASE

BASE COURSE

BUILDING FENCE

With the wall laid out and the footing trench dug, the real challenge begins. Now you can start building.

First step is to sort your stones by size, thickness, and shape. You may not actually divide rock into piles by size and shape (a mason's helper does this in the trade). But you'll catalogue each stone mentally. With experience you'll find that when a certain peculiar opening occurs in a course, you'll remember that there's a stone that should fit at the bottom of that little pile you made back where you left the thermos of iced tea. In time you'll find that you automatically memorize the configuration of every unusual rock you handle. And you'll find a place in the wall for almost every one. Indeed, it becomes a challenge to make a spot for an unusual shape, and you can enjoyably waste great amounts of time fitting and refitting the oddballs.

You'll come to value certain oddities – such as the "lock stone": a rock with a sharp notch in it that will accept and hold a corresponding point on another. Or the "course-binder": a stone that has projections in three dimensions, so it will lie flat in one course but intrude into the course above or below. If properly placed, each of these oddities can add strength to the structure; if poorly set, they will challenge stability.

You will discover that the more bricklike its shape, the easier a rock goes into a fence and the better it looks. You'll save especially fine stones with a perfectly flat, square side for outer faces exposed to public view. You'll put aside your heaviest thin stones to make a fine, flat top. And you'll come to view as a particular treasure a large flat stone with two adjacent 45-degree corners so that it will top out an end or corner.

The rounder and odder-shaped a rock, the harder it is to fit into the wall. So, put your biggest and worst stones in the first course at the bottom of the trench, rottenest side down. You may have to dig out holes at the footing bottom to accommodate wobbleknobs in the real stinkers. Or you can knock them off.

Set below-ground stones so their outer margins meet to form a solid, straight line along both sides of the wall. But leave an inch or so between their inner junctions. Fill the spaces with small rock or rubble; this is to let water percolate into the ground with minimal obstruction. And arrange this first course – and all others except for a flat top – so that the outer edge of each stone is a little higher than its inner edge. Rocks will make a shallow V shape, with the midline of the wall – its spine – slightly lower than its outer edges. That way gravity not only pulls the rocks down, but it pulls the wall in and on itself for greater stability.

With part of the first course laid, your affinity for the craft and your own style will begin to develop. You may find it more satisfying to lay the entire bottom course first. Or you may want to lay several courses at once – always keeping the lower courses out ahead of the upper by a few stones. Some people find in their character a need to build a minimum of open space into a wall, working for

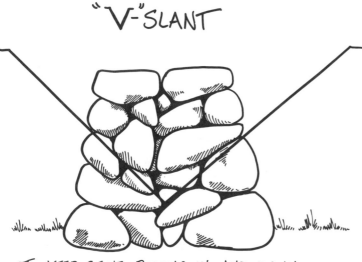

"V-"SLANT

TO KEEP STONE PUSHING IN AND DOWN ON ITSELF.

BUILD AROUND "MONOLITHS"... AND UNEVEN STONES

hours to create as closed and bricklike a surface as they can. Others can tolerate a lot of gaps; still others like gaps but will want to fill them with rubble and shims. The wall won't care either way, so long as the bigger rocks are laid properly. Do it however your sense of order dictates; the wall will stand for a century or two so long as you truly enjoy each other's company.

A Fair Warning

You may find you don't like working with stone once you've tried it for a bit. You have to enjoy hard manual labor and find satisfaction in solving three-dimensional problems. Wall building is dirty, often sweaty stoop-labor that can leave you sore, bleeding, and grubby. Rock is a coarse artistic medium, demanding little fine motor control and permitting few precise furbishes. If you don't like it, if you find that you don't get real, visceral gratification from turning a rock pile into a proper fence, don't force yourself. Use the rock to floor a patio or garden path, fill your trench with compost, and plant asparagus and rhubarb, which will last almost as long as a wall and provide satisfactions of a different sort.

Building steps in a stone garden wall.

A builder found a good place for an irregular giant.

THE BASIC RULES

After the base course is laid comes the fun. Following are the elemental rules of building fences of stone:

Don't set stones in the fence; drop them from a small height.
If you try to lay stones in gently atop one another, you'll crush a finger in the middle. Drop the rock and move your hands out from under, quick.

Lay stones flat, and two-over-one, one-over two.
Always set stones with the narrowest dimension in the horizontal plane—laid flat in other words, and always according to the old-time formula: one-over-two, two-over-one. Put still another way, always cover an up-facing joint between two rocks with the solid under surface of another to minimize the number of inter-course joints, or *run*.

Build with your eyes first.
Don't lift a large rock till you have measured the space by eye or with a length of twine or steel tape if need be, found a rock to match, and laid in any shims needed for a solid bed.

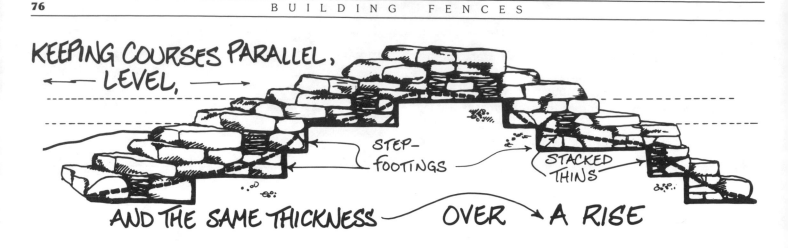

KEEPING COURSES PARALLEL, ← LEVEL, → AND THE SAME THICKNESS → OVER ↘ A RISE

STEP-FOOTINGS

STACKED THINS

Avoiding Run, Keeping Level, and Tying Faces

Ignoring the one-over-two, two-over-one rule, so that you permit joints between stones in successive courses to line up one over another, creates *vertical run*, a serious fault in any masonry construction. The wall will fold at the crease. Properly lapped, the rocks in a dry wall will shift back and forth with the seasons but not fall out too quickly.

The one-over-two rule applies in the horizontal dimension as well: put one beside two, two beside one. Where you have a lot of little stuff you must use, try to alternate stacked thin rocks with thick single rocks in a course. Pile thin rocks on each side of a single thick one, and avoid backing multiple thins against one another where possible. Adjacent stacks of thins will slide over one another, permitting the wall to slip off itself much as a deck of cards will slough over when pushed with the palm of your hand.

As the fence goes up, raise the guide line and sight along it frequently to keep the courses as horizontal as possible.

Perfectly level courses are not critical on flat ground and on any terrain are hard to maintain precisely unless you have perfect table rock that is 6 inches thick or better. Maintaining consistent courses with really thin rock is possible, but it takes more time than it's worth to most builders; lifting, adjusting, and shimming a thin stone takes as much time as setting a thick one, and building a fence of straight, true, level, and parallel 1- or 2-inch-thick courses takes forever.

With any rock supply, thickness of courses will be dictated by what comes up in the rock pile and will vary as you go. Sometimes a course will unaccountably dip or rise despite your best efforts. But, especially on rolling land, do your best to keep gravity pulling straight down. If you slope the course lines, particularly going over a rise, the wall will want to slide off itself along the slanting juncture lines.

From time to time, (say, when you've laid a horizontal run of stone equal to twice the fence's width) and as the rock permits, *tie* the faces of your wall. That is, lay a long rock across the width of the wall in an interior course, so as to cover all the rocks in the course below. That adds lateral stability.

ROCK LAID FLAT WITH GOOD "ONE-OVER-TWO" PLACEMENT:

TOO MANY SMALL AND IRREGULAR ROCKS, POORLY SET:

TOO MUCH "RUN"

Chinking – In or Out?

No two rock fencers agree as to the best way to *chink* a wall – to shim with small pieces to fill gaps or to lodge rounded or odd-shaped stones in place. Do you chink *in* or chink *out*? That is, when rock ends don't mate well in the flat or there is a substantial gap in the interior of the wall or in a face, do you fill with rocks laid big end *inside* the wall so as not to work out? Or do you hammer in a wedge-shaped shim, large end *out*? I do it both ways. So will you, I imagine, though hammering shims *in* is easiest and most appropriate in a finished, ornamental flat-rock wall such as an in-town front-yard retaining wall, where appearance is important.

As you build try to imagine the effect of gravity on each rock as you set it. In time you'll develop an intuitive feel for how best to place each stone to keep gravity pulling straight down on it. Just as in the bottom course, I like to have the rocks in each following course angling down slightly toward the center of the wall, so that all the rocks in each face slope in and down toward the midline a bit. Together with a nice angle of batter, it helps the wall to hold itself together.

Ends and Corners

The sections that make your wall-building reputation are the ends and corners that butt up to public ways. I've known wall builders to haul good stones for miles to make a lasting impression on posterity.

You want the ends to hold up unaided; there's no more wall beyond them to rest against, and the rocks behind are constantly trying to push the end stones out as weather expands and contracts them. So save the biggest and best flat-faced and square rocks you can for ends. Then, tie alternating courses, first face to face and, next course, back into the length of the wall. For a really permanent end, extend your footing out in a wedge for several feet in front of the wall.

A corner is a pair of ends woven together, and it's more complicated still. Seasons will have the wall heaving at a corner from both lengths, so a corner should be stronger than a simple end. Tie alternating courses into first one then the other flight of wall. Within the wall, avoid any run at all; try not to let the edge of any rock line up with the joint where two rocks match above or below. Save the best tie stones for corners, and save giants, which may have a place in the base of a corner if not in a length of wall.

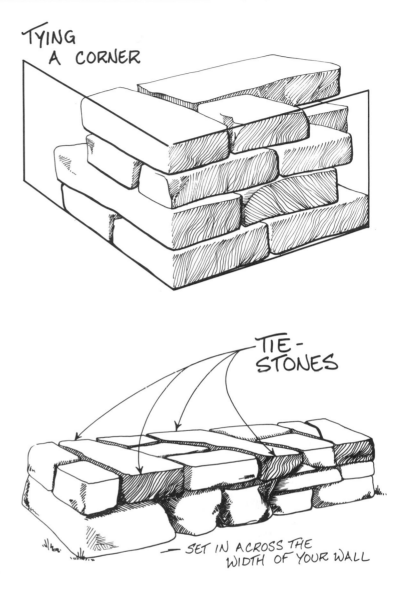

TYING A CORNER

TIE-STONES

— SET IN ACROSS THE WIDTH OF YOUR WALL

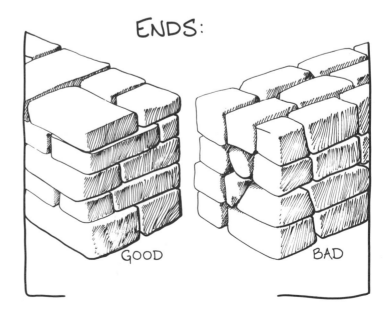

ENDS:

GOOD   BAD

Topping Out

The finishing step in a rock fence is the top. If your stone is nicely stratified sedimentary or metamorphic, you should save the biggest, most perfectly flat, square-sided pieces for a flat top. It takes a practiced eye to bed table-rock top stone at the first try. First you must match the upper surface shapes of top stones so they make as perfect a plane along the fence top as possible. I like to lay out the top as I build courses, laying the best flat stones out in the top pattern alongside the rising fence, as in a giant jigsaw puzzle.

Then you must match the bottom of the top rock with the top of the next-to-last course. Flat stone likes to wobble; to install the top rocks, you must tip each to see the bottom, then lay well-bedded shims as needed on the bed course so the top stone will rest solidly. I like to establish three solid mounting points – two at the outer edge and one inside – to make a triangular perch for top stones. Then shims can be hammered in around the edges to shore up the basic three-point mount. I find that if I try to arrange a four-point or more bed, the top rock wobbles forever – and trying to cure it is like trying to level a chair by sawing bits off successive legs. There's no wobble to a three-legged stool.

WORKING WITH IRREGULAR STONE

If flat stone is in limited supply, you can build perfectly satisfactory fences of rubble fill. Use your best stone for the outside and the top, and fill the center with whatever is available. Build the outer faces as independently standing mini-walls, and fill the interior as each section of outer shell is completed. Don't use mud or sand as a filler, though; it will run out after a few good rains unless you mortar the top and point the side joints.

Building with rounded stream- or field stone is harder than with flat rock, and the fence won't stand as long. Ground motion tends to roll the ball-shaped rocks around atop one another, and without regular maintenance the structure quickly rolls apart. But the building

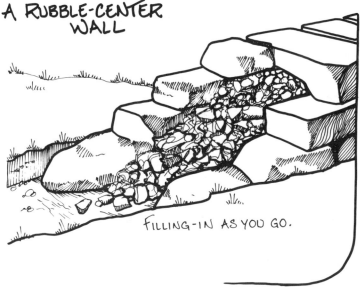

A RUBBLE-CENTER WALL

FILLING-IN AS YOU GO.

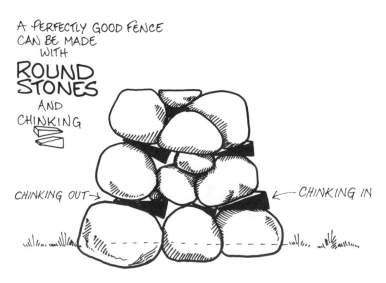

A PERFECTLY GOOD FENCE CAN BE MADE WITH

ROUND STONES AND CHINKING

CHINKING OUT →

← CHINKING IN

principles are the same: two over one, one over two; avoid run, and tie in when you can. For optimal stability, try to lay each rock so that its flattest faces meet matching faces on adjoining rocks. Mate as much rock-to-rock surface as possible to reduce potential roll. In many fieldstone walls, the best looking flat sides of individual stones are hidden away. It is the most contorted surfaces that greet the open air. The fences may not be as pretty as they would be if the flat faces looked out, but they are stable.

Angular and wedge-shaped chinking stones are particularly handy in a round-stone wall. A chip of flat rock under a rounded one acts much as a chock under a wheel; it will keep the rock from rolling. I use a big sledgehammer to split as many large hardheads as will break (you never know till you whack one), then distribute the cheese-wedge shims within the wall. Here, I always chink *out* – that is, with the larger end to any wedge rock inside the wall. Chinked the other way in round rock, the wedges would work out in no time.

DRESSING ROCK

The finest ornamental walls are made of flat stone laid with the least open space between rocks – except perhaps for openings left intentionally to contain rock-garden plantings or vines. These are not made of found rock, but of flat, easy-splitting stone that the mason cuts on the spot. Sandstones and limestones can be readily split into almost square blocks; some walls look almost as though they have been made of sawn stone. Many soft shales split out into thin layers, and their fine grain permits easy and even cutting for square corners and edges.

A pointed sledgehammer is good for gross splitting, but gentler tools are needed for the fine work. I use the mason's chisel and a hand maul for splitting large stones along the grain. To cut off sides and edges, I lay the flat rock over an inverted L angle iron (an old fence post) and score and trim it with a hand ax. A roofer's chrome-plated hammer-headed hatchet is the latest addition to my rock-working kit.

With these tools plus time and ambition, you can split and trim small rocks and shims to chink into all the cracks and crevices in your fence, and the finished job will present a nearly smooth face to the public. The finish you give to the unseen, inner face of your wall is for your own satisfaction and price of craft. I judge another mason's workmanship not by the what shows on Main Street, but by the inner faces that are out of public view.

Splitting shims.

Trimming rock with roofer's hatchet.

CROSSINGS AND THROUGHWAYS

Stone fences have more trouble crossing paths and waterways than simple wire or wood fences. Ground water will flow under or through a conventional fence, and gates can be hung easily from fence posts. But opening and closing and making waterways through a stone structure takes time and thought.

Crossing a stream is easiest if you stop the fence at one side of the water and restart on the other. Just build a pair of ends, perhaps with a wooden water gate or a barbed-wire grid hung from posts sunk right beside the end stones.

Periodic freshets can undermine a wall as water courses through, bounces off the stones, and gradually digs out the soil from around the footings. A section of drain tile, or, for a large stream, a corrugated-steel or ceramic culvert, will direct the water and support the fence.

A stone bridge with an unmortared arch is something that I have wanted to try for years, and I will do it if I ever find the time. You must dig a sound foundation for piers on each side of the arch, then put up a wooden support to lay the perfectly-cut and matched rock on. The keystone fits in at the top, permitting gravity to hold the bridge together just as it keeps stone fences in place. Books on Roman and Medieval European architecture give the dimensions and details of construction, and you'll find them in the library. If you get your arched-stone bridge built before I get to mine, let me know, will you?

GATES

To make an opening in a wall, you simply build in a pair of facing ends. Wooden hinge and latch posts will permit you to install any gate you prefer. PT wood posts can be sunk deep at the ends just as with a wooden fence. Or you can affix a creosoted hardwood board to the vertical inner face of each end with long through-bolts that you mortar in as the wall goes up. Again, long-shanked hinge straps and eyebolts to accept a latch can be mortared directly into the wall. As illustrated, put large washers on threaded bolts through drilled keeper plates to give the mortar a good purchase. Be sure to use all-

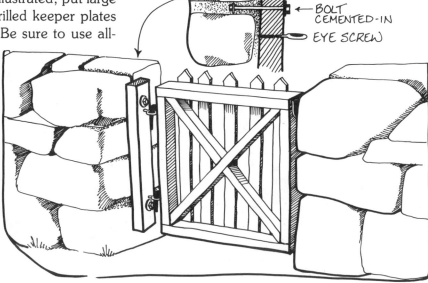

BOLT CEMENTED-IN

EYE SCREW

A nice end mated to a wood gate post, but too much run just to the left of the corner pier of stones.

galvanized hardware, and put especially heavy stones on top of the hinges' attachments to prevent the gate from sagging.

Stone fence just naturally asks for a black metal gate with creaky hinges. You can get one of those lightweight and attractive tubular sheet-metal gates that accompany modern black metal fencing. But the hand labor you've put into the fence deserves a hand-wrought iron gate. Making one takes a forge and anvil and a blacksmith's hammer and forearm, and I refer you to the library again, and to nineteenth century ironmongery books.

If you are tempted to try your hand at smithing, farm-supply firms still sell 800-pound anvils (rail freight charges collect, and you'd better be prepared to handle the thing at your end), but I haven't seen a farm-scale forge for sale anywhere in years. For the small amount of metal work that I do, I use a firebrick-bottomed backyard charcoal barbecue with a blower cobbled up from parts out of a surplus electronics-supply catalogue. Keeping a fire takes practice, to say nothing of heating the metal and shaping, cutting, and punching it between stokings.

See chapter 10 on local iron fabricators or write one of the custom-ironwork firms that advertise in the old-house journals. They make wrought-iron fences and gates and will design one to your measurements or follow a design of your own. It won't be cheap, however.

Iron fence can be attached to wood posts or hinge boards or hung on mortared-in hinges and latches. More traditional is to cut holes in the end stone itself with a star drill. You drill an entrance opening double the diameter

of the hinge and latch bolts. Then enlarge the hole inside the rock to make a pear-shaped chamber. Finally, the bolts are inserted and jammed into place with lengths of lead that are tamped around the bolts with a punch. To be a bit more modern you can lodge bolts in with an epoxy matrix such as fiberglass boat patch.

STILES

A purer form of rock-fence gate is a stile – either a slot opening or a series of stone steps built into the wall. Through-stiles are found in European sheep and cattle fence. Facing ends are build midway in the wall to leave a narrow slot that is large enough to let a person pass but too narrow for the animal being fenced to squeeze through. They are best built near a corner, and aiming at a diagonal away from the corner itself, so a beast passing by and looking straight at the opening through its side-mounted eyes sees nothing but more stone.

Step stiles for stone fences that are tall enough that they can't be easily jumped can be made as a stair rising on one side of the fence and falling down the other. They can be simple stone stairs jutting out from the wall in a line perpendicular to the fence. A little more elegant is a stair built into the wall itself, either up and over straight ahead in a very wide wall or with up- and down flights placed side-by-side. A stair can also be built with the stairs rising and falling parallel to the fence line. Most in keeping with the craft of stone work are *wing stiles*, long stones inserted in the wall so that a foot or so of rock extends out from the wall face, forming steps that rise and fall as they march along opposing sides. The steps must be of a durable rock so they don't split under your weight, and must be well weighted by large top rocks in the wall itself.

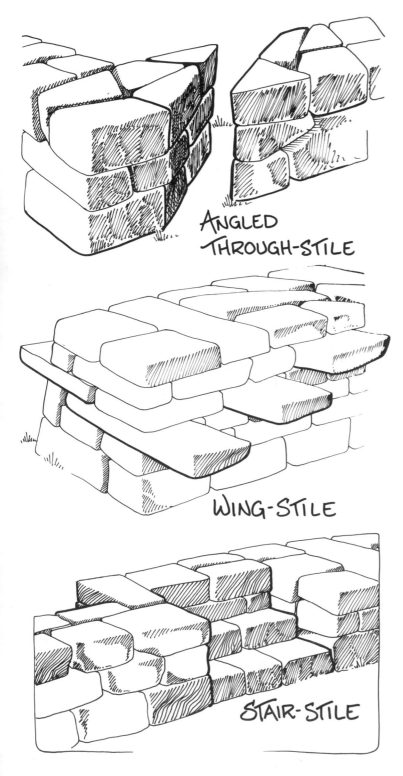

ANGLED THROUGH-STILE

WING-STILE

STAIR-STILE

RETAINING WALLS

A line of stone fence makes a most attractive retaining wall – a tier of rock that fronts and holds a bank of soil. It can be anything from a foot-high curb bordering the lawn beside the sidewalk to a 6-footer that reduces the slope of the yard in front of a house located up a steep rise from the street.

High retaining walls require special building techniques, construction permits, and the services of a qualified engineer, contractor, or mason. For details, see chapter 10.

A dry-laid retaining wall of up to a yard in height, though, is little more than a conventional stone fence with soil piled behind it. The wall can be built before the fill is added or it can be dug into an existing bank.

Be sure to build in a good degree of batter to resist the push of wet fill. One inch of rearward slope per foot of height is a minimum for a high wall (10 inches of batter for a 10-foot wall), and a garden wall can slope at both front and back in almost a pyramid shape to provide excellent soil retention.

But a low retaining wall facing a street looks best if the face to view is straight up and down. Compensate for a flat front by increasing the slope of the rear face. Increase the width of the footing, and build the rear, buried face at a definite angle – 45 degrees is not too much – to give the wall maximum holding power. Especially for a wall in a lawn or garden, where you wish to create a feeling of tranquility, put your larger rocks in bottom courses. Decrease average thickness and width of stones as you build up. Doing so takes less heavy lifting and is good stone masonry, but it also adds visual stability and an intangible sense of balance and permanence to the wall and it surroundings. Built the other way around, with big stones at the top, the wall would be just as sturdy if well laid but would appear to be teetering on its base, making a vaguely unsettling impression on the observer.

If the wall rises much over 2 feet, dig a deep footing, pack a face of gravel up to half as thick as the wall is deep behind the rock as you build, and lay tie stones back into the bank as if you were tying a corner. The gravel will aid in drainage, and each tie stone will give the wall an additional anchor. Place a *weep tube* – a length of 2-inch plastic plumbing pipe is good – every 5 or 6 feet along the bottom of the wall. Slant it at an upward angle from the face and back into the gravel layer. To make sure that sand and soil don't clog the uphill opening, pack it well in a bed of good-sized gravel. Water will drain out freely,

This stone retaining wall has held a steep roadside soil bank for over 200 years.

and the wall won't have to withstand the tremendous pressure exerted by a bank of waterlogged soil.

You can build stairs, stepped sitting walls, or rock planting boxes into a stone retaining wall; look through the landscaping and home-and-garden books and magazines for photographs of walls that will make your hands itch to begin placing stones. But, don't be in a rush. Stairs take the right stones, correctly placed. I've been working to perfect a stone stair for five years now.

Rock-garden plants or climbing ivy will root in the fissures between the rocks. And intentional gaps in courses, each with a long rock acting as a ceiling stone, or *header*, can be filled with rooting medium to hold large plants.

RETAINING WALL

SOIL FILL

WEEP TUBE

DEEP FOOTING

A MINI-WATERFALL

My favorite retaining wall is a vertical rock garden with a tiny waterfall, hidden away in the back garden of a gracious colonial home. The wall, built against the incurving bank behind a half-shaded flower garden, is made of native stones placed so that their weathered, lichen-covered faces protrude in a craggy, natural-appearing fashion to form a real grotto. The owner planted dusky-green rock-garden plants and clumps of native moss in the niches. Then she ground up leftover lichen and moss, mixed the slurry in buttermilk, and splashed the mixture on bare stone and into narrow crannies to inoculate the raw-looking spots with the beginnings of life.

During construction she had the mason install a length of inexpensive, semirigid PVC pipe behind the rocks. A garden-hose connector was joined with plastic

pipe cement to the downhill end of the pipe at one end of the wall. The other end was fitted with a plastic L fitting arranged to poke out between stones above a tiny pool. The pool is floored with flat slates that disguise a waterproof plastic-sheet bottom.

In the summer a hose is attached to the pipe and turned on when anyone visits the garden. Drainage is no problem. Flow is never more than a musical trickle, and when the pool fills, the overflow drains off among potted begonias nestling amid native ferns. When the leaves turn color in the fall, the hose is detached and the down-sloping pipe drains itself. But during the growing season, with water dancing down rugged and moss-covered rocks to splash into the pool hidden in a mass of greenery and bright flowers, the place is magic.

4

BRICK, BLOCK & MUD FENCE

To anchor a fence post so it will stay put under any conditions, or to build a really permanent fence or wall of tiles, brick, or cement blocks, you need to immortalize your work in concrete or mortar – *mud*, as is called in the trade.

The bonding agent that is the basis of all mud work is a formulation of natural mineral-rich materials, such as limestone, oyster shells, and iron ore, that is *calcined*, or heated in a kiln to 2,700 + degrees. Water is driven out, the materials fuse, and they are grounded into a fine powder: *cement*. The cement powder is mixed with varying amounts of naturally-occurring *aggregates* – sand and/or gravel – to make the dry base for masonry compounds. Those compounds are *concrete*, the plastic mix that hardens into skyscrapers and roads and is molded into cement blocks; and *mortar*, which is used to bond together individual rocks, vitrified clay bricks and tiles, or precast blocks.

When water is added, it combines chemically with the cement powder (recombines, really) in a process called *hydration*. The mixture of cement powder and water, now properly termed an *hydraulic cement*, solidifies within an hour, binding in the aggregates (sand or gravel) and adhering to almost any solid inorganic material. Over a period of three days it cures and hardens, and in a month or more it returns to rock. Here's how to use cement to build a monolithic structure that is as rock-solid as nature's own.

KNOW YOUR MUD

You can get Type-N cement some places, and you may find it congenial. Type-N is made from local clay rock that varies in quality (and reliability) but lets you work mud the old-fashioned way. Check building codes before using Type-N in a high fence or retaining wall; it may be prohibited for use in any architectural structure.

More consistent than Type-N is an assemblage of rocks containing alumina, iron, lime, and silica that was first concocted by an early-nineteenth-century British mason named Joseph Asphin and named after its resemblance to a rock from near the English city of Portland. Portland cement is sold in 94-pound, moisture-proof bags containing 1 cubic foot loose volume for about $6

per bag in small lots. The American Society for Testing Materials sets standards for cements, and ASTM Type-I is the general-purpose Portland cement you'll get unless you live in an area like the Far West where the soil is high in sulphates, which leach ordinary concrete, or you have a need for special curing times or temperatures because you are building a large structure.

Type-IA Portland cement is Type-I with an air-entraining compound, a kind of soap powder, added. Whereas large bubbles impart critical weakness to concrete and mortar and must be worked out of any architectural cement product, air entrainment adds several thousand tiny bubbles per cubic inch of finished material. The bubbles add resilience and resistance to freezing and chemical damage. In the Snow Belt, most commercial concretes are air-entrained.

The only other common cement is ASTM C91, or masonry cement. It goes only into mortar, but it's hard to come by outside the trade.

Type-1 Portland cement is what you'll find in most hardware and building-supply outlets, and it is fine for any home-scale project.

To get the terms and ingredients straight:

Cement is the bonding agent common to all mud works. It is sold by the 94-pound sack. Each sack needs about 5 gallons of water to undergo hydration and shrink back to rock. (Each cubic foot of dry cement powder plus almost as much water becomes ⅔-cubic foot of new-made stone.)

One part cement and a half-part water (by weight) mixed with two to three parts sand and three to five parts gravel becomes **concrete**, a plastic mix that is poured into molds on site or in a precasting facility. You mix your own or purchase it premixed by the cubic yard.

Portland cement and water mixed with equal parts of hydrated lime and two or three parts fine sand make **mortar**, which is used to create a bonding layer between rock, fired ceramic bricks, or precast concrete blocks. You always mix your own as needed on the job. It is easy to confuse the terms: cement, concrete, and mortar. If you call a commercial-aggregate company and order a ton of cement as a footing for your garden wall, you're liable to be charged double.

Premixes

In addition to pure Portland cement, which you *must* combine with sand and gravel (alone, with nothing to bond to, it has no strength), any building-supply or hardware store sells premixed cement products. To use premixes, all you have to do is add water, stir, and use. You'll find 25-, 40- and 85-pound sacks of a conventional sand/cement/lime *mortar mix*, a general-purpose *concrete mix*, and a *sand mix* that is used as a concrete patching/refinishing compound or stuccoing agent.

Sacrete is both a proprietary brand name and the generic term (like *Kleenex* or *Coke*) for all bagged cement mixes. A bag costs about $3.50 – too costly for large jobs, but fine for small projects. You can learn a lot about making good mud from a bag or two of premix, and I suggest that before tackling any major project you get some premix and play with it. Buy a 40- or 85-pound bag of concrete or mortar mix (surprisingly small to be so heavy,

and a defining example, if you need one, of "dead weight"). With it, buy a mason's trowel, and get hold of a barrow, cement mixer, or a 4- by 8-foot sheet of exterior-grade plywood. Make the plywood into a mortar box or mix your mud on the sheet directly. You'll also need your fence-maker's twine and a line level, plus hammers and chisels or concrete-working tools as appropriate and described below.

PREMIX AS A TRIAL MIX

If it is to set properly and last for a hundred years or more, cement must be mixed with the right amount of sand or gravel and water. Pros always make a trial mix of any new combination of materials to determine the best proportions for the application at hand, and so should you and I. To see what concrete should (and shouldn't) look like, trial-mix a bag of premix. Set up your first small project (see below), clean out a steel barrow, make up a mortar box or rent a cement mixer, and combine the dry mix with about ¾ of the amount of water specified on the package. Try to work with the resulting too-dry mix. The concrete will be gravelly; when you pat the top of the mix with a trowel, the rocks won't slide effortlessly into the sand-and-mortar matrix to give you the smooth presentation you want along molds and on top.

Now mix the balance of the water into about half of the too-dry mix. It will be too wet, and watery sand will slop away from the gravel. A trowel pushed into it will smush in, and when you slide it sideways, it will press gravel down and make a wave in the sand-mortar matrix. Now that you know what concrete *shouldn't* look like, mix it properly. You may need a cup or two more water than specified; add it in small amounts. The result should give you a sense of relief. It just feels and looks and flows right. With a light troweling, gravel will slip into the matrix, and the matrix will bounce up easily into a firm, smooth surface. Still, the concrete will have a dry look. When poured in small quantities, it won't quite flow but will want to hold together. It will fall in blobs and make a satisfying plop when it lands . . . like a well-fed toad. Piled in a cone, it will slump perhaps a third of its height.

SETTING A POST HOLE

Anchoring a mile of fence posts with premix and burying $3.50 in each post hole isn't economical. If you have that big a job, you'll still have to purchase cement by the sack, but you should buy sand and gravel in bulk – by the truck load. Using Sacrete to make a concrete anchor for a single post is a good practice project, though.

Let's work through installing a gate post: eight feet of 4- by 4-inch pressure-treated wood sunk 2½ to 3 feet down. Dig holes and compact the bottom with the post (as directed in an earlier chapter). Unless you have a flowing, sandy soil, compact the sides too as much as possible by wiggling the post back and forth; soaking the soil can also help it firm up. The concrete anchor can work loose in time if the soil surrounding it is loose. Now, put 4 to 6 inches of coarse gravel in the bottom and compact that, or lay a flat rock on the hole bottom.

Gauge the volume of the hole; if it's a small, post-hole-digger-dug hole no more than 8 inches across, and if it's in firm soil, I use all concrete for the anchor. Wider than that (as when you must dig out rocks), I interlayer rocks with the concrete. Assemble enough concrete (and rocks) to make a solid ring in the hole around at least 8 inches of the post's length; the concrete mass needn't fill the post hole to the top.

The easiest mixing board is an old 4- by 8-foot sheet of plywood. On a level board or in your barrow, mound the dry premixed concrete and scrape out a dent in the center to make a doughnut shape. Add water (3½ quarts per 85-pound bag of Sacrete, plus up to 2 more cups of water to make a full gallon if needed to get a flowing mix). Use a hoe to mix in the water by pushing the inside of the dry-mix doughnut out away from the puddle, then pulling dry mix from the outer perimeter back and into the water. On a board don't let the round doughnut of mix break, or all your water and much of the cement will flow off from the gravel and sand. The concrete will be weakened, even after you add a correct amount of new water. Masons' hoes have a hole in each side of the steel blade to make the mixing easier; garden hoes don't. Mine has no holes but always carries a rind of dry cement on the shaft.

LIST OF TOOLS AND MATERIALS FOR SETTING POST HOLES

Post-hole digger
Gravel
Spirit level
Tamping tool (long prybar)
Concrete mix and water
Mixing board or barrow
Mixing hoe
Shovel

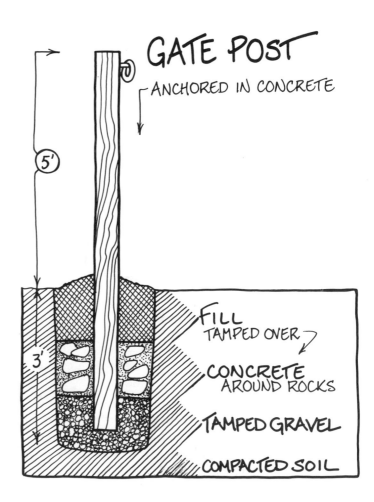

GATE POST
– ANCHORED IN CONCRETE

5'

3'

FILL TAMPED OVER
CONCRETE AROUND ROCKS
TAMPED GRAVEL
COMPACTED SOIL

Set the post in the hole, put another 6 inches of gravel or small rocks around the bottom of the post, and tamp it well enough that the post stands straight without support. I find that the long steel prybar I use in stone-wall building makes a good tamper in small-diameter holes. That rock layer is to let water drain; if you set a post in pure concrete it would be sitting in a basin, become waterlogged, and rot faster.

Now set the post plumb with a spirit level and shovel in your concrete around its base. You may find that, once mixed, the concrete obtained from a single sack would make a very small dent on that cavernous hole. If so, add in rocks if you have them. Clean the rocks; cement won't bond to soil. And be sure that each rock of any size is surrounded by concrete. I make a puddle of concrete, add rocks so they aren't quite touching, then top up with concrete. I build up in layers like that, punching the concrete in each layer down around the rock and working out any air bubbles with a stick or my fist.

Let the concrete set up overnight. Then fill the hole with the soil you removed, tamping it hard to set post and anchor to stay. Mound soil around the top to encourage water to run off.

To set a line of fence posts in concrete, buy the sacks of cement plus the sand and gravel and mix as needed. I find it easy to cement-anchor gate posts, the mailbox post, and such things as kid swing sets around the house. Trucking dry mix and 5-gallon jugs of water out to the fields is work – but worth it to anchor corner posts in pasture fencing and know they won't move for fifty years. If you live in an area of loose soil, deep post holes and cement anchors may be the only way to put up a fence to stay. Check with local fencers to see how much concrete should go in how much of a hole.

A FORMED SLAB

Can you think of anywhere you'd like a level, solid rock to step on – say under the gate in your new poultry-netting garden fence where the chickens are already trying to tunnel out? Build a small reinforced-concrete slab as practice for making wall footings. Dig out the sod in a rectangle a little more than 1½ feet wide by 1 foot across. Dig 6 or so inches deep – down to firm soil. Use a sledge-hammer, a wood beam, or bricks to compact bottom and sides well. Fill the hole to within 4 inches of the top with gravel, make it level on top, and tamp well. Now, build a rectangular form – two 2-foot-long and two 16-inch-long planks of scrap 2- by 4-inch lumber with four 8-inch stakes nailed on the outside at the ends, stake tops level with the tops of the form boards.

Nail the ends of the form boards together and tap the stakes and form down into the gravel so the top of the form is level with the soil. Use a spirit level or the leveling board with your fence-maker's line level laid on top to level the form all around. Made with nominal 2-by-4s set on edge, the top of the form will be about 3 inches above the level gravel bed; that's a correct thickness for a thin concrete slab.

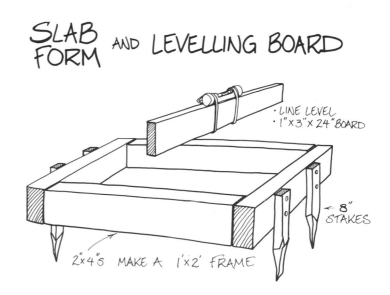

SLAB FORM AND LEVELLING BOARD

· LINE LEVEL
· 1" X 3" X 24" BOARD

← 8" STAKES

2"x4"s MAKE A 1'x2' FRAME

To give the slab the extra strength it needs, you can find a length of old wire fencing, metal lath, or even several thicknesses of chicken wire folded and stomped flat. Lay in the reinforcement, mix the concrete, and pour it in so the mix just overflows the form. With a stick or hooked garden cultivator, dig down into the bed of wet concrete, snag the reinforcement, and pull it up off the bottom of the form and into the concrete, but not to the top.

Now, rest a straight-edged *strike board* – the leveling board you used before you poured the concrete will do – on the sides of your form and *screed* the concrete: saw the board back and forth over the surface, moving forward slowly, agitating the overflowing top like so much jelly till a thin surface of cement and sand rises around the gravel to give you a smooth surface. Don't overwork it on any one pass or you will bring up too much water. If you do create a puddle of water, resist the temptation to sprinkle on dry mix. Wait till the water is absorbed, then go over the surface again, leaving it rough for a good foothold. Professional concrete workers would trowel the surface smooth, then score it for a good foothold, but you needn't bother.

Don't pull the forms for several days lest someone step on the edge of the uncured concrete and break it down. Cover the new slab with plastic sheet, and leave it on as long as you can. Three days is a minimum.

When you've removed the plastic and pulled your forms, you have made a reinforced, formed slab – a small version of the footing you'll need for a mortared wall.

EVALUATING PROJECT SIZE FOR DO-IT-YOURSELF CONSTRUCTION

Any cemented structure is a rigid monolith that will crack if the ground beneath it is not rock-solid. It *must* have an immobile footing strong enough to support weight of 100 to 400 pounds per cubic foot.

Low garden walls in warm climates can have footings as little as 1 foot wide and the same deep if the soil is solid, and shallow footings are okay in snow country if you reinforce them and build in expansion joints. But a tall wall must rest on a footing that is 6 to 12 inches thick and 4 inches wider on both sides than the wall it supports. To prevent cracking, the footing must be dug down to solid subsoil or 1 foot below frost – whichever is deeper.

Don't plan to skimp on the foundation. Any mortared structure you erect will outlive your need of it, and building codes are very firm on footing depths and dimensions and on materials and methods for a masonry wall. You'll need an approved design and a building permit for any substantial mud works. For a large mortared fence or retaining wall the code will probably require a qualified mason or aggregates contractor at least, to oversee the job.

If your wall is 30 feet long, and frost goes 2 feet deep in your part of the country, excavating a yard-wide footing trench will have you removing about 7 cubic yards of soil. You'll need to hire heavy equipment if you don't want to spend the hour needed to hand dig each cubic yard of average soil plus whatever time and effort is needed to remove it from the site.

For projects needing more than a yard of concrete, you are almost surely time and money ahead to call in a cement mixer unless you have a large and willing work crew with strong backs and a great deal of time on their hands. Bought concrete costs about $50 a yard – professionally mixed, delivered, and poured on the job. Buying all raw materials for mix-your-own may not save you much. (Figure five $6 sacks of cement per yard = $30 to begin; then you have to add in trucking costs for the aggregate, at least $5 a yard where I live.) Buying only the cement and digging your own aggregates and gravel in quantity from a sand bank and gravel pit will save a bit more, but at the cost of hours of very hard labor.

Do you really want to hand-mix concrete? Each yard of concrete must be handled five times. You must: (1.) Transport materials to the work site; (2.) Apportion components into dry mix; (3.) Mix thoroughly dry; (4.) Mix thoroughly with water; (5.) Haul to form and pour. That's *almost ten tons* of shoveling for each yard of concrete if you are doing it by hand. Steps 2, 3, and 4 can be done at once in a small cement mixer. All steps plus the transporting are done for you if you buy ready-mixed concrete.

I'm not trying to dissuade you from building your own wall from the ground up. But digging footings and hand mixing even a single yard of concrete is a whole lot of work. A backhoe can do the digging in a day, and all you need tell the aggregate firm is that you need concrete for a wall footing. Then you pay the bills.

MIXING YOUR OWN CONCRETE

Making mixes for prestressed, reinforced-concrete skyscrapers, interstate highways, and bridges is a precise science. But, for post holes and wall footings, you don't need an engineering degree.

For post holes, I make a freehand mix that consists of:

1 shovel of dry Portland cement,

3 shovels of clean sand (no soil or leaves and twigs in it),

4 to 5 shovels of clean gravel, and enough water to make the mixture flow properly.

Footings are more demanding, and you should measure more carefully. First, use the largest-size gravel practical, but no larger than 1/3 the thickness of the slab being poured.

The most important measurement is your cement-to-water ratio; water is added in proportion to the cement in each batch of concrete, not to the total mass of cement plus aggregate. Add 5½ to 6 gallons of fresh water to concrete mix incorporating each bag of Portland cement. The pros mix concrete by weight: at 8.33 pounds/gallon of water, you will add 46 to 50 pounds of water to each 94-pound bag of cement.

To be exact, figure proportions by mixing a trial batch of sand and gravel by weight, then add the exact amount of water needed to make the proper cement paste. Get a bathroom scale or spring scale, and measure ingredients out into a bucket. Record how many shovelsful are needed of each component to come up to the weights listed below to make the mix you want from the materials you have on hand. My little muscle-power cement mixer will hold a cubic foot and no more, so the following numbers are for 1 cubic foot of concrete. Multiply by 3 if you have a large motor-driven mixer available. Multiply by 27 to get amounts needed for a yard.

Most of the hobby masonry books dutifully tell you to follow traditional mason's practice, make up a cubic-foot measuring box, then weigh up cubic-foot measures of dry ingredients as though you were going to charge someone for the work. It's a waste of time for a home job. I measure by the shovelful. Last time I wrote it down, using my old garden shovel plus a new sack of bone-dry Portland cement, fine-grained sand, and river-run gravel,

MIXING CEMENT

FOR EACH CUBIC FOOT OF CONCRETE

POUNDS OF:

FINE CONCRETE	DRY CEMENT	WET SAND	WET GRAVEL	GALLONS OF WATER
½″ gravel	27	51	55	1⅔
My actual shovels:	(2½ plus ⅓)	(4½ + a bit)	(6 + a scant 7th)	
¾″ gravel	25	47	65	1⅔
COARSE CONCRETE				
1″ gravel	24	44	70	1½
1½″ gravel	23	38	75	1½

I measured as follows:

Cement weighed 10 pounds per shovel – shovel stuck in, lifted, and held till all loose powder had run off. That makes a very low pile on the shovel, as cement runs off easily when dry. Sand weighed 11 pounds per shovelful. It was a muddy sand that heaped up on the shovel; I had to tap the bottom of the shovel off the ground twice to lower the pile to a consistent measure. Gravel weighed 8 pounds; as much of the rounded 1/16- to 3/8-inch rounded stone as would stay on the shovel.

To get the number of shovels needed to make up each batch of concrete, I divided the weight of each shovelful into the numbers in the table below. The number of shovelsful needed to reach the indicated weights with my ½-inch-average-diameter gravel are in parentheses and bold-face type. Your weights and measures will be different. Keep the water-to-cement ratios precise, though.

Make up a trial mix to get the water right, as all combinations will vary with water content and specific gravity (weight to volume ratio) of sand and gravel. Sand stored in the open will hold about 5 percent water. Gravel will hold 1 percent. Make up a sample batch and pile a shovelful up into a cone (12-inches high is the standard, and the pros have metal cone-shaped molds they use). The cone should naturally slump more than a quarter but less than half of its height. It should look and behave as did the packaged mix. Too gravelly, add sand; too sandy, add gravel. If it is more sloppy than needed to get the mix into the mold, reduce water; too stiff to work properly, add water. Measure the additions carefully and modify measurements to make up the final mix. Measure and modify carefully the first time, and the rest is all shoveling.

PREPARING TO BUILD A MASONRY WALL

Whether made of field stones, cement block, or brick, a masonry wall demands precision. Sides should be straight, courses parallel and level, and layout and footing preparation must be exact. Brick masons work for years to perfect the skill of laying those perfectly squared chunks of ceramic into perfectly squared walls. You or I can't hope to approach a mason's speed or accuracy, but with care we can build a fence that only an expert can tell is amateur-made. (And then only because it is too carefully worked.)

You can build a wall only one brick thick, put buttresses in it, and it will stand just fine. In 1929 future British Prime Minister Winston Churchill built a retaining wall of that design at the back of his garden at Chartwell, his home in Westerham, Kent. He did well enough that the Amalgamated Union of Building Trade Workers gave him an "adult apprenticeship" card. Throughout a tumultuous political career, Churchill often reminisced that the summer he spent building that wall was the most peaceful and satisfying of his life.

For a free-standing brick fence, it is best to erect a pair of brick walls side-by-side to make a sturdy 8-inch-thick dry-cavity wall. A fence made of a single width of cement blocks makes a finished wall of the same size; it is just as sturdy and goes up a great deal faster. You can also mortar up a stone wall if you must, but don't just plan to slosh mortar in to speed dry-wall construction. Design a mortared stone wall to be as wide as the typical tie stones you will be using (see the chapter on stone building). With any masonry construction, lay out carefully and dig a good foundation for a proper footing.

Footings

Conventional size and depth of footings – the below-ground concrete pad that all masonry walls must rest on – are based on rules for making earthquake-proof residential buildings and are a bit much for a garden fence. The theoretical minimum footing is as deep as the wall is wide, half-again as wide as the wall, and at least half as thick as the wall, resting on 6 inches of well-compacted gravel atop stable subsoil. However, in frost country, the wall will crack if it isn't anchored well and deep enough that front won't heave it. For a retaining wall that will be holding back a substantial amount of fill, you must go well *below* frost.

To be practical, digging a footing for a 3-foot-high wall to below 4-foot frost level in the Great White North is a little silly. Dig your trench down to solid subsoil – at least 1½ feet deep. If the soil freezes solid during winter in your part of the world, 2 feet is better. If you need a block heater to get your car started in February, 3 feet is best. I'll show how to build in expansion joints to discourage cracking, but for best information on footing depths that are needed for your climate and soil type, telephone a local masonry contractor and ask how far he sinks footings for walls like the one you plan.

Plan to dig the footing trench 3 to 4 inches wide on both sides than the base of your wall. You must put a 4-to-6-inch thick layer of gravel under the footing for drainage. Minimum thickness of the concrete pad should be 3 inches for a low wall, 6 inches for a 4-foot wall, 8 to 12 inches for a 6-footer. If any masonry wall is going much over a yard high however, consult the local building code for footing specs.

Now lay the wall out with stakes and the level line just as with any other fence. You will be using this line to keep courses level, so be sure your stakes are as high as the fences will go. Don't tie the line tight to the stakes; tie loops on the ends and slip them over. Place the line on the side of the job opposite from where supplies will be coming from and where you will be working.

With a cutting spade, remove sod and topsoil in a trench a bit wider than the footing is to be, and add it to the garden compost pile. Remove subsoil to a level base (run a measuring line with a weight on one end, the other end looped on the level line, to get the base level). If the wall is going up a hill, arrange both layout line and the base in level steps. The rise of each step must be a multiple of the thickness of building materials: 8 inches for block, one or several brick thicknesses, or thickness of typical stone for a rock wall.

Preparing the footing.

Use a flat tamper or a 4 × 4 fence post to compact the soil well. Add in a 4- to 6-inch layer of gravel or crushed rock and tamp well.

Now decide whether you want to fill the trench almost to the top with concrete or lay a minimal footing and build up from that (and do your masonry bending down for the first few courses). Bear in mind that an 18-inch-wide footing trench dug 1½ feet deep with a 6-inch gravel layer can hold 1½ cubic feet of concrete per running foot. That's a bit more than a yard of concrete for each 20-foot section of wall. Filling the trench with concrete is easiest if you buy premix and must dig deep. A minimal footing is best if you are mixing your own for a shallow footing (and even then, you may have to widen the trench to get working room).

A FILLED-TRENCH FOOTING

To fill the trench with concrete, inset wooden top frames nailed to thin stakes into the sod along the top of the trench. Set the forms before adding gravel if soil is crumbly; stakes may shove dirt out into the trench. You may wish to make a ladderlike frame, with spreaders nailed on top of the form boards to keep them separated. Inset the form boards so their tops are just below sod level (you don't want the footing to show – especially with a stone or brick wall), and level the forms with a spirit level. Another approach is to stake 2 × 4 form boards on top of the sod along the top of the trench, and shave sod or shim the boards as needed to get them level. Then, fit your strike board with a blade that sticks down 3 inches into the trench so you can level the concrete to just below sod level.

A MINIMAL FOOTING

For a minimal footing to go in the bottom of the trench, make up forms from 6-inch-wide lumber. Set the forms in the gravel at each side of the bottom of the trench and tap them level. You may need spreaders to keep the forms straight. Tack the spreaders across the tops of the forms so they can come out as the concrete goes in. Top up gravel to make a 4- or 6-inch-thick footing, depending on height of your wall.

If you're stepping the footing up a hill, nail a cross member across the open ends of forms as they step up each rise to contain the fluid concrete.

Now put in your concrete. If possible, pour it all at once. If you're mixing your own, it's best to have one crew dry mixing, another adding water and mixing the wet stuff, and a third finishing. Work the concrete in the form by wading in it with rubber boots or sloshing up and down with a stick to get out bubbles, and screed immediately.

Reinforcement isn't essential in a footing, but it can discourage cracking – especially if you suspect that you could have dug deeper. Old steel fencing will work; trim and bury it just as with the paving stone made earlier. More professional is to use reinforcing rods. You aren't building a skyscraper, though; get them in the least-expensive size and lengths at any masonry-supply store. Two or three rods laid side-by-side in midfooting will compensate for some (but not all) slackness in digging out a footing trench.

If you buy premixed concrete, have plenty of helpers on hand. The cement-truck driver will arrange his chute as needed to help you do the work so long as you don't take all day. If any of the job is more than 15 feet from somewhere the cement mixer can drive easily, rent or borrow several fat-tired, shovel-nosed, metal-tub mason's barrows and plan to wheel the concrete quickly from truck to forms. The barrows will be heavy, and the ground may be soft, so have planks on hand to lay as a roadbed. The driver may help you distribute the mix, may not. For sure he won't help with any wheelbarrowing.

Don't be tempted to set your masonry into the wet foundation. Cover the new footing with plastic sheeting and let it cure for a week.

RAISED-FOOTING FORMS ON A SLOPE

"SCREEDING"

STRIKE BOARD; MOVE BACK AND FORTH

MORTARING STONE, BLOCK, AND BRICK

Once the footing is cured, you can begin laying fence. First, I'll discuss a mortared version of the stone walls detailed in chapter 3, and I'll cover mortar itself. Then will come block and brick fence.

The Dry Run

First step in mortaring a stone fence is to test-lay the foundation course dry, bedding each rock as solidly as you can. You're laying the bottom rocks on a concrete footing, and you'll find that with that flat, solid foundation, you will just naturally want to select only the best, most regular rocks and lay your courses to be as even and level as you can get them. There's more sighting along the level line and more shims that go into a mortared stone fence than into a fence dry-laid, and you'll find yourself chipping and splitting rocks that you would accept as-is in a dry-laid wall. Also, the more chips and small rubble you put in, the less mortar you'll need.

Only after the first course of stone is laid should you mix the mud. Make no more mortar than you can use within a half-hour, and it is best to underestimate at first. *Be sure to wash off your trowel, carrying bucket, and mixing equipment after each mix. Half-set mortar from a prior mix will accelerate setting of a subsequent batch.*

Mixing Mortar

Mortar is lovely stuff to work with. Buy a small bag of premix and make up a trial batch using the water quantities given on the package to see how it should look. Make it up too dry and too wet, then just right as described above for premixed concrete, and try working it in all modes. Too-dry mortar will crack when you throw it on the mortar board rather than flowing out in a lovely svelte line. If it's too wet, instead of sitting up proud it will sag into a puddle and drizzle over the edges of the trowel blade. Proper mortar has a crisp consistency – plastic and fluid, but not sloppy. It will give out a *tssssst* when you dig the side of your trowel in, then will stay together on the blade. Hold the trowel properly, with your thumb pointing directly at the tip of the blade. When you tip the

trowel by rotating your wrist and pulling back to lay a line, the mortar will roll off deliberately and land convincingly without cracking or puddling. Gently sling a wad of mortar at the vertical surface of a clean, moist (but not wet) stone or a concrete block. Good mortar will splat into a disk and adhere. Too dry, and it will bounce off; too wet, and it will stick but then slough off leaving a wet spot.

You can purchase mortar mix for $3.50 to $4 per 80-pound bag, or you can make your own from: one part Portland cement; one part hydrated lime (at $3.50 per 50-pound bag); and 4 to 6 parts moist sand. Add water as needed to make up a good-working mix.

To start, figure on 1 pint of water per 10-pound shovelful of dry mix. I wet the old plywood sheet used as a mortar board, dump on a shovelful each of cement and lime, add in five shovels of sand, and dry mix it well. Then, I make a little volcano of the dry mix, fill it with a bit less than 1 gallon of water, and stir. I add more water at the end to make it flow nicely. I find that this amount of mortar is about all I can use without rushing before it begins to set – and I still have to stir it each time I come for a load. That is working solo, now. With a helper mixing and carrying hod, the work goes four times as fast.

Back to the stone wall. . . .

Set the base course of rocks on the footing in a ¾-inch-thick bed of mortar, spread on and pressed down and smoothed out with the trowel. Remove a dry-laid

---

**TOOLS FOR LAYING
A MORTARED MASONRY WALL**

Layout stakes, twine, and line level

Mason's trowel

Straight-edged spirit level
  (a long mason's level is best)

(Long straightedge—one made of steel is best)

Mortar mixing board or cement mixer

Striking or joining tools

Mortar board or carrying bucket

A good running-water supply

Tools of the mason's trade: cement mixer, hoe and shovel, bricks and blocks, pre-mixed concrete and sand.

rock or two, spread mortar on the footing, and reset the rocks, tamping each well to create a perfect stone-mortar-footing bond.

I work on one course at a time, waiting for the mortar to dry to lay following courses; unlike brick and block, which are four-square in all dimensions, even well-shimmed stones can wobble in soft mortar, breaking the bond. Let each course dry for a day.

When the second course has been well dry laid, mix your next batch of mortar. Remove each stone, fill the hollow places inside the wall with mortar and rubble, and replace the stone in as little mortar as needed to bed it completely – but be sure there is a minimum ¼-inch mortar bed between stones.

Each rock should rest solidly on stones below it; the mortar shouldn't be an excuse for laying a poor stone wall.

After a few minutes' sitting undisturbed, the mortar will lose its wet sheen and begin to firm up. Before it hardens, you must tool each joint, compressing and finishing the surface to exclude water. As soon as you can poke a finger in and the print remains firm (within a half-hour, minimum), use your trowel edge or a jointing tool to scrape out each joint to be slightly concave. Press the mortar in a little farther at the top of a horizontal joint than at the bottom, to make a down-and-out-sloping lip to guide water out of the wall. Press hard so the mortar bonds solidly in a well-feathered lip to both upper and lower rocks. Mold joints smoothly in both horizontal and vertical dimensions – as if you are making water guides

for the many years' rains that will be running down and off your wall; leave no little ledges or pockets that water can puddle in.

Be sure to cap a mortared wall well. Water – especially the acid rain we seem to be getting these days – will seep into an imperfect top and leach the alkaline mortar. In cold country it will freeze and push the mortar out. Lacking enough flat top stones to cover most of the surface, you can build a box similar to a ladder-shaped footing form, set it on top of the wall, and trowel in a 2-inch-thick *concrete cap* (never apply mortar over ½-inch thick). Or, make up or purchase precast concrete paving blocks and mortar them on. Get that top course of rock perfectly level: lay in as many shims as needed, don't skimp on the spirit level, and refer to the layout line constantly. Those square-ended, flat castings look awful unless they are laid level and their sides are aligned perfectly all along the wall.

Slip-Form Construction

Another approach is to build box-shaped wooden forms atop your footing and lay mortar and stones using the box as a giant mold. Arrange the most attractive stones so that the flattest faces are exposed to public view. Have all materials on hand and build fast so you can remove the form before the mortar hardens from exposed rock faces. Such a fence can have sides as perfectly flat and vertical as a brick wall.

Concrete Blocks

The quickest masonry fence you can build is made from concrete blocks—inaccurately called "cement blocks" by everyone, myself included. A standard block is 15⅝ inches long and 7⅝ inches high and deep. Figuring a ⅜-inch mortar layer between blocks, you plan a structure in 8-by 16-inch segments and courses that are 8 inches high.

Blocks contain two or three through-holes, or cores, which reduce weight. A common *stretcher*—the main building block—is shaped like an elongated H to reduce the size of mortar joints between blocks in the vertical dimension. Blocks cost about $1 singly or delivered in strapped "cubes" of ninety blocks that will make up 80 square feet of one-block wall. One cube will make a wall 20 feet long and 4 feet high at an approximate cost of:

Block: 90 @ $1.00 =	$90
Mortar	5
Cap blocks 20 @ $.50	10
Footing concrete: 1 yd.	50
	$155
COST PER RUNNING FOOT:	$7.75

The approximate number of stretchers you need is easily computed;

1. **Divide the length of the wall in inches by 16 (15⅝ inches per block plus mortar joint),**

and

2. **Multiply the result by the height of the wall in inches divided by the height of a mortared block: 8 inches.**

Example: for a 20-foot wall:

1. **Divide 20 feet × 12 inches/foot or 240 by 16 = 15**
2. **Multiply 15 by the wall's height (4 feet × 12 inches = 48) divided by height of a block, or 8 = 6 and, 15 × 6 = 90 (close enough).**

For ends, you will need to replace some stretchers with end blocks that have one smooth end face. You will need one full and one half-sized end for each course.

The day before you plan to build, break the straps that compress the blocks into a cube, so water will flow through freely, and wet the blocks, especially if they've been stored under cover. If blocks are too dry, they'll suck the water out of the mortar, and hydration won't be complete. At this time inspect the blocks to learn top from bot-

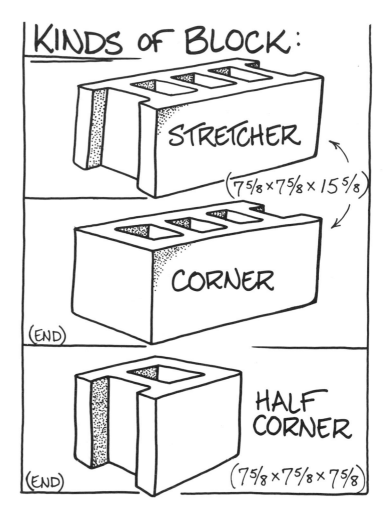

KINDS OF BLOCK:

STRETCHER

(7⅝ × 7⅝ × 15⅝)

CORNER

(END)

HALF CORNER

(END)

(7⅝ × 7⅝ × 7⅝)

tom; the core holes are tapered slightly to a cone shape so the molds used to make them can be extracted. The broader or thicker face should go up, to provide a larger mortar bed.

Next step is to make a dry run, laying out the entire first course of the wall without any mortar, a half-sized end block at one end, a full-sized end block at the other, and regular stretchers in between. Space all blocks a precise ⅜-inch apart. Set the line-up twine at precise block height, level it on the stakes, and remove the line level so it won't get in the way. Line the blocks up precisely with the line almost touching their outer edge, but don't crowd the line; any block that touches the line can create a bulge in the wall. Snap a chalk line or scratch a groove in the footing top along both sides of the course in case you kick a block out of alignment.

Once the footing is in and the first course is dry laid with the level line in place, I mark off 8-inch distances (or block thickness plus ⅜-inch) up one of the stakes, to determine the level of future courses and to be sure that mortar joints are all an equal thickness. Real masons dispense with stakes and use experience to adjust mortar levels, but I need all the help I can get.

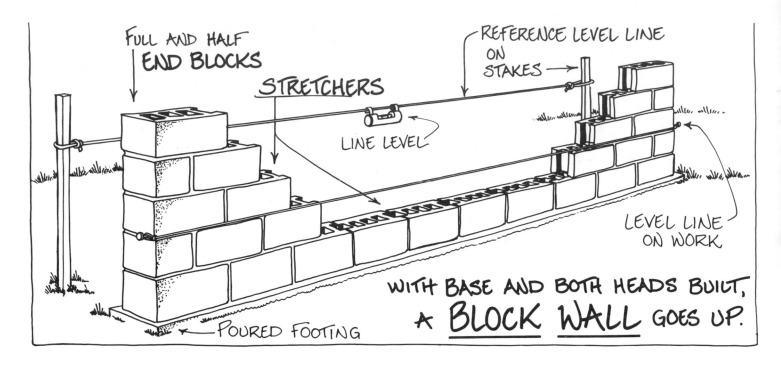

FULL AND HALF END BLOCKS

STRETCHERS

REFERENCE LEVEL LINE ON STAKES →

LINE LEVEL

LEVEL LINE ON WORK

POURED FOOTING

WITH BASE AND BOTH HEADS BUILT, A **BLOCK WALL** GOES UP.

LAYING BLOCKS

To bed blocks on the footing, raise the level line on your stakes to exactly the height of your block plus ⅜-inch. Be very precise. If you keep the line singing tight, you needn't keep the line level in the center of the course; rather, you can read it accurately from right beside any block in any home-place-sized wall.

Remove an end block and the stretcher next to it, and lay a generous ½-inch-thick, block-sized pad of mortar under the end block only. Mound the mortar pad into two rails (so block sides will bed well) by making a groove down the center of the pad with the trowel, and set the block back in place. With one eye on the level line and using a spirit level to check and the trowel handle or a hammer to tap the block gently, adjust till it is aligned perfectly with the twine and is level and square in all dimensions. The end block will be a mortar-bed higher than the rest of the dry run.

If you find yourself fiddling with adjustments for more than a minute or two per block at first, you are asking for a poor bond. Admit that you are a novice, pull the block, discard the mortar, and hose off foundation and block. Have a cool drink of lemonade and try again at the other end. When the footing has dried, lay a fresh block, and appreciate the skill of an experienced mason.

With the first corner block set perfectly, on go the stretchers. Set the next three or four blocks in the dry run up on end to one side of the footing. Lay down a pad of mortar, and groove it. Butter the twin butt ends of a standing block with ½-inch lines of mortar and set it in

against the corner, dropping the block onto the mortar bed from an inch or so in the air and aiming with enough forward momentum that the vertical mortar joint is the correct ⅜-inch thick and that only a tap or two with the trowel handle is needed to align it with the level line and square it up in all dimensions with the spirit level. You can butter ends of both blocks if you like; it is more work, but it does make an easier joint. Scrape up mortar oozing from the joints with the heel of the trowel and use it to butter the next block, but discard any mortar dropped on the ground and contaminated with dust.

Take your time in setting the base course. Don't be afraid to waste mortar; be sure to get the mortar pad on thick enough so you can adjust the block by tapping and squishing out mortar from the sides. But keep the block *level* as you squish! Any time you have to remove a block (usually because you've laid too thin a mortar bead and one end has dipped too low) hose it off and get a new block that is thirsty for mortar. You can add another dollop of mortar to the old bed so long as you haven't worried it for more than 60 seconds.

The secret of good block- and brick laying is to get the mortar joint together quickly – ideally in a single drop and with a tap or two on each end – so the thirsty blocks or bricks will glom onto the mortar (and one another) in a permanent bond. Every extra wiggle you apply to adjust the masonry threatens to weaken the bond. But better to tap and adjust over a thick bed of mortar than try to cram mortar into an open joint of half-dry mortar. The patch is bound to make a poor seal and work out.

BUILDING LEADS

After the base course is laid, it is best masonry to build a wall from a succession of *leads*, where you stack up the beginnings of several courses at each end first – four blocks in the first course above the base, three in the second, then two, then one – leveling them very precisely with the layout twine and line level. When the courses between those leads are filled, another set is built. All the precision measuring and leveling is done at the leads; then a length of mason's twine is laid right on the work – so it runs just off the far side of the course where you want the egde of each block to line up. If you look hard enough you can get proper mason's twine with special corner blocks or cups that will grab to corners of brick or block. Once his leads are set, a skilled mason can fill in the center of each course as fast as a helper can sling the blocks. It's a wondrous thing to see.

Ends are laid up with long and short blocks alternating as courses rise. That way, stretcher blocks in successive courses are staggered in *running bond* so that each joint is covered top and bottom by solid block (unless you want to put in a vertical slip joint to compensate for differential expansion and an inadequate footing. Details follow).

Turning corners, you must lay out guide lines along each flight of wall. Don't use half-blocks to end each odd course. Lay full-sized corner blocks in alternating directions so each block always covers a mortar joint below. If the angle is a perfect 45 degrees, the corner will be knife sharp. With any other angle, or turning corners in a curve, you'll have partly open joints – with little corners of block jutting out along the vertical edge at each corner. This will cause no structural weakness and will admit no water if the mortar is well joined to the blocks.

To establish the level of each course above the base, rather than continue to raise the level line on stakes, you can make a *story pole* – a stick marked at 8-inch intervals to indicate the precise elevation of the top of each course above the footing. You must have a clear strip of footing to set the pole on, though – hard to attain by a mortar-spilling amateur like myself.

Check level as you lay each block.

LAYING BLOCK-ON-BLOCK

Once the base course of blocks is laid, you will be setting block on block. Lay the mortar in twin ¾-inch-deep lines along the outer rails, or the long ends, of three or four blocks at a time. Don't bother laying mortar *across* the courses; it adds nothing to strength. Set three or four blocks up on end, and butter the two face ends with an even, half-inch-deep line of mortar. Holding the block by the partitions between core holes, set it into the mortar bed as accurately as you can by eye. As you set a block in, tip it slightly toward you so you can see where it will meet the lower course. Use the level line or story pole to adjust for correct mortar-bond thickness. Use the spirit level to adjust for level and plumb, and employ the level (or better, the longest straightedge you can find) to be sure the face of each block is in a perfect plane with all blocks adjoining it.

Adjust each block by tapping gently with the trowel handle. Blocks will settle gently into new mortar and slide back and forth easily. Do all adjusting now. If you move a block once the mortar is set, the bond will unseal, weakening the wall and admitting water. With your trowel, cut off mortar that protrudes from joints and use it to butter the next blocks. Any that falls to the ground should be discarded; catching mortar extruding from joints just as it is about to fall becomes a most satisfying skill.

You'll have difficulty at first setting in the *closure block* – the one that goes in the opening left at midpoint

of each course. The opening is only one block wide, and both ends of the block must be buttered. You only have one chance to set it in; misjudge your alignment and the butter will shear off one or another joint. You are best advised to remove and scrape mortar off that block, hose it down, and let it rest for a day or two. Butter up a new one with fresh faces thirsty for mortar. You must push the block down at just the right speed, so that mortar sticks to the moving ends but slides along the stationary faces. If you take too long with the mortar in the closure itself, scrape it out, hose it down, and come back in an hour. The knack will come with practice. Don't even think of making a *slush joint*, where you dribble mortar down into the space between stationary blocks. The mortar will not be compressed against the blocks, the bond will fail, and the shades of generation on generation of masons past will shudder.

Within a half-hour of laying each course, finish the joints on both sides of the blocks. Without good jointing, the wall will leak. Water in the wall will freeze in cold winters and break the joints. Even in mild climates it will gradually eat out the mortar. Use the trowel tip, a straight pointing tool or a mason's S-shaped jointer to *strike* vertical joints: press in hard on the soft mortar to create a firm, water-tight seal between mortar and block. Discard all of the partly-set mortar. Tool horizontal joints deeper at the top than at the bottom so that the mortar slopes down and out to guide water out. Strike the vertical joints in a smooth concave curve, and don't leave little dams to retain water where joints intersect. I strike the up and down joints after tooling the horizontals to assure a good water flow off the wall face.

EXPANSION JOINTS

To build in an expansion joint, build facing ends in the middle of the wall, beginning alternate courses with half-stretchers to create a continuous vertical joint or a straight seam up the middle of your wall. Mortar that joint as usual but weaken the bond by scraping out mortar to a depth of ¾-inch in the vertical joints between blocks on both sides. Fill the joint with painter's caulking compound. That will permit the wall to shift without breaking.

Put expansion joints in every 10 or 20 feet if your weather is extreme and you fear your fence's footing may be too shallow.

GATES

Design in a gate anywhere you like. (The width can be any multiple of 8 inches). You'll need more full and half-size end blocks to close up every other course in the gate opening. Set bolts in the mortar joints between end blocks to hold on a wood frame. I make the frame and a wooden sill for the gate of 8-inch-wide-by-2-inch-thick hardwood lumber and drill it as needed to set anchor bolts into both frame members and mortar joint as the courses rise. A heavy wood gate goes well in a block wall.

If you don't want to use a wooden sill, fill the sill blocks with mortar mixed with enough extra water to make a slip or grout that will flow easily into the cores. If the sill course rests on a lower course of block rather than the footing, place a mortar-support over the joint between them – metal lath is conventional, but a length of

Striking the joints.

hardware cloth will do. Otherwise, you will be pouring grout down successive cores all the way to the footing.

Use the same technique to seal the top of the wall, making a slight ridge – a peaked roof – on top. Or, set 1-inch-thick cast-concrete paving blocks on top of the top course. Flat rock, slate, or 16- by 8-inch paving or patio blocks will do fine, too. Lay a mortar bed along the faces and on the midribs under joints in the top course of block. Arrange the top pieces so that joints in the top are not over joints in the course below. Butter ends and set in the top blocks. If a top joint falls over a core hole, put a length of hardware cloth over the opening and lay a line of mortar on it so the joint will be fully supported. You will finish up a wall needing half a top block and will likely have to split one. Use a masonry blade for a circular saw if you have one. Otherwise score the block deeply with a chisel all around and tap it gently along the crack till it breaks. You may have to try breaking several before you get a clean fracture. Put the broken end in the mortar joint.

FURBISHES

Once you get a footing in and learn the knack of setting in blocks, your wall will go up very quickly, but raw cement block isn't very attractive. You may want to prepare in advance to decorate it. You can buy or make (from nonrusting aluminum wire) wall ties or keepers that are set to protrude from the joints. You can attach vines to them or use them to wire on wooden trellises.

For a smooth wall, plaster the blocks with mortar. Wet the wall down one evening and the next day mix up a thin plaster of mortar and water and trowel it on. Getting a plaster-smooth surface isn't hard, but you can put in intentional swirls or pat the surface as you trowel to produce a rough texture that will disguise imperfections in your plastering technique as well as hide the joints in the wall.

Most elaborate is to veneer the block with decorative brick or stone that is cut or cast thin for surface decoration. These lightweight veneers have a thirsty backside that will stick happily to mortar plaster; you simply trowel on the plaster, stick on the veneer, and tap thoroughly with the trowel handle to ensure a good bond. Most masonry veneers come boxed with good application directions.

Concrete block is also made in open-lattice designs that are good to let air through. And you can substitute fired tiles in any number of designs and colors, both solid and in open-work designs. Laying them is done the same way as laying block; only the dimensions are different. Just be sure to clean spilled mortar off tiles immediately (unglazed tiles in particular).

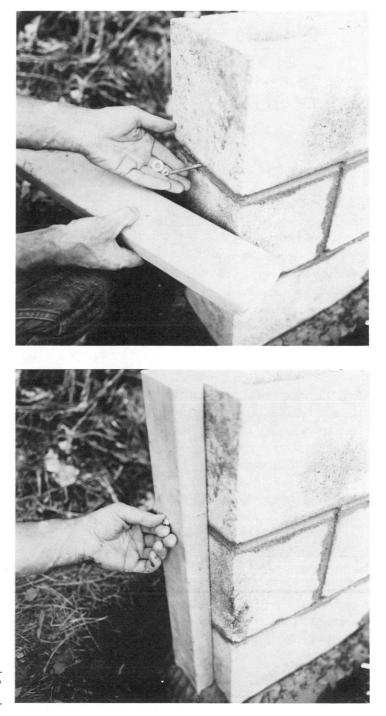

Attaching wood post to bolt cemented into a block wall.

Brick

Laying brick is the self-same process as putting up concrete block, only it's more exacting and time-consuming – and a great deal more costly. Like block, brick comes in "cubes" – of 544 bricks, which will build half the amount of 8-inch-thick wall as a cube of block. But bricks cost several times as much as blocks. For comparison, to build a 20-foot-long, 8-inch-thick, 4-foot-high wall of brick (twin faces of dry-cavity wall), you will spend:

Brick: 2 cubes @ 180 =	**$360**
Mortar:	**20**
Footing concrete: 1 yd.	**50**
	$430
COST PER RUNNING FOOT:	**$21.50**

That's almost three times the cost of a block wall and five or six times the cost of the most elaborate custom-built wooden fence.

I doubt that you'll want to spend over $4,000 in materials for 100 feet of 8-foot brick wall to fence off the back alley when a top-quality stockade fence can do the same job for less than ten percent of that cost. If you do, you can get the services of a professional mason thrown in for not a great deal more.

Still, a little, low brick wall can fence off the front yard or provide a space-divider and low sitting space at the side of the garden, and it can do so with a style that no other material can provide. Brick is classy-looking stuff, no question about it. It's *substantial*. Banks are made of brick. You can design with brick too – in a way you can't with big, cumbersome block or even with fence boards; look in the home-and-garden design books and magazines for ideas.

Finally, working with brick is more fun than pulling taffy. You shouldn't wear gloves; start slowly to let your hands become callused enough to enjoy the feel of baked clay. When you get into the flow of it, the mortar lays out in sweet lines, and you sweep off drippings from the joint laid just before and use them to butter the end of a new brick, which you slip firmly in place, and tap twice before moving on. There is a graceful rhythm to laying brick that is very satisfying. I suggest that before tackling a brick fence you seek out a construction project and watch the smooth and effortless technique of pros who can lay two cubes a day.

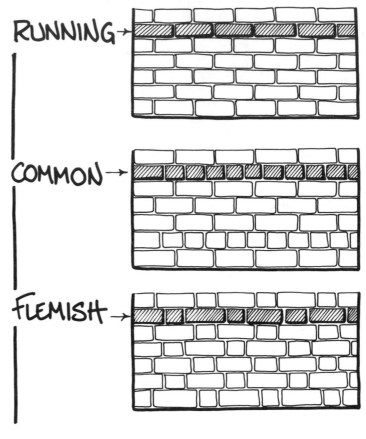

PATTERN BONDS:
RUNNING→
COMMON→
FLEMISH→

PICKING BRICK

Visit a building- or masonry-supply store to choose your brick; it comes in a greater variety of color and surface textures than you might guess. In addition to the masonry tools listed above you will need a *bolster* or *brick-set* – a wide-bladed, hardened brick-splitter available at any hardware store. A *mason's hammer* is useful for trimming or splitting brick; one end is a square-faced hammer, the other a curved, pointed chisel you can use to score brick on both sides to get a good break.

So long as you avoid laying bricks with the joints lined up, you can arrange them in any pattern you see fit. Some of the variations are illustrated. On your own footing, (or before it goes in) I suggest that you dry lay several feet of wall. Try it in standard running bond, in Flemish, English, and common bond.

For a single-face wall, you can use simple *running bond.* Try weaving in buttresses or two- to three-brick piers at the ends and every 10 to 15 feet along the wall. Build in a gate with square pillars at each side, a sitting bench, a stair, or an arched alcove at mid (focal) point along the wall. Use your imagination. The Building codes may specify footing depths and will regulate how bricks are laid in dwellings, but any brick arrangement will make a good fence so long as no two joints line up in bond.

Most bonds contain twin faces (*wythes*) of brick, and alternate bricks laid sidewise in the wall – stretchers – with bricks laid endwise: *headers*. Those make the most common and sturdy wall, with an open cavity between the two wythes to drain moisture. The headers connect wythes for strength, and a top course of headers makes a simple cap. If you build a twin-face wall in running bond, you'll need wall ties – 6-inch lengths of corrugated sheet metal or wire – to set into joints along every even-numbered course from the second one up. I make wall ties from fence-wire pieces 6 inches long with a hook bent into each end.

As you should with all fencing, try to live with the brick design for a while before setting it in cement (literally). Design trends these days lean toward simplicity. Though they are more fun to build, the more involved patterns can become irritating, especially if you are using an ornamented brick. I've seen brick work where the headers are all dark, the stretchers all light, and it looks like a checkerboard to me. Perhaps such a pattern will fit your place and your own good taste; just be sure before you mortar it up.

STRUCTURAL BRICK BONDS:

STRETCHER

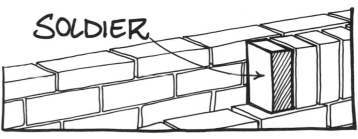

HEADER

SOLDIER

Setting brick into a mortared bed.

BUILDING WITH BRICK

Here's how to put up a twin-face wall in *common bond*, which isn't as simple and common as the name suggests. Common bond consists of three course patterns: common stretchers, headers with bricks cut to ¾ length at the start and end, and stretcher courses begun and ended by headers. The differing sequences of headers and stretchers are to ensure that no joints line up. I'll suggest again that you cut bricks and dry lay a full section of this or any other brick fence before you begin laying – to get the patterns straight and be sure you like them.

Put in your foundation. If you want to bury several hundred dollars' worth of brick instead of concrete worth small change, you can make the footing of bricks too. As far below grade as needed in your climate, tamp soil, lay 6 inches of gravel, and on that your mortar pad. Set in a base course of two columns of headers laid end to end (for a 16-inch-wide base). Repeat for a double thickness. Center on this a course of headers and stretchers butted together for a 12-inch layer, and on that lay a full course of headers. At current prices (about 33 cents a brick) that's $8 or $9 dollars a running foot buried for now and forever, and with a foot or more yet to rise to see daylight.

The strongest mortar thickness for brick is ¼-inch – though you may have to double that for warped bricks. To lay the wall, set your guide line at a height of brick width plus ¼-inch above the footing, and dry lay the base course of each wythe so that the outer faces are 8 inches apart – the length of a brick laid as a header. Scratch the bedding pattern on top of the footing with a nail and pull the lead bricks. Lay a solid mortar bed for three or four brick lengths and groove it down the center of each wythe just as for blocks. Set in end bricks along the guide line, and tap to proper mortar depth. Then butter the ends of the next brick and begin laying the foundation course. Continually check with the level line to keep alignment and mortar depth correct. Brick masons adjust by *eye* (and if you look closely at some new walls, you'll see a lot of waves: seasick brick work). To minimize the problem, I do a lot of squinting down the wall and check plumb and square *every* so often with the spirit level.

When the base is laid, set up five-course leads to be filled in between as the wall goes up:

1. **Three stretchers on the bottom of each wythe;**
2. **A ¾-brick followed by four headers;**
3. **Two stretchers;**
4. **A stretcher course led off by a header and one stretcher; and**
5. **A single stretcher to start another stretcher course.**

Put in a header course just above the base course and in every fourth to sixth course as you rise. To start a header course, cut the lead bricks to ¾ length, then lay in headers so that the center line of a header brick coincides with the joint above and below. Another cut brick will be needed at the other end.

Build in from the leads using the guide line, just as with blocks. When the first leads are filled, raise a new set of leads – as always, measuring, aligning, and leveling carefully.

It gets to be a real kick to lay brick rapidly; you slice out a wedge of mortar, lay and groove it down the center in two fluid motions, butter the next brick, and slide it in, tap with the trowel handle, and catch the extruding mortar to butter the next brick. It makes you feel at one with masons going back a thousand years. But don't get so carried away with your new-found proficiency so that you build in a sag or lean. Stoop down to check that *every* brick in a low course is flush with the guide line till you are sure you are getting it right. Be sure you aren't crowding the line, and double check that the twine is perfectly taut.

Closure joints in brick are easier to complete than in block walls. The base mortar is already in place. Butter ends (or sides in header courses) of both bricks already in place. Butter the closure block too, and squash it in. Mortar will ooze out all around, which is what you want to effect a good seal.

The final part of the job is tooling the joints. Use the trowel point for flush, struck, or weather joints. A rounded jointing tool is needed for concave or *beaded* joints and a square-edged tool for the deeply-inset *raked* joint. However you do it, press firmly to seal the mortar. Finally, before the mortar is set, scrape the inevitable blobs of mortar off the brick, then take a rough brush to brick faces and joints. If the brick is permanently stained by mortar, muriatic acid from any full-line paint or hardware store will clean it. Use the stuff with caution!

MORTAR JOINT FINISHES:

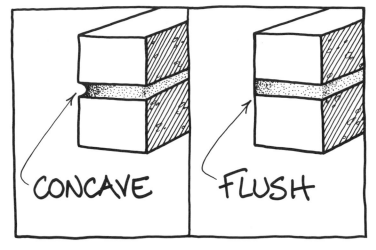

CONCAVE   FLUSH

STRUCK   WEATHER

THE CLEAN-UP

Finally, after every session, clean up. Hose wet concrete or mortar off every tool that isn't going to be used within the hour. Cement will stick forever to almost anything hard. Wash mortar boards down to bare wood and hose the barrow to slick metal. If you leave a concrete mixer uncleaned overnight it will be ruined, a pod of hardened and adhering concrete settled in what will ever more be the bottom of its now-off-weighted drum. Any time you don't plan to use steel tools for a while, oil the metal surfaces; steel scoured by cement and sand will be totally unprotected and begin to rust immediately. Cement's caustic action drys wood, too, so when you're done for the season, apply a liberal coating of linseed oil to wood handles of trowels and shovels and hoes, and rub it in well. You'll want tools of the trade in good condition the next time you get the urge to play in the mud.

5

LIVING
FENCE
&
HEDGEROWS

The second-best thing about a living fence is that it is practically maintenance-free. It doesn't need painting, and you never have to patrol it to replace fallen rocks or repoint breaks in the mortar or fix broken wires or split boards. You will have to tend the plants when they are very young, but only till roots are deep enough to stand up to wind or passing creatures and to survive dry weather. Once it is established, a hedge or hedgerow needs no more than occasional trimming.

The first and best thing about a living fence is the vibrant, ever-changing life that it sustains – especially if planted to a mix of flowering and food-bearing plants. Forsythias in our newest tall hedge announce spring with their sun-gold blossoms and are followed by old-fashioned mock orange and red honeysuckle that draw ruby-throated hummingbirds as well as several types of bees and nectar flies. I swear that it's the fruit of the Russian olives that attracts a pair of cardinals that don't normally nest in our cold climate. Chipmunks and squirrels scrabble for fallen cones in the mulch beneath the evergreens, flocks of migrating finches nibble their way through the hedge fall and spring – and the growing season through, we snack from bush cherries, tall-bush blueberries, and dwarf apples planted in the hedge.

Our first live fence was planted along the front of our farmhouse the same summer and for the same reason that we put a lath-and-furring fence out back – to restrain an energetic young son. I put in that fence using a low-cost system of succession planting that I dreamed up, and the scheme is as workable now as it was then.

A TEMPORARY FENCE IN A PERMANENT FENCE'S TRENCH

We wanted a quick-growing barrier to keep the children safe and serve as a privacy screen for a distance of about 40 feet along the road. A tall-enough wood fence would have been out of character on a narrow forest road, and we lacked the cash and the inclination to buy a ready-made hedge of prepruned foundation plants. A woods home needed a woodsy living fence, but most plants appropriate to a permanent hedge take years to grow.

To serve the first year or two, we decided to put up a temporary screen of chicken wire and cover it with quick-growing annual vines. It would come out easily as the permanent hedge plants took over.

Single planting holes dug into sod are satisfactory for setting large hedge plants that will shade the grass immediately. But we would be putting in seeds and small plants, so we dug up a trench that could be cultivated like a garden. I got out the rotary tiller and prepared a trench to satisfy the old rule: "Dig a ten-dollar hole for a five-dollar plant."

I scattered a thick layer of soil-sweetening wood ash atop a 2-foot-wide strip of land along the fence line and used the rotary garden tiller to chop the sod, mix the ash, and loosen the topsoil as deep as the tines would go. Then I dug out the dark loam, piling it in a bank alongside the trench. A good 6-inch layer of the lighter-colored clay subsoil and rocks came out next, and I carted them off.

I shoveled the sod/topsoil/ash mix back into the hole, tromped it well, and topped up the trench with the richest soil on the place: pure, composted litter from the chicken house, which had already been brought to a neutral soil acidity with scatterings of ground limestone. A length of 4-foot-high poultry netting was strung loosely from tall poplar poles set 6 feet apart along the trench in front of the house. Louise planted seeds of annual vines along the wire line.

Thinning green bean seedlings in a temporary screen.

Seeds for a Quick Fence

To provide a quick screen offering foliage, flowers, and edibles, Louise interplanted the following:

BEANS

Several seeds of Kentucky Wonder and Scarlet Runner Pole Beans went in around each pole. The Kentucky Wonder is a fast-growing vine that produces broad leaves, an innocuous white flower, and wonderfully-flavored green snap beans on vines that will grow to 15 feet with support. Scarlet Runners, not so vigorous, produce bright-red flowers and beans that are good eating if you catch them young. When germinated and showing two true leaves (first leaves following the fat, half-bean-shaped cotyledons or nursery leaves), the bean plants were thinned to two plants of each variety per pole. The first climbing tendrils from each plant, which will grow upward to the sun any way they can, were trained up the pole. As side shoots appeared, they were strung out along the wire – by carefully unwinding each day's upward spiraling growth at the tip of each vine end and extending it lengthwise.

MORNING GLORIES

We always start a dozen or so pots of Heavenly Blue morning glories (*Ipomoea*, called "moonflower" in Britain) in March for heavy bloom all summer and fall. I use a stout knife to make a nick at the base of the tear-drop-shaped seeds and soak them overnight in warm water. Five seeds are poked two seed-thicknesses deep into sterilized compost or commercial planting mix inside 4-inch planting pots made of pressed peat moss. To plant, you just set the pots in the soil along with the young seedlings and forget them, as the pots molder down in time. The seeds never germinate at the same time – given a soaking or not. After two weeks the three most vigorous plants in each pot are kept, and the pots are placed together in a sunny window and watered well till time for setting out.

When the vining tendrils of our fence-line morning glories appeared, Louise poked a thin, yard-long stick into each pot so they would climb straight up and not wind around aimlessly to knot together in a Medusa's snarl. For the new screen Louise placed a pot each few feet along the wire, poked the sticks into the wire, and as the vines grew, spread the tendrils out in a fan shape much as she did with the beans.

VINING NASTURTIUMS

My dad introduced me to nasturtiums (*Tropaeolum* species) as a salad garnish when I was a toddler, and we always plant them to brighten up the vegetable garden and add a peppery crunch and bright color to summer salads. For our hedge we bought several mixed-color packets of the vining variety, which will brighten a wire-mesh fence if you show the growing tendrils the way and tie them as they climb (then let them droop at the top to cascade their flowers downward). Only when soil was dry and warm did a solid row of the rot-susceptible, pea-sized seeds go in an inch deep and 2–3 inches apart along the wire.

Vining nasturtiums are getting hard to find. These days I buy them from the United States representatives of the British seedsmen Thompson & Morgan (P.O. Box 1308, Jackson, New Jersey 08527), whose free catalogue lists the largest variety of flower seeds on the retail mail-order market as well as a selection of hard-to-find vegetables.

CUCURBITS

Any squash, cucumber, or gourd vine will climb a fence with training; as with nasturtiums, you must lift the new growth daily so the little spiraling tendrils that sprout from the stems will grow around the wire; otherwise they will spread out rapidly along the ground in their normal growth habit. We had cukes and squash in the garden, so chose a packet of varied small summer gourds for the fence. Germination of these seeds is always skittish, and every seed in a gourd mix seems to have a different size, color, and shape, promising a grand variety of round and flat, dipper- and turban-shaped fruit in shades of dark green, yellow, brown, and gold to dry for table center-pieces. We planted each seed in its own 3-inch peat pot and waited till the plants were showing a second pair of true leaves and wanting to climb. Once sure that the season was advanced enough for these tropical annuals, we put them into the compost on the sun side of a screen that was already half-covered with young bean, morning glory, and nasturtium vines. (I suppose that, like most seeds, gourds are grown by one or two specialists and sold through all the seed merchants. But, I buy ours from the free catalogue of cold-country specialists Johnny's Selected Seeds, Albion, Maine 04910.)

Harvesting Hansen's bush cherry.

Starting the Quick Fence

For the first few weeks we trained the hedge vines to the top of the chickenwire screen, snipped back too-adventurous plants, and tried to give every plant equal sun room. But the growth soon got beyond us, and by midsummer the screen and ground all around were a riot of competing flowers: a red bean blossom poking out here, the vibrant blue trumpet of a morning glory or the brilliant yellow of a squash blossom there, and nasturtiums twining in and out everywhere.

Without any help at all, the beans spiraled up the poles and soon were waving long fronds 10 feet up in the air. To keep the plants making bushy growth from nodes between the leaves, I'd snip the tips of the longest vines and would go searching through the leaves to remove the pods before they began to set seed. Our screen became a great rank jungle of searching vine tendrils, but it provided the privacy we sought. Indeed, I needed to prune it back to keep the compost-nourished vines from shading out the hedge plants I was putting into the main breadth of the trench.

The living fence kept little Sam in bounds, too. Each morning he enjoyed picking flowers and bringing them to his mom, preferring the biggest gourd blossom he could find. He tried tasting the spicy nasturtium flowers – just once. But he did take to picking young beans and nibbling them raw. It's a habit he's retained into teenhood, though most cooked vegetables are ignored.

PLANNING A PERMANENT HEDGE

For our permanent living fence, I went prospecting in two places: in the woods and through Gurney's seed and nursery catalogue.

Our woods is full of young native evergreens, mostly pines. I looked in the clearings for hemlock, fir, or white (five-needle) pines about 6 feet in height, with live branches and dense growth down to soil level. I "ditched" a half dozen of them, using a flat-bladed cutting spade to slice the root-packed forest loam a foot down in a circle about 8 inches out from the trunk of each tree. Over the summer the newly root-pruned trees packed the circle inside the cut with new root growth. When I removed the trees that fall, they were about as ready for transplanting as a plant you'd find with roots tied in a burlap sack in a nursery.

Lacking a handy woods, you can purchase nursery stock and select from a vastly greater variety of far bushier plants than I could find growing wild. A nursery can also stock larger hedge plants than those I ordered by mail as seedlings from Gurney's, a mail-order supplier of just about anything that anyone could imagine for lawn or garden. Mail-order economics dictate that only young stock can be sold, most of it sent in full winter dormancy and bare-root (without a heavy ball of soil). If you don't know Gurney's delightful, large-format, full-color catalogue, send a postcard with your name and address to Gurney's Seed & Nursery Company, Yankton, South Dakota 57079. Gurney's will sell anything legal that grows, and I've tried oddballs like bamboo and paw-paws and crowder peas and six-shooter sweet corn from them for the fun of it.

I sent off for a selection of economy-size rooted cuttings or seedlings of plants that would grow quickly to about 6 feet in height and would flower, bear fruit, or both. My order included a half-dozen each 1-to-2-foot-tall honeysuckle, Russian olive, lilacs, blueberries, and forsythia, plus pairs of offbeat fruiting plants with names like sand cherry and buffalo berry.

Before the plants arrived, I measured out locations for the six evergreens I'd ditched, planning to space them 6-7 feet apart initially, with the nursery plants scattered between. I assumed that the shrubs would grow quickly to their full height, to provide a living fence for a decade or more. Evergreens grow slowly, but in time, and if we kept the shrubs from crowding them out their first few years, the evergreens would grow to full-sized trees, crowding out the shrubs to provide a living fence that would last 100 years. The trick would be careful spacing and frequent pruning to achieve the maximum screen effect as the several plant types made growth.

I marked out the spots where the evergreens would go and dug planting holes every 2 feet between the evergreens' locations. I stuck in the various woody shrub plants, more or less at random. Despite frequent watering, most of the offbeat fruiting plants failed to survive; I probably ordered the plants too late in the year. Only one buffalo berry (whatever that was) flourished.

The honeysuckle and forsythias proved the most luxuriant of the shrubs and in just a year needed pruning lest they crowd out the slower-growing lilacs, blueberries, and Russian olives. The olive has a lovely gray-green foliage, and we came to prize it the most, though the plants do need top pruning; left alone they grow to become large trees. The high-bush blueberry plants with their glossy green leaves put out a few flowers the first season, and though I did not acidify their soil for peak growth and fruit production, we were enjoying a few large, plump berries by the second year.

Each of the transplanted evergreens lived, though all but the hardy white pines sulked for two years, stubbornly refusing to put out new growth. The pines loved their new home, and I had to tip prune them to keep them in check while we waited for the others to take hold, which they did in their third year. By that time we had a good 4-foot-plus living fence of deciduous plants, and I took down the wire mesh.

After five years, and in the hands of new owners, the hedge was a lush thicket, a good 8 feet tall. The forsythia had lost out to the honeysuckle, the lilacs were being crowded out by the Russian olives. Today, some fifteen years after planting, the evergreens are shading out the lower shrubs, and the fence is assuming its mature configuration. All in all it has been a successful experiment. The hedge has been a lure for wildlife and a source of privacy and an occasional snack for a decade and a half, and its service has just begun.

Before planting a hedge of your own, take time to think over all the conventional fence-location criteria, plus the requirements of plants that are to serve as a living fence for generations.

Sun

Light availability is the hardest horticultural influence to control: you can't just remove a building or a neighbor's shade tree. Assess sun availability before locating a living fence or choosing plantings. Most broad-leaved hedge plants prefer full sun: unscreened sunlight from dawn to dusk. Eight hours of sun are a minimum for most – though I must admit that the hedge described above grew to a jungle on less than five hours of light during the height of summer and received practically none once the sun dipped below the tree line in winter.

Lacking sufficient light to fuel the photosynthesis that is the basis of plant life, living fence plants will put their energy into trying to reach the sun. They'll grow "leggy," rising into great long-stemmed giraffes of plants with little leaf growth low down to provide the bushy habit you want from a screen.

A SHADE FENCE

With good light you can choose from a world of planting stock, but if you don't have much sun you can plant a shade fence with slow-growing evergreens that don't need full sun to fuel a complete change of leaves each year. Many needle-bearing evergreens actually need shade to develop from seedlings and will tolerate it into maturity. Broad-leaved evergreens such as hollys and rhododendrons will provide a shade-loving hedge of year-round greenery plus spring flowers in every climate.

In frost-free and properly humid areas, camellias are planted in shade to preserve their fragrant blooms. Mountain laurel, with its year-round cover of small, glossy leaves and a bower of pink or white flowers in early summer, prefers partial shade and will tolerate winters to −30 degrees. (Just don't let your goats browse laurel leaves; they're toxic.)

Water

If you live in Bermuda grass country, you already know the problems that summer heat and drought bring to lawns and ornamental plantings. Many indigenous and commercially propagated plants are drought-tolerant; your nurseryman will have suggestions, and garden books are full of ideas.

In well-watered areas, few hedge-type plants will need irrigation after the first spring. If water is needed, periodic soakings under a thick mulch or trickle-irrigation with a drip-pipe laid in the planting trench are the most water-conserving techniques.

It is an excess of water – too much stagnant water pooling around roots due to poor soil drainage – rather than a dearth that is the more common problem in ornamental fence plantings. The soil beneath a hedge located by your walk or road is liable to be compacted, and the gravel or rammed-earth underlayments of walks and roadways themselves can obstruct underground water flow. If water movement is poor, so is air transfer, and plant roots need to breathe as much as you and I.

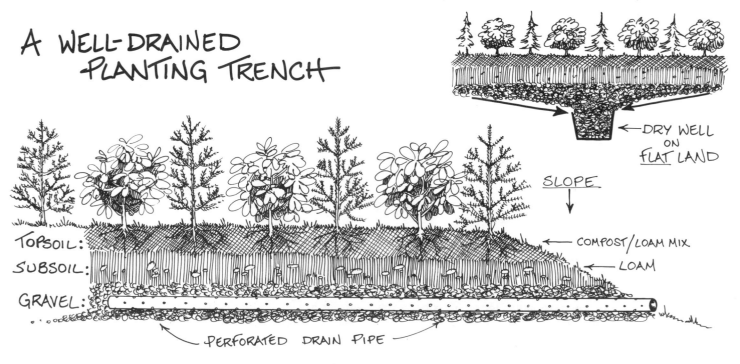

A WELL-DRAINED PLANTING TRENCH

←DRY WELL ON FLAT LAND

SLOPE

TOPSOIL:
SUBSOIL:
GRAVEL:

← COMPOST/LOAM MIX
← LOAM

PERFORATED DRAIN PIPE

To see how well the soil under your fence line drains, perform a "perk test." Dig a hole a foot around and good 2 feet deep, and fill it quickly with water. If it percolates off at a perceptible rate, your drainage is good. If the water puddles in the hole – say, in a pit of the hard clay you find as subsoil in many areas – but goes down slowly, drainage is okay. But if a pool of water remains in the bottom of the hole after a half-hour or an hour, you have a drainage problem. Plan to dig your planting trench at least 2 feet down. A yard or 4 feet deep is better. Then, line the bottom with crushed rock or gravel, and if drainage is really poor, install a perforated drain pipe. Lead the drainage trench or pipe to a dry well or downhill outflow. For an excavation that complex and a long fence, particularly if drain pipe or a dry well is involved, you will probably want to hire a backhoe, and you may need a municipal permit to dig. If so, I would turn the whole project over to a landscaping contractor or architect who knows local hydrology and can recommend a drainage system that is suited to your area. They'll also know what plants are best as well as where to get them and how to plant them in a problem soil.

Of course if getting water to or from a living fence is too much bother, you may decide that an inanimate fence is best for you. You can still liven it up with an easily watered grape vine or with annuals.

Fertility

Most any proven lawn or garden soil will support a conventional hedge with little modification; just set the plants into a trench or well-prepared planting holes. An average soil will do for an average hedge, though you may be restricted to the hardier plants. But for best viability and fastest growth – for a super-hedge – treat the fence line as a garden. Test and treat it for acidity and increase its nutrient content.

You can buy small soil-test kits at the nursery, have a landscaper test your soil for you, or send a sample of your soil to the local land-grant university. For the latter service (costing $2 to $5), consult the nearest agent of the cooperative extension service, U.S. Department of Agriculture. There's an extension agent in every county seat in the U.S.A.

Test kits or garden books will tell you how much of what to add to your soil: lime or wood ash to reduce the acidity that is typical of most North American soils, plus bone and mineral meals and composted animal manures or chemical mixtures for plant food. And compost. You can never add too much pure compost – plant matter

that has been let rot down to pure humus. Its fibers help to both hold and drain water, will permit roots to penetrate easily, and act as a reservoir of plant fiber to break down and nourish your planting over the years. For the best hedges, enrich your top-soil and replace as much of your own subsoil as you can – as I did in the hedge described above. Use compost for soil enrichment if you have it. If you don't, mix in peat moss and/or artificial soil conditioners such as perlite or vermiculite and fertilizers.

GOOD HEDGE SOIL

If you're building up marginal soil, here are three good plans. Use them as a basis for adding soil sweeteners and fertilizers determined by soil test.

1. Fair Soil (supporting good lawn, garden, and tree growth)

Remove topsoil in the trench or planting holes and set aside. Dig up and loosen subsoil to a depth of 18 inches to 2 feet. Remove any rocks and roots and mix the subsoil (in the trench or in a box or barrow) with equal parts of peat moss and either an artificial conditioner or coarse sand. Add as much conditioner as you can manage, up to the volume of the subsoil itself.

It is best to measure soil additives precisely according to soil-test directions. For any but the most perverse soils or finicky plants, however, it is safe to add a light sprinkling of ground limestone, bone meal, and 5-5-5 garden fertilizer. Mix well. Put on just enough to give the soil a light dusting; too much of any fertilizer is worse than none at all. Put the enriched subsoil in the bottom of the trench. Now enrich the topsoil the same way, return it to the trench, and plant the hedge.

2. Poor Soil (worked-out farm fields, development fill)

Do as above, but discard the subsoil. Mix topsoil with the peat, etc., and place in the bottom of the hole. For the top layer, order a load of good loam, supplement it per above directions, and put that in the upper layer of the planting hole.

3. Terrible Soil (sand, hardpan, clay)

If you have any of these garden disasters at the surface, the lower soils will be worse. Dig out the entire trench or planting hole and replace it all with imported loam, supplemented as above.

Soil enrichment calls for a lot of digging and some expense, I'll agree, though the cost need not be great. In most areas a truckload of loam is not prohibitively expensive, and it is a good investment. Don't be tempted to try organic-gardening-style surface soil-conditioning methods with a hedge. Adding mulches and digging in compost and encouraging earthworms over the years is fine for a garden of annual flowers or vegetables that you fork or till up each fall. But most hedge plants have shallow roots, and you can't dig more than a half-inch into their soil without harming the roots. The bed you make for a living fence is the bed it will rest in for life. Make it as deep and rich as you can manage.

A Last Recourse

If your planting situation is terminally grim: if your home borders a parking lot or is located on rock ledge; if you have impossible soil or no drainage at all, or live in a multistory building and have only a balcony for outdoors, consider giant planting boxes or raised beds.

While traveling on Uncle Sam's account some years ago, Marine Corps buddies and I built a raised planting bed of coral chunks in front of our bivouac on the beach of a tropical island where the sand bordering a blue-green lagoon was a gorgeous and glistening light pink but was salty, nutrient-poor, and unsuitable for growing anything but beach prickers. The young coconut palms just emerging from the nuts, palmettos, hibiscus, bougainvilleas and unnamed flowering vines made the place seem more like home when we unearthed and Jeeped them out from the interior for planting in jungle soil that we'd sweetened with seashells crushed under combat boots.

You should dig deep to remove as much offending soil as possible and replace as above. Then, using railroad ties, stones, concrete blocks, or other soil containers, construct a giant window box along the fence line. Top up with garden loam or fill the bed with planting medium purchased by the bale. A bed that is three railroad ties high and a yard wide should support most evergreens and hedge plants up to 6 to 8 feet in height.

A hedge made from all imported parts – soil included – will be expensive, and most fence budgets will find it appropriate only for short expanses. But where a raised bed is a necessity, the touch of life or color that it provides will justify the cost.

CHOOSING HEDGE PLANTINGS

I suggest trips to the library and then the nursery to select your hedge plants. The list of plants and details of their culture could fill a book – indeed, they do fill dozens. But here is a list of the most common and widely grown plants for hedging.

A List of Ornamental Hedge Plants

SHRUBS

Abelia (*Abelia grandiflora*). Hardy to Zone 6. A round, prunable shrub which grows to 4 feet, has glossy leaves, and bears white or pink trumpet-shaped flowers all year long. Needs good soil and some sun.

Barberry (*Berberis* species). Hardy to Zones 4 or 5. The "prickerbush" with dark green, narrow leaves and red berries that is common in city hedges. Dense branches with plentiful thorns grow to 6 or more feet. Prunable to any shape. Evergreen in the south.

Beauty bush (*Kolkwitzia amabilis*). Hardy to Zone 4. A shrub which grows to 10 feet and is covered with small, fragrant bell-shaped flowers that drive the bees wild in late spring. Has a nice gray-green foliage and thick woody stems that grow out of bounds if not pruned. Grows in any soil, tolerates shade, prefers full sun.

Boxwood (*Buxus sempervirens*). Hardy to Zone 5. The dense hedge plant that can be clipped like a poodle in spheres or squares or any shape you like and still remains covered with small, dark, evergreen leaves. A slow grower, box demands well-drained soil and good sun.

Euonymus (*Euonymus* species). Hardy to Zone 6. A semievergreen shrub which grows to 7 feet but is prunable to any height. Common hedge plants with glossy dark green leaves that stay on the plant all winter, and white or pink fruit.

Firethorn (*Pyracantha* species). Hardy to Zone 6. Will grow to 20 feet or prune to any lesser height. Has evergreen leaves and showy red fruit that lasts through winter.

Forsythia (*Forsythia* species). Hardy to Zone 4. A moderately dense shrub that grows to 8 feet with long whips bearing yellow flowers before the tulips bloom. Will tolerate partial shade but blooms best in full sun. For dense hedge growth, prune only after flowering is over and by removing whole, old stems from center of plant.

Honeysuckle (*Lonicera* species). Hardy to Zone 4. Dense, woody shrubs with fragrant and colorful trumpet-shaped flowers in the spring.

Hydrangea (*Hydrangea* species). Hardy to Zone 5. Familiar rounded, dense shrubs with round flowers in summer that can be made pink or blue with soil additives.

Lilacs (*Syringa* species). Hardy to Zone 2. With white to purple, fragrant spring flowers, this old reliable will grow to 20 feet. Grows in any soil and sun conditions but needs pruning. Remove old flowering spikes and cut out overgrown trunks at the base; new suckers will replace it (but leave only the suckers you want).

Mock orange (*Philadelphus* species). Hardy to Zones 4 or 5. Grows from 6 to 12 feet, with white flowers that (in most varieties) smell like orange blossoms. Grows in any half-decent soil and tolerates shade.

Mountain laurel (*Kalmia latifolia*). Hardy to Zone 4 and north with shade. Slow-growing, spreading and gnarly-trunked shrub with evergreen leaves and pink flowers. Must have acid soil.

Pieris (*Pieris* species). Hardy to Zones 4 or 5. Broad-leaved evergreen with long leaves arranged in a star and clusters of off-white bell-shaped flowers. Dense shrub growing 6 to 10 feet. Prunes well. Does best in acid soil and partial shade, and will survive city life better than most shrubs.

Rhododendron (*Rhododendron* species). Some rhododendrons are hardy to Zone 2. There are thousands of species of this broad-leaved evergreen with showy flowers. Grows slowly to 6 feet or more. Needs acid soil and shade. Azaleas are classed with rhododendrons but are usually smaller plants that lose their leaves in winter.

Sweet pepper bush (*Clethra alnifolia*). Hardy to Zone 3. Familiar spikes of white, spicy-smelling flowers in summer. Grows to 8 or 9 feet, prefers dry soil

and full sun but will grow anywhere. Good for coastal areas.

Roses (*Rosa* species). Hardy to Zone 2. Thorny and vigorous canes of rambling roses can be trained along the outside of a hedge to good protective and decorative advantage.

Viburnum (*Viburnum* species). Hardy to Zone 4. Rounded shrubs that grow to 8 feet or so. Have rounded leaves with finely toothed edges, bad-smelling but showy flower clusters, and red fruit. Grows in any soil, but likes moist habitat.

Yew (*Taxus* species). Hardy to Zone 4. There are many varieties of this fine foundation planting, which has spreading evergreen foliage. A dense shrub that will grow as high as you let it. Prefers good soil, sun or shade.

SMALL TREES

Dogwood (*Cornus florida*). Hardy to Zone 4. A native American tree which grows to 10 feet or more in sun. Tolerates shade and crowding. Has white-to-pink blossoms in spring, purple-red leaves in fall, and red berries in fall.

Crabapples (*Malus* species). Hardy to Zone 4. Flowering crabapples are low trees with twisting branches that can be pruned to hedge size. Brilliant spring bloom and fruit that birds like and that makes jelly.

Gingko (*Gingko biloba*). Hardy to Zone 4. A low tree with interesting fan-shaped leaves. Can't tolerate water-logged soil. Adaptable to sun or shade and will survive in urban conditions.

Golden chain tree (*Laburnum watereri*). Hardy to Zone 5, grows to 30 feet, likes moist, neutral soil. Drooping grapelike bunches of yellow, pea-shaped flowers in spring.

Hawthorn (*Crataegus* species). Hardy to Zone 4. Dozens of species. Low, thorny trees that flower in spring and have red fruits through the winter. Needs good soil and full sun. Prunable to an impenetrable hedge.

Hemlock (*Tsuga canadensis*). Hardy to Zone 3 or 4. Dense feathery evergreen. Canada hemlock can be pruned to any shape, and the Carolina hemlock grows naturally in mounds that will fill a hedge. Likes shade and wet soil.

Holly (*Ilex* species). Hardy to Zone 6. English or American hollies have dense, prickly, dark evergreen foliage, and females bear the red berries you see in

Christmas wreaths. Grows large, but is prunable to any height. Prefers partial shade, acid and sandy soils.

Japanese snowbell (*Styrax japonica*). Hardy to Zone 5. Has spreading branches and clusters of white blossoms in spring. Grows in sandy soil. Needs sun.

Shadbush or Serviceberry (*Amelanchier canadensis*). Hardy to Zone 4. Prunable or will grow to 25 feet. A rounded tree with silvery foliage, white flower clusters in spring, and purple fruit that birds adore. Tolerates any but the worst soils.

Silk tree (*Albizzia julibrissin rosea*). Hardy to Zone 5. A low tree, 15 to 25 feet high with spreading growth, lacy foliage, and pink puffball flowers. Tolerates the worst, dry soils.

Redbud (*Cercis canadensis*). Hardy to Zone 4. Low, shrubby tree with lovely coral-pink flowers in early spring and large, heart-shaped leaves. Prefers a mildly acid soil that is well drained.

Witch hazel (*Hamamelis* species). Hardy to Zone 5. Low scrubby trees which grow to 15 or 20 feet. Have odd red or yellow flowers in spring or in fall when leaves are off. Grows in any soil.

PLANTING

It is best to plant bare-rooted plants in the early spring when they are in winter dormancy but preparing for a rush of spring-season growth. Late-fall planting is next best, though few plants will make meaningful root growth during the cold, low-sun months, and some can die or be severely set back by dry winter winds. You can plant balled nursery plants or wild or home-grown stock that has been ditched months earlier most any time of year, though spring is best for them, too.

Decide in advance how high and wide each plant should grow. You may want a uniform hedge of same-size plants, or you may prefer to alternate tall evergreens with spreading deciduous bushes. Some species take to crowding well and will fill out; others will get leggy. Be sure you know each plant's growth habit before setting it in.

Then make your layout. Carefully draw the size and shape of each specimen as it will appear at maturity on a photo or elevation drawing of the house or landscape. Mark the planting holes in the lawn or prepared planting ditch. If you want a fast screen, put quick-growing annuals or expendable perennials in the interplant spaces and plan to remove them before their foliage grows to compete with the permanent plants'.

The day before planting, soak the ground well if it is dry. Any excess water will drain down overnight.

Wait till after the sun is low the next afternoon (so drying sun and heat will be at minimum) to set plants in. If planting nursery stock with roots balled in burlap, follow nursery instructions. They may tell you to put the plant in at the same level at which it was growing in the nursery row and pack soil around the bagged root ball. Others may suggest that you cut off the burlap, spread the roots, and pack soil around them. Much depends on the variety and how the plants were grown and harvested.

It is easiest to leave the burlap in the planting hole; roots will grow right through, and it will molder away. But if plants are wrapped in plastic be sure to remove that.

Most bare-rooted mail-order stock these days is sent ready to plant. If not, follow shippers' instructions as to top- and root pruning. If there are no instructions, trim off all broken or bruised roots and trim off at least a third of top growth to compensate for roots lost in digging.

Determine from the dark, buried area of the trunk how far up soil reached on the stem or trunk in the nursery row; that is how deep the plant should go, and you should fill your trench or hole accordingly. Make a little mound at the bottom and spread the roots out as evenly as you can in a cone around it. Pack soil well around roots, then fill the hole, leaving a small catch basin around the top, and water the plant well. A drink of weak manure tea or fertilizer solution (1 tablespoon per gallon of a water-soluble fertilizer such as Stern's Miracle-Gro) is allright, but don't overdo it and overstimulate a plant that needs time to acclimate to new surroundings.

If the plant is a tall one, stake it. Hammer a hardwood tomato stake or sapling pole in the soil several inches from the stem (avoiding buried roots) and tie the stem and trunk to the support at the top and every 6 inches down to soil level with strips of soft cloth. Do not use those plastic-wrapped wire ties. They can saw-cut a soft, young trunk as it sways in the wind. And if you forget and leave them on too long, they can girdle the growing bark. Cloth can't abrade and will rot away if forgotten.

AFTERCARE

Keep the soil moist all the first year. If a fingernail scratch in the lighter-colored, dry surface of the soil shows dark, the earth is moist enough. Don't let soil dry out much deeper than ¼-inch, and never let the topsoil dry so much that it cracks.

Many hedge plants are shallow rooted by nature, and you want to encourage them to dig down as far as they will to gather nutrients and resist drought. So, always water deeply once a week, lacking a good drenching rain. Put a tin can out and let the sprinkler go till there is an inch of water in it. Or let the hose trickle for a half-hour at the base of each plant.

Water is best conserved by a mulch: any material that will cover the bare ground beneath plants to reduce evaporation and moderate soil temperature. Some landscapers use the black plastic sheeting that you can get in rolls at garden-supply stores. Indeed, you can weight a length of plastic over a strip of live sod and just plant through slits in it. The plastic will kill the sod and nurture the hedge. It's ugly, though, unless you camouflage it with a layer of natural materials, and it can retard both water penetration and air circulation.

More attractive are natural materials: ground bark and old hay are common mulches in our area. I've seen ground corncobs used in the Midwest, peanut shells in the South, pine needles in the North, and leaves and grass clippings most everywhere. A gravel layer, flat rocks, or tiles make good mulches, though weeding them can be a nuisance. I prefer a natural mulch; you can pull or hoe weeds through it easily, and the material rots down to plant food in time.

If you want a great shaggy bear of a hedge, let it go, and don't prune off growth till you trip over it. For a more formal appearance, you'll want to keep the plants in trim, and it's best to start early. Prune often and lightly. After the first year, any time an errant whip deviates from your plan, snip it off.

Especially with mixed-species plantings, keep the more aggressive plants from overwhelming the slower growers. Prune rank-growing shrubs freely from the second year on. If you have forsythia, wait till late winter to cut them back, bring the cuttings inside, put them in water in a dark, warm place, and they will produce sweeps of golden bloom – a promise of spring in February.

Be prudent in trimming evergreens. A whole year's growth appears all at once as light green sprouts at stem ends. Take off tops of the main trunk, or "leader," with care. Trimming many species produces a split leader or double trunk, which can ruin the tree's appearance if you want a slim and elegant hedge. A split tree will be bushy, however, and that can be desirable if your plan calls for a more rustic fence.

Mixed evergreen hedge overgrowing a barricade of snowfence on posts.

A WEATHER FENCE

Open-country or shore-side dwellers will welcome a barrier that protects living space or stock-holding areas from wind, wind-blown snow, or encroaching sand or dust. No weather screen serves so well as a living fence. The roots hold soil, the top growth breaks up wind but doesn't cut off air flow altogether, and no tree can be blown down by any but the most severe storms.

A weather fence can consist of a single line of medium-tall shrubs set 20 feet from a lane to act as a snow fence, a mile-long file of cottonwoods along a stream bed to intercept and soften the winds blowing across 100 miles of dusty prairie, or a file of hardy evergreens placed at the back of the yard to protect tender ornamentals from winter winds. Gardens in Britain are frequently protected by a three-tier planting system. Tall native trees set in a line – often two or three staggered lines – are followed by a line of medium-sized trees that are "pleched" or trimmed to a uniform height. The final barrier row is a low hedge, also trimmed to uniform, formal shape.

Lombardy poplars.

A weather barrier is often located well away from the house and is the most utilitarian of living fences. Sturdiness, long life, and hardiness are important; appearance often isn't. You can temper soil for exotic, imported windbreak plants, but my advice is to stick with what grows locally, even if it runs to little but cottonwood or aspen. Take a drive through the country, and see if you can't identify the best-looking trees in the best-established local tree lines. If you aren't a tree expert, collect a few leaves and see if the nearest nursery can match them.

The Midwestern plains are prime windbreak country. Early settlers planted two- to ten-row windbreaks from a variety of native and imported tree species. Lower, bushy-growing plants went in the row nearest the house, with rear files of increasingly tall plants placed 10 to 20 feet apart. A well-established windbreak is a strip woods that's arranged like so many Boy Scouts in a troop photo: short ones at the front, tallest to the rear. For best growth, place trees in evenly-spaced rows so you can cultivate and remove competing underbrush easily for the first several years. Tractor tillage is quickest, though a rotary tiller or sickle-bar brush cutter will do the job if you don't have miles of hedgeline to tend.

Any of the following traditional windbreak trees – alone, mixed together, or mingled with native deciduous or evergreen trees – will make a fast-growing 25–50 foot weather barrier that will last two centuries or more.

Cottonwood. The widespread eastern cottonwood (***Populus deltoides***) and the several localized western subspecies are traditional windbreak trees on plains ranches and prairie farms. New strains of cottonwood are "cottonless." They don't litter the ground with cotton-candy-like male flowers each spring as do native varieties. All are fast growers, but the new varieties will grow as much as 10 feet in a year in good soil and are hardy and attractive. Cottonwoods grow naturally along streams and are water-hungry. Don't plant them around a septic system (they'll clog the outflow with roots) or near a well that gets low in October (a cottonwood will drink it dry).

Lombardy poplar (*Populus nigra* var. *italica*) is that tall, skinny tree you see in lines along fence rows in France and in parts of North America. Cultivated for thousands of years, it was imported from Europe by early settlers to add a civilized touch to the raw landscape. The lombardy poplar is a natural genetic sport; only male trees are known, so they must be propagated from cuttings. Looking best when planted 5 feet apart in groups, lombardy poplars make a fast-growing wind screen that is attractive for a generation or so, but they don't last long by tree standards. Dead branches become unsightly, and a single dead tree in a fence line looks like a missing tooth in an otherwise perfect smile.

Osage orange (*Maclura pomifera*) is native to the south-central U.S. but is found throughout the East and Northwest. A low thorn tree with orangeish bark and thick branches, it makes a dense hedge. If you enjoy Indian crafts, you can make its supple wood into bows and the inner bark into a yellow fabric dye. The Osage people used it that way and loaned the tree use of their name. You can find young trees in some Midwestern nurseries, and seedlings grow anywhere the species has naturalized. The lumpy and inedible grapefruit-sized fruit make a squashy, bug-infested mess on the lawn or barnyard, so don't plant Osage orange near the house.

Russian olive (*Elaeagnus angustifolia*) with densely arranged branches bearing attractive gray-green foliage, has a high degree of cold and drought resistance. It was brought to the Americas by settlers to serve as an ornamental windbreak. It is still widely planted in the prairie provinces and states. The tree can be pruned to a low shrub or let grow to up to its tree height of 25 feet. The ½-inch-long yellow fruit, covered with silvery scales, is attractive to birds.

Flowering shrubs for front rows. Flowering hedge plants that will grow tall and fit well on the house side of a hardy windbreak include lilac, honeysuckle, any of the witch hazels, smokebush, dogwoods, the snowball bush, pussy willow, forsythia (that grows to 10 feet in full sun and good soil), old-fashioned mock orange, and in the South, magnolias and hydrangeas. In the East you can transplant staghorn or smooth sumac if you take care to keep it in trim; copses of those soft-wooded weed trees will advance at an alarming rate. I like sumac because the long, berry-red fruiting spikes provide midsummer nectar for my bees. But it can become a fast-spreading nuisance if the area in front of the planting isn't kept mowed. Be sure you don't transplant poison sumac, which isn't a sumac at all but has a similar look and growth habit. Poison sumac bears fruit in drooping clusters of whitish, waxy berries rather than up-pointing red spikes. Poison sumac causes a poison-ivy-like skin rash that can be severe in some people.

Bringing up the rear. In the rear files of the windbreak, you can try planting (or as in my own experiments, transplanting) any young native tree or shrub that looks promising. In New England I've had success with soft and hard maple, oak, ash, beech, and the conifers mentioned earlier. I always ditch wild trees to let them grow roots in a compact bundle for a season before moving – as detailed above. Don't try transplanting nut trees if the nut they sprouted from isn't still in evidence; walnuts, butternuts, and others have a single large taproot that is impossible to dig out, and the tree will usually die if you try but take a deceptively long time doing it.

The Gurney catalogue has for years sold a selection of bargain-priced windbreak trees. If they are suitable to Gurney's North Dakota environs, the trees should thrive anywhere. The catalogue lists over a dozen deciduous varieties and some ten evergreens, and offers 1- to 2-foot seedlings for as little as 17 cents apiece. The selection includes green ash, honey locust, walnut, hackberry, and the Siberian pea tree.

Rosa rugosa. My favorite weather fence is a thick barrier of beach rose or *Rosa rugosa*, which thrives along the sand coast of York County in southern Maine. It is a characteristic rose plant with prickly canes bearing dark-green leaves and yellow-centered white or pink blossoms that are followed by large, seedy, but succulent brick-orange rose hips. The hips offer a tasty energy boost when eaten out of hand on a beach run, make a mild jam, and when dried, steep into a tea rich in vitamin C. A rose hedge will grow almost anyplace so long as it has good drainage and plenty of sun to keep down aphids, powdery mildew, and other typical rose ailments. Growing as much as 2 feet a year, it rises to 6 to 8 feet in height if not wind-truncated. Growth is dense if plants are set in about 2 feet apart, and the prickly stems make an impenetrable hedge.

However: Rosa rugosa was widely disseminated by the Department of Agriculture as a soil-holder in erosion-control programs during the 1930s. It spreads through seeds disseminated by hip-eating birds and also by sending out underground shoots – which can turn a single plant into a thicket in a few years. It has become a weed and a serious problem in many areas. In the South, where it can grow year-round, it has taken over acres of grazing land, and even here in New England, it competes with aspen and juniper as the pioneer plant in natural reforestation of abandoned farmland.

HEDGEROWS

Living plants have been used as protective fence by mankind for millennia: African plains dwellers still build *kraals* of thorn bush and you'll find bamboo planted around dwellings and stock compounds in the tropics. Europeans were building hedge fence before Roman times. Veterans of ground combat in the European wars can tell you how difficult – nay, impossible – it was to penetrate the hedgerows of France. In parts of Great Britain, farmers still tend hedgerows that have divided land holdings for a thousand years and more.

Hedgerows and the small fields they enclose were designed for animal-powered tillage, and many English and European hedges are being bulldozed out to accommodate mechanized agriculture. Some landowners are trimming sides and tops of the hedges that remain with mechanized flails rather than renewing the hedges in the traditional ways. Still, there is a place for the old-fashioned hedgerow in the English and continental European countryside, and a move is afoot to preserve as many as possible as historic relics.

Reviving an Old Craft

If you would like to join me in reviving a bit of ancient fence practice on your own place in the New World, put in an experimental hedgerow. Skimpy little hedge-rows have sprouted up along stone walls between mowing fields in much of New England, along streams in the Midwest, and up from bottoms of watered gullies in the Far West. Rosa rugosa, Russian olive, and other hedging or windbreak plants have been planted thick enough to act as de-facto livestock fences in some areas. But inside their leafy, sun-side border growth, those thickets aren't thick. Limbs aren't dense enough to keep man or animal from passing. Little effort has been made to create truly impenetrable hedgerows in North America.

A new hedgerow could be started as a triple row of dense-foliaged trees and shrubs that do well in your locale – much as we made our own first attempt at a front-yard living fence. Set the hedge plants windbreak-style in multiple rows. Try a mix of evergreens and tall trees in the middle, lower trees and shrubs along the perimeters. Plant both rows and plants within rows close together, acknowledging that many individual plants will be crowded out in time. Top prune deciduous plants at first to encourage strong, dense, and uniform side growth.

The secret to creating a living fence so dense and strong that it will retain livestock is upkeep. Left to their own devices, plants will reach for the sun, and in time your hedgerow will be a linear forest of bare trunks. This strip forest will sport a fringe of leafy shrubs along the flanks, but in the interior all the woody growth will grow tall, reaching for the sun. Large trees are permitted to

Tying down shrub stems to create a hedgerow in back of the low stone fence.

grow in the middle of some European hedgerows; indeed, the last vestiges of Britain's once-great oak forests grow in hedgerows. But the perimeters of hedges are kept in lower-growing plants that are pruned and trained. Each year the hedge keeper patrols his rows, climbing up on the hedge if need be to pull down new sun-trending growth to renew a robust outer layer of living wood.

To start hedgerows in Europe, limbs are traditionally pulled down and bound to hazel stakes thrust in the ground. I've had some luck cutting green willow poles and jamming them as deep into the soil as I can. Then I pull down up-reaching limbs of such bendy trees as black cherry, ironwood, and young sugar maples. I pull hard enough to crack the limbs if need be; they almost always heal and grow back fine. A pair of limbs from the left and right of the willow pole are pulled together, hauled to ground level, and bound to the embedded pole by twining slim branches around each other three or four times in a "bowerman's" knot. Take about a 1-foot length of two whippy young twigs and cross the right one over the left. Now wind the end of the left twig front-to-back over the right one; wind the right twig back-to-front over the left one. If twigs aren't cooperative, you can bind them with cotton twine, which will rot away before it can girdle the limbs. More often than not, the willow anchor takes root, entwining itself to the other branches, which quickly adopt the bent growth pattern for life. The outside of the hedge becomes a profusion of competing twigs and leaves as each plant sends out new growth to find sunlight.

Annual renewal of hedgerows is essential. If they are let go, new growth quickly heads for the sun, shading out the lower matted growth, which dies out, leaving the flanks of the hedgerow bare and doomed to die. In succeeding years, branches are pulled down and their ends are pushed into the hedge and bound around handy branches anywhere an opening appears. Inside the hedge, the twisted branches of living and dead wood make a real snarl. My hedges are small-scale in concept and merest babies by European standards, but they show every promise of growing up to be genuine impenetrable hedgerows – fences that retain their holding power as long as the owner tends them annually. If you decide to try a hedgerow of your own, let me know how you do, won't you?

Staghorn Sumac.

6

PRIMITIVE FENCES

ABE LINCOLN'S FENCE

I t was probably as much for the sake of campaign publicity as was the story of his log-cabin birth, but President Lincoln always maintained that the hardest work he ever did wasn't debating Douglas or preserving the Union, but splitting out fence rails during his youth in pioneer Illinois. Lincoln's Midwest, like much of the continent, was covered with forest that had to be cut to clear fields for crops and pasture. Logs provided the raw material for everything on the frontier farm from ox yokes to birch brooms. The Lincolnesque split-rail fence was a true New World invention, incorporating that most abundant natural resource into the farmer's single greatest time- and capital investment in early animal-based agriculture – fence.

Trees grew straight and tall, and logs up to 11 feet long – a good length for fence sections – could be gotten from easy-splitting trees such as first-growth heart pine, white oak, locust, cedar, and chestnut. A rail splitter would wedge a new-cut tree in place on the ground and start a vertical split along its center line with his ax. The wet, green wood would crack readily. The woodsman would insert a steel wedge in the crack and hammer it home with a maul or sledgehammer (never with the ax, for fear of warping the handle hole or *eye* of the ax head). When the split was large enough, he'd insert a dogwood *glut*, a wedge- or cone-shaped piece of dogwood or other nonsplitting timber. He'd hammer it down with a large hickory maul or a club-shaped billet called a *beetle*. When the split was opened up several inches, another glut would go in, to be hammered home till the first loosened. Then the first glut would be leap-frogged over the second and into the growing split – and on till the log was halved. The ax would be used to keep the split straight around knots and twists in the trunk and to sever any thin withes connecting the halves. Then each half would be turned on its flat side. The half-logs were split into quarters, and with a small tree the job was done. Larger logs needed further splitting; quarter sections of medium-sized logs would be wedged upright between X-shaped poles and split into eighths.

With really large trees the half- or quarter-sections would be subdivided both horizontally and vertically. First to come off was the rot-resistant heartwood rail from the knife-edged inner edge of a quarter piece. Then the log was sectioned as grain, size, and the splitter's whim indicated. Some would split the sections horizontally, "board fashion"; others split vertically, "bastard fashion." Some split out all pie-slice-shaped rails, others made them mostly square or rectangular. Practice differed from one section of the continent to another, too, but it all made good fence.

The Virginia Rail Fence

The earliest rail-fence design – and the fence that Abe Lincoln split rails for – was the simplest: interlaced ricks of six to ten or more 4–8-inch-thick rails set one atop the other in a zigzag or rick-rack pattern in a bed about 5 feet wide. A good fence maker would lay two stones together to form waterproof stands for the ends and the center of an 11-foot heartwood bottom rail laid at a shallow, less-than-45-degree angle to a fence line running through the rail's middle. A foot or so from each end of the base rail, more rails were laid on at a wider-than-90-degree angle to the base rail, aiming in a lazy-Z-shape

Zigzag or rick-rack split-rail fence in Indiana.

pushed well into the soil about 2 feet back from each junction on opposite sides of the fence, then angled up toward the junction to form an X over the top rail. Ends were crossed over the top rail at the junction to lock the joint. The props pressed against the rails and held them down at the same time, providing a sturdy brace so long as the wood remained sound.

Stakes were pairs of heartwood poles hammered in the ground perpendicular to the fence at each junction. Some builders placed them in the wide angles made by the interlaced ends on opposite sides of the fence; others locked them against the shallow angles made by protruding ends on the same side of the fence. Stakes were pulled together with lengths of cord or soft wire wrapped on at the top and midway down to clamp rails firmly between them.

For high fences, long props were placed to lean against (and make an extended X over) the top rail. Then, the zigzag pattern was recommenced with another run of rails called *riders* placed atop the crossed stakes. Stake-and-rider fences could go to 6 or more feet in height, with more riders added as needed.

Corner of a New England split-rail fence. Note smaller rails at bottom to restrain small animals. Bottom rail rests on stones to resist rot.

back toward the fence line. Down went others repeating the base-rail orientation, then on went more pairs facing back, and so on in a *snake, worm, zigzag* or *rick-rack* pattern.

Bottom rails were selected from the thinnest splits so the slot between could be narrow enough that small livestock couldn't wiggle through. Sometimes a spacer would be inserted between the thin lower rails to prevent sag and maintain spacing; short lengths of heartwood were poked in from the outside of the fence midway along each section, free ends resting on rocks.

Props and Stakes

The heaviest rails went on top to weight the fence securely. But once it got much higher than four or five rails, the fence tended to be tippy and easily shoved over by large stock or blown apart in high winds. So in went *props* or *stakes. Props* were full-length heartwood rails

Abe Lincoln's fences were quick to go up and easily moved as fields expanded, and splitting rails for them required a minimum of tools and no time-consuming skilled labor. If bottom rails were held clear of the ground and undergrowth was controlled to keep the wood dry and prevent rot, rail fences lasted two generations or more.

Of course, most eighteenth- and nineteenth-century rail fences are long gone. The originals were recycled into more timber-conserving mortised post-and-rail fences, burned for firewood when the once ample timber supply began to run out, or let rot. You can still find the green and moldering remnants of a few rail fences wandering through the woods of Northern New England and the Carolinas, and historical museums such as those at Salem, North Carolina and Old Williamsburg, Virginia, have preserved some miles of antique fence for posterity.

I don't know that anyone but an historical buff with a really big woodlot would be interested in making a stacked-rail fence. But splitting rails is as good a back-muscle exercise now as it was in Lincoln's day, and you can split your own lengths for a post-and-rail fence with the proper wood, tools, and ambition.

Split rails set into auger-drilled mortises in front of this eighteenth century home.

HURDLES

Along with the new European immigrants to North America came the original of today's hog-panel or steel-mesh calf/sheep cribs – the hurdle. Hurdle making was an established trade in the farming regions of Britain and the Continent. Two types are easily reproduced by those interested in old-time hand crafts: the open split-wood sheep hurdle, and the opaque woven-screen wattle-hurdle. Either design makes a lightweight, easily transported temporary fence or screen. Several can be connected to form a pen suitable for corralling small children, pets, and livestock, or a portable sheep fold for holding placid livestock or rotating them on pasture. A suitably well-aged hurdle hanging from pegs on a wall of your new barn will give the place an instant aura of antiquity.

The split-wood sheep hurdle was made to be as long as available timber would split consistently and as high and with as many posts, rails, and braces as were needed to maintain rigidity and contain the beasts in question. A common size was about 8 feet long and 4 feet high with 1- to 1½-foot-long sharpened stake ends to each of the three vertical members.

Hurdle makers would cut small ash or white oak trees, divide logs into 8- to 11-foot sections, remove bark with a spoon-shaped *bark spud*, and section the tree as its size dictated. The heartwood would be split out, and the good-splitting sapwood divided up with a *froe* (a long, thin splitting wedge about 2½ inches wide that is fixed at a 90-degree angle to a short hickory or ash handle). Splints were made ¼- to ⅜-inch thick and 3 to 4 inches wide.

Thickest lengths would be used for verticals. A spoon bit was used to drill out the top and bottom of mortises, the holes into which horizontal rails were placed. Then a chisel or a rocker-shaped, hook-and-knife hurdle-maker's tool was applied to pry out the waste between holes. Snug-fitting horizontal rails were jammed into the mortises of each end post, and the central vertical member and the two Y braces (see the photograph) were attached to the rails with pegs or clinch-nails.

Pegging isn't difficult; you drill holes through the joint and hammer in slightly oversized oven-dried hardwood pegs (obtainable from any hardware store) or your own hand-whittled locust pegs. Leave ¼ inch of peg protruding from each side of the hole. Moisture in the green splits will soak into the dry pegs and swell them tight. When the wood around the peg dries and pegs loosen, split the protruding ¼-inch of the pegs with a chisel and pound and glue in small hardwood wedges (whittled or bought) of the sort used to hold on ax heads. Slivers of wedge in each peg – inserted in a + pattern so the wedge on one side goes with the grain and the opposing wedge goes in the opposite direction – will lodge the peg in place forever. As well they should; this is an easy but time-consuming sort of old-time joinery.

Nailing is a great deal faster. You can still get easy-bending cut-style clinch nails by special-ordering *clout nails* from the hardware store. Cut flat so they are wide and thin, they slip easily between the grain of splittable woods (after you master the trick of hitting them square enough that the soft steel doesn't bend). When hurdles are hammered up on a hand anvil or on a length of rail-road rail or a granite rock, the emerging nail will hook over to form a staple and curve its tip back into the wood, clinching the joint.

Four sheep hurdles, with sharpened post ends pushed into the ground, protruding rail tips interlaced, and a hoop or loop of rope tossed over meeting verticals at each corner, will contain a couple of sheep on good graze for a day. Once or twice a day, or more, depending on the graze – you go out to the pasture with water buckets. The hurdles pull easily from the soil, and you move the crib and sheep along with them, just far enough to reach fresh graze. Push down the posts, put fresh water in the bucket tied to one rail, and the sheep are fenced, fed, and watered for another little while.

WATTLE HURDLES

In the Europe that early North American settlers came from, wood was already scarce in many areas, and portable fence panels were made of rushes or of hazel or willow sprouts woven wicker-like through vertical poles. That *wattle-hurdle* was a free-standing version of the foundation that was plastered with a mixture of mud, straw, and manure to make a wattle-and-daub building wall.

As with the split-wood hurdle, you can make a wattle screen to any dimensions that suit.

You'll need forms to hold the vertical saplings, or *sails*. For the bottom, you can dig holes in the soil and anchor well a thick plank that has been bored every 6 to 12 inches with 1- to 1⅕-inch-diameter holes. (The smaller diameter your vertical poles and weaving materials, the closer you'll want the poles. Also, build in an even number of verticals if you plan to weave in a twilly *hole* or carrying port as described below.) To keep the poles from wobbling as you weave, make up a top form from a length of thin board with holes drilled through in the same pattern as in the bottom form member. The top form too must be anchored securely, or you can forget

Erecting a maple sapling pole framework for a wattle-hurdle.

the top form and fasten the vertical poles to any horizontal crosspiece – the header over the barn-door opening on our place, for example.

Cut 3½- to 6-foot lengths of any sapling. I use aspen – "popple" in local usage – a pioneer tree that's the first species to invade abandoned fields. It cuts like soap and dries hard, though it's brittle unless oiled. It's best to hang or lay the end poles out straight in the sun for a few days to dry a little so they won't bend in easily as *weavers* are bent around them. Poke the large ends of the sails into the holes in your form, lodging wobbly sticks with small wedge-shaped whittling shims. Slip the top form over the sails, wedging up those holes too if needed.

For your weavers, or *withes*, use any easy-bending new growth. The old-time European hurdle makers used European hazel saplings or especially cultivated plantings of a fast-growing indigenous willow species, *Salix viminalis*, or osier willow. This is the lovely, round, nonsplitting material you see in real wicker furniture – some of it still sound after a hundred years' service on the front porch of someone's summer house. *S. viminalis* was imported to America by early wicker furniture makers and has naturalized in a few damp spots from Pennsylvania north along the Atlantic coast. I've read about how well it bends and how fast it regrows after cutting, but I haven't yet met anyone who could point out a stand in North America.

The European hurdle makers, using hazel or osier saplings with bark carefully stripped off, made a fence that would hold up to the weather for ten years or more. But for a less ambitious screen you can use any slender branch that won't break when bent double; weeping willow works for me. Small branchlets bend easily, and any new growth up to pencil-thick can be persuaded to cooperate. Any material that can be used in rustic basket making is good; black willow is common along streams in the East, and you can bend possumhaw viburnum (not the possum haw itself), *Viburnum nudum* or withe-rod viburnum in the South and the cottonwood poplar in the West. Nearly all trees whose spring branchlets bend into wattle are fast-growers in damp or swampy land, though I've woven up leggy spring growth from overgrown forsythia bushes and other long-twigged ornamentals with good enough results.

Testing Branches for Wattle

1. *Break off a long, slender branch from a likely tree or bush and strip off twigs and leaves.* **Hold the tip end and strip leaves and twigs down toward the base—against the grain. The more cleanly the small stuff strips, the faster it will weave into neat-appearing wattle.**

2. *Try bending it double; if it snaps, you will have to try working in a bend. Squeeze about an inch of branch between your fingers. Work, bend, and twist it by degrees to separate an inch of lengthwise plant fibers. If bark but not interior fiber splits, that's okay, though if it breaks, the bends will be frizzy looking.*

4. *Try bending—continuing to twist back and forth as needed—till the branch bends double with no breakage of internal fibers.*

5. *Twist the loosened fibers moderately tight till they reform a solid cord, but not so tight they rupture. Then bend the branch double and tie it to retain the bend.*

6. *Let the withe dry in full sun and open air, and check in several days; if the bend is strong and tight and the branch has not become breakable you have good prospective material.*

Weaving Wattle

You can weave withes with the leaves and twigs in place for a wild and rustic look. Leaves will drop off in time to leave a prickly-looking screen that begs to support a fast-growing vine. For the most finished appearance, remove twigs and bark and split the withes in half with your pocket knife or the bill hook of a pruning knife. Weave so the cut surfaces are all on one side and the rough side and all tag ends are on the other.

Begin weaving at the bottom of the pole frame with your thickest branches. Starting part way in, weave the branch around one side of a sail, then around the other side of the next, in an in-and-out pattern till you reach the end. Then twist the withe at the bend, first loosening, then retightening fibers to prevent breakage at the sharp 180-degree turn around the end sail. Bend the withe around the pole so it is just barely snug – not so tight as to create inward pressure, which will either bend the end sail or cause a warp. Then weave your way back, in an alternating weave pattern. Add new withe as needed, lodging loose ends of the withes down through several lower strands.

It isn't pure wattle art, I know, but before removing a screen from the form, I like to tack small brads or put long gun-staples through bottom and top withes and into the sails to keep the weave straight over time. It isn't a bad idea to nail withes to sails in a horizontal line across the middle, too. It takes more time and experience than I have to learn how to weave consistent pressure into each turn of each withe as it bends over each sail. I can tell you from experience that screens made by amateurs (by this amateur, at least) can warp and twist, and the sails get all whee-whawed as they slip around in inexpertly-woven wattle.

A Twilly Hole

If you'd like to make a really authentic wattle hurdle, weave in a *twilly-hole* near the top. Bend withes back around the two center sails to leave a several inch high opening between. Then, be sure to make the weave above the hole especially sturdy. Several added mini-sails can be woven in to add stability; drill holes for them in the top frame and lodge their bottom ends in the lower runs of weave. When done, cut out the free lengths of sail running down through the twilly hole (unless you like the barred jail-door effect).

The hole can be used to peek into or out from the enclosure. Traditionally, a pole was strung through so the shepherd could carry several panels at once. A whole fence could be hauled around if end sails of several hurdles were bound together top and bottom to make an accordion-fold, multipanel screen. Set yours up in a circle, and fold (sic) your sheep in for the night.

I've seen loosely-woven, 8-foot-high hurdles – twilly holes and all – used as privacy screens between the back gardens of city townhouses. They were roughly made and wonderfully rustic looking. Morning glory vines adorned them in summer but, unlike a perennial vine, died out in winter so the wattle could dry to resist rot. The open weave let plenty of air circulate, though you couldn't see through. The eye-height twilly holes were screened with a small matchstick curtain on a bamboo rod to maintain privacy – except when neighbors on either side wanted an invitation to the next-door chablis-and-brie party.

METAL FENCE

"**Y**ou *do* have to fence them, you know!" the lady dog breeder said. But the miniature Yorkshire terrier puppy was so adorable, and the kids so instantly attached to him, that no one paid attention.

As Max the Terrible grew to his full 14-inch length, he became a fierce defender of his home territory and a marvelous watch dog. But the breeder had been right; if his leash was dropped or the back door left ajar, he'd take off like a small furry tornado and stay gone for hours protecting the family against every sentient creature within a mile. After a winter of twice-a-day Max walking, we decided we needed a fence.

A COMMON PROBLEM

The design constraints were complicated, and our long-debated decisions may suggest solutions for problems you will face in designing and building your own area fences. The easiest design, a conventional, full-yard perimeter fence, didn't seem neighborly. Traditional pickets or black iron would have matched the colonial architecture of our New England college town. But there just

Max behind his namesake fence.

weren't many fences of any kind in evidence other than the requisite wire-mesh or grape-stake fences around pools and tennis courts, plus a few garden enclosures. The town is heavily treed and be-shrubbed, and living fences are common. But we lacked the years needed to grow a hedge thick enough to conceal a Max-proof wire fence. Besides, any fence planted or built to acceptable design would have cost more than the dog.

At last we decided to fence just enough of the yard to serve Max's needs with the least expensive and most innocuous fence we could find. That dictated an area of at least 25 by 25 feet, for a fenced area of 625 square feet, surrounded by low wire fabric on lightweight steel fence posts.

We decided to fence the portion of the back yard off the rear porch and around the segment of lawn occupied by the woodpile and equipment shed. The fence would extend off the house (which would provide most of one side of a 1,250-square-foot area – doubling the fenced area at half the fencing costs). It would surround two segments of lawn and, properly gated, it would not infringe on traffic through any important area. A ramp would extend to the ground in the fenced area from an opening in the back railing, and we'd install an accordion fence at the steps of the porch.

CHOOSING MATERIALS

For all his ferocity, Max hasn't much weight behind his yap. He wasn't going to be hard to fence. Yorkies aren't diggers, but they can jump. Therefore, a lightweight fence on lightweight posts would do, so long as it was fairly high but low to the ground and tight enough along the bottom that he couldn't work under. Nor need the fence be permanent: the day would come when Max would be superseded, and chances were that at that time the fence would go also. So we went looking for easy-in/easy-out posts and relatively inexpensive fabric, gate, and latch materials from the local hardware stores.

For posts, I chose light, forged-steel, U posts designed to hold wire fabric – they have alternating holes and wire hooks for attaching the fabric, and a small spade foot spot-welded to the bottom. (Don't get posts made exclusively for electric fence; they have holes, but no fence hooks.) The posts are painted grass green and come in 3- and 4-foot lengths for $2.25 to $3 apiece. You can buy longer lightweight posts, but – as I discovered – they are too flimsy to act as ends or corners for even a 4-foot-high fence, and I'd not use them again for anything but interpost stays. The posts are steel-strapped into bundles of 10, but are usually sold individually unless you need 50, 100, or more stakes.

I'd had enough experience with small animals' worrying escape holes through the cheapest fence material you can get – wound-wire poultry netting – that I looked for genuine welded-wire fabric. Available in any hardware store was the Yard-Guard type of 1/16-inch-diameter wire fabric that comes in 3- or 4-foot heights of 2 × 2⅝-inch mesh and is coated with grass-green vinyl to match the fence posts, resist rust, and appear less conspicuous in summer (but stick out like a sore thumb in snowy winters). The vinyl coats any scratchy wire ends but increases the cost of the fence from farm-economical to consumer-expensive.

Three-foot-high fence is too low to restrain a determined jumping dog, so I opted for the 4-foot fabric. A standard 50-foot roll, sheathed in an easy-sliding plastic sleeve, costs just under $40.

An equal length of a slightly sturdier, 1 × 2-inch mesh, galvanized fence fabric, uncoated and unsheathed, sells for about $10 less. The only other fence that I could find in hardware stores was 3-foot-high, uncoated galvanized that came in 100-foot rolls for about $50. Either height of the heavier, larger-gauge fence must be mechanically stretched if it is to look at all good and remain tight enough to restrain even a small animal. That requires strong, anchored end and corner posts and fence-stretching equipment – a whole dimension more complicated than a simple temporary lawn fence should be.

I opted for the Yard-Guard. The coated fabric is lightweight, and the wire is soft and easily crimped for tightening and to negotiate slight rises and dips in the yard. On lightweight posts, the fabric isn't strong enough to keep in an animal the size and strength of a boxer or springer spaniel, and I would restrict its use to fencing in small children and small pets, or to keeping rabbits from demolishing the pea vines.

LAYOUT AND INSTALLATION

TOOL KIT

To install the Yard-Guard steel post fence, you'll need:
Layout twine
Hand sledgehammer
Hammer
Flat-blade screwdriver or stout knife
Long-nosed pliers
Wire cutters (standard weight)
Spool of soft wire

To fabricate and install braces:
Hacksaw
Wood saw
Hand drill (fitted with bits and a grinding wheel)
Wood screws
¼-inch × 1½-inch bolts and nuts
U clamps
Extra posts and wood as detailed in text.

Though the label on Yard-Guard fence says you can "Hang It – No Stretching," you must install it on securely buried posts and pull it tight enough that the top wire is good and straight, or it will sag and look sloppy. If the bottom is not tight, small creatures can wiggle out of a play yard or into a garden, in which case you might as well have no fence at all.

First step, as in all fencing, is to lay out fence lines with twine and stout, well-sunken stakes. Run the twine line at the same height as the planned fence, build in loop-ended twine gates, and live with the layout for a while. That trial period is particularly important in area fencing that cuts through your property and so can disrupt established traffic patterns in ways you may not anticipate on paper.

Once the layout is decided and the twine-fence tested, decide on the placement of gate-end-, and corner supports. Best as always are 4-inch-square or larger PT wood posts sunk at least 2 feet deep in concrete anchors. Heavy-duty steel posts with anchors and guy lines will also do, if you don't mind their crude appearance and high cost. But no lightweight steel post will support a gate or end for long. As I found out, if the little post doesn't pull loose, it will bend.

Installing and Bracing End Posts

Posts should go in just deep enough that a full fence-height length of post is exposed, and they should be aligned so that the outside of the U, and the little protruding finger flanges that will hold the wire-mesh, face the outside of the fence. Set and brace your ends and corners first.

I was able to use the house to support each end of Max's fence. The post nearest the gate butted to the porch at 3 feet above ground. A 1½-inch sheet metal U clamp and two wood screws served to hold it to the floor rail. The end post at the other end of the fence ran into foundation rubble when I tried sinking it close to the house, however, so it had to go in about 18 inches out from the building. I connected its top to the house corner with a 1½-foot length of laminated plywood made by gluing three 1½-inch strips of inexpensive ¼-inch exterior-grade Luan ply together with Elmer's Carpenter's (waterproof) glue and weighting them overnight with several bricks. These flimsy little attachments wouldn't hold a stretched fence for a second, but they support Max's fence admirably.

Corner posts, where the fence turned 90 degrees, proved that I'm not the fencer I'd thought. For the most visible corner, I sunk one of the lightweight posts and braced it with a 2-foot length of angle-iron pounded into the soil at a 45-degree angle so that it met the post about a foot above the soil line. I assumed that this small bottom-brace (similar to corner braces I'd put into farm fences on heavy-duty posts) would suffice. But when I strung on a 30-foot length of wire and pulled it hand-tight to hook it onto the opposing corner, the flimsy little post bent double where it met the brace.

I had to replace the laboriously hand-hacksawed length of angle-iron with a longer brace – another lightweight post hammered into the ground so that it slanted down at a 45-degree angle, this time from the top of the corner post. I used a circular grinding wheel on the electric drill to cut a notch in the edge of the upright to accept the top of the brace, then wired the top of the brace to the corner post with soft fence wire, looping the wire through holes you'll find punched at the top and each two or three inches along all steel fence posts. The wire will keep the angled post lodged in its notch, well braced against the corner once the fabric is stretched on. Plus, the angled corner brace gives the fence a more substantial look, as though it was put in to stay.

The far end of the fence was hidden in a line of lilac bushes, and for the distant corners I used some surface-rusted but serviceable 7-foot heavy-duty spade-foot U posts from our old poultry yard. Pounded down 2 to 2½ feet, they were adequate corners for the Yard-Guard fence when braced with the short lengths of angle-iron I'd cut originally for the lightweights.

If I were to do it over again, I'd plan on heavy-duty posts for all ends, corners, and gate posts, even at double the cost – and I'd advise you to do the same even if it means a trip out of town to a farm-supply store. (Ordering from hardware-store catalogues, or from Sears or other mail-order sources, you have to buy an entire bundle of stakes – an unnecessary expense for a Max-type fence.)

THE GATE

Lightweight posts call for a lightweight gate, and several fabricators manufacture skeleton gate kits of aluminum tubing for the frame of the gate, hinges and a latch to fix on U posts, plus brackets and bolts to stretch and hold a piece of your chosen fence fabric onto the gate. Our gate kit from the hardware store cost $27 and change. It came without the fabric, of course, and also was missing a couple of essential nuts. Finding replacement nuts was a minor nuisance.

The gate kit I used, by Beacon Industries, Inc., of Westminster, Maryland, is the best design I've seen – missing nuts or no. The frame is made of thin aluminum tubing – two shallow U-shaped pieces connected by two short, straight lengths. Crimped ends of the straight pieces slip into the open ends of the Us. You cut a piece of fence fabric to fit the opening and attach it with pairs of flat plates that bolt together, clamping corners of the fabric between them. The paired plates then attach to holes drilled at corners of the gate frame with threaded bolts that run through little flanges bent in the ends of one of the plates. Tightening nuts at each corner tightens the fabric.

Hinge pins are a pair of L-shaped threaded bolts with a set of clamps on one end that fit perfectly over the edges of a normally-installed, U-shaped steel gate post. The gate hangs from them on eye bolts that are attached through predrilled holes in the frame.

The latch is a simple U-shaped stamping that also bolts to the frame; it will tilt up to open the gate, but when released it rests extended at a 90-degree angle to keep the gate latched.

It is a ten-minute job to assemble the frame, cut and attach the fabric, and bolt on the hardware, but don't do it last thing. That's important. Put in the fence – complete and tightened, up to one gate post. Install your gate on that gate post, then put up the other gate post, and carry the fence on from there. In other words, don't leave gate installation to last if you're working with bendable steel posts. A gate must fit its opening precisely if it is to latch securely. The eyehooks and L bolts of these kit gate hinges can be moved along their threaded shafts to adjust the gate back and forth within the opening up to an inch or so, but if the opening is still too large or small you'll have to pull posts and restretch fabric to make the gate fit.

Bracing the Gate Posts

Gates in lightweight fence are best hung off a building, but we needed an opening in mid-fence for Max's enclosure, and we found the posts were too flimsy to hold even the lightweight aluminum kit gate. The alternatives were to install heavy-duty, hard-to-remove gate posts, put in a stockade-type door frame to box the gate, use steel braces as in the corner posts, or tension the gate posts by tightening the fabric against some sort of horizontal frame along the top of the fence – much as chain-link fence is tensioned.

I elected to rig horizontal wood rails along the top of the fence at each side of the gate. I cut lengths of nominal 1 × 3 furring strip equal to the distance from the bottom of each gate post to the nearest braced post or corner. The boards attached with wood screws inserted through the holes in the tops of each steel post. I trial-fit each board carefully so that when installed, it kept the gate post perfectly vertical and plumb. A carpenter's level is helpful in getting gate posts square, though you can drop a weight from a length of twine to fashion a plumb bob and align the post with that.

Next, I cut lengths of fabric to fit the flights of fence at each side of the gate, cutting them enough longer at each end so I would have enough of each horizontal wire to wrap around the post with a couple of inches to spare.

You'll find little flanges stamped every 2 inches into the outside face of U posts designed for wire-mesh fence – just right to fit standard fence fabric. The bottom two flanges point down, the rest point up. You have to fit bottom horizontal wires onto the bottom hooks and pull up on the top wires to hook them on the tops of the posts. Or perhaps you'll find it easier to slide the majority of the wires into the up-facing top flanges first and force the lower wires into place: I find that I need pliers to stretch the wire down and using pliers it's hard not to scar the vinyl coating. So I apply the pliers to the bottom wires where scars on the coating won't show.

To attach cut ends of wire fabric to the posts, starting from the bottom, pull the cut end of each horizontal wire tight around the post, twist it back around itself, and wind it tight. Long-nosed pliers are almost a necessity for a taut fence.

LINE POSTS AND ROUTINE FENCING

With the ends, the gate, and adjacent fabric pieces attached and braced, the rest of our Max fence went up in a snap. The fabric turns easily around the sharpest corners; you need only squeeze each horizontal wire around the corner post with your hand to create a sharp bend.

Along the layout twine strung between corner posts I set line posts so there would be a vertical fabric support every 6 to 8 feet. The ground was gently rolling, and to avoid having gaps between fence bottom and ground in dips and having the bottom of the fabric flare out as it traversed rises, I made sure that there was a post at the bottom of each dip and the top of each rise even if it meant slightly unequal distances between posts. Each post was sunk perpendicular to the layout line so that 48 inches of post were exposed and the bottom fence-hook flange was just 2 inches above ground level.

Each horizontal wire of one cut end of fence fabric was wrapped securely to one end post. The fabric was unrolled, stretched hand-tight, and hooked around the post at the far corner. Next I went from post to post, pulling horizontal wires tight with pliers and hooking them over appropriate flanges. Slack produced was accumulated and taken up at the far corner post. Then I turned the corner, continuing to unroll fabric, till I reached the far end. The post-to-post tightening was repeated – producing a good, taut fence.

Whether from manufacturing inaccuracies or being bashed in transport (in the back of my truck as likely as in the common carrier from factory to retail outlet), many of the little hook flanges on the posts were smashed into the post and had to be pried out to accept the fabric. A twist or two with a stout flat-bladed screwdriver did the job. I'd hate to have to do it for heavy-duty posts surrounding a 40-acre pasture, though.

Dips and Rises

Unrolled fence fabric can't bend up or down in its flat, horizontal dimension any easier than a length of board can; you must take tucks in the fence fabric to negotiate rises and dips in the land. It is easy with soft-wired Yard-Guard. Through a dip, hang the fence with the bottom wire tight, then crimp the upper horizontals at the post to take out the slack. Over a rise, do the reverse: hang the fabric so the top wire is tight, then crimp the wires below.

Martha did the crimping as I stretched Max's fence. She'd catch a wire right beside the post with the end of the needle-nosed pliers; then, using the side of the post as a levering fulcrum, she would twist the wire around the pliers' nose at the same time she bent it in and back to-

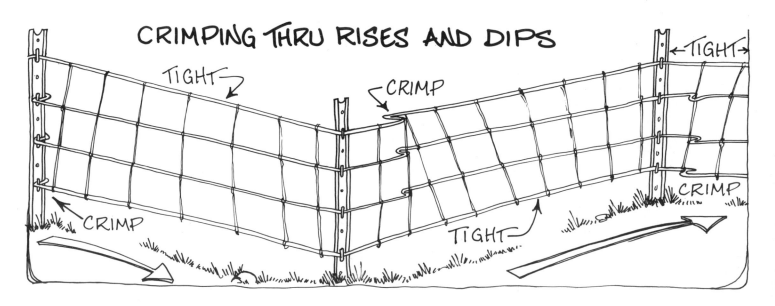

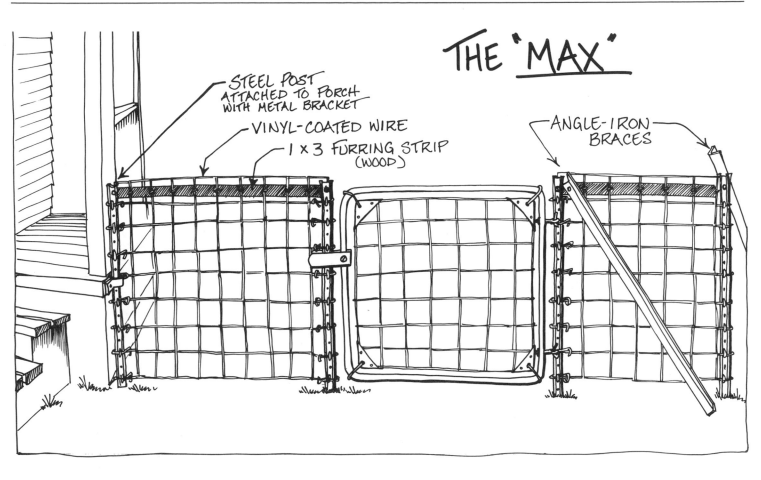

THE "MAX"

STEEL POST ATTACHED TO PORCH WITH METAL BRACKET

VINYL-COATED WIRE

1 × 3 FURRING STRIP (WOOD)

ANGLE-IRON BRACES

ward the post. The crimps are little S's in the wire and aren't noticeable unless you are looking for them. If crimping wire at one post doesn't tighten the fabric thoroughly, you can take up the slack at the next post.

After the fence was tight, I went around with the sledgehammer, hammering each post in far enough to snug the bottom of the fabric well into the grass. That loosened several lengths a bit along the bottom, and to prevent Max from working under, I put in crimps at each post till the wire was retightened. At one spot along the back of the fence where there is a thick growth of ferns and I'd been in too much of a rush, the fabric was a good 2 inches above the ground. When I tried to pound it in, the guilty post hit a buried rock and wouldn't sink further. Rather than unfasten and rerig the fabric, I laid lengths of firewood along the several feet of inch-high opening. Not a very elegant solution, and a reminder not to rush fencing – but the logs don't show in the greenery, it was getting dark, and Max doesn't know the difference.

TIME AND COSTS

Max's fence took perhaps three hours to erect, but the job was spread over a week and more as I made up special braces and pulled in one tool or another from the distant workshop.

One hundred linear feet of lightweight Yard-Guard fence with stakes, one gate, and braces to fence 625 square feet (or as in our own case, some 1,200 square feet when a building forms one side of the fenced area) costs out as follows:

Fabric: #2 48-inch × 50-foot rolls of green (or white) vinyl-coated galvanized wire in 2 inch × 2⅝ inch mesh @ $40 each: **$80.00**

Posts: located each 6- to 8-feet, plus extras as braces:
24 @ 2.50 each: **$60.00**

Gate: # 1 @ $30.00   **$30.00**

Misc. wood and hardware: **$5.00**

                              $175.00

COST PER RUNNING FOOT: **$1.75**

8

WIRE LIVESTOCK FENCE

The principles I learned the hard way in putting up Max's Yard-Guard fence apply to any other wire livestock or garden fence you'd care to install. The posts must be of strong enough stuff and dug deep or braced well enough to withstand the tension needed to keep the wire taut so the beasts being fenced are restrained. The rules remain the same whether you will be stringing spools of barbed wire, rolls of welded- or woven-steel netting, reels of the high-tensile electric fence mentioned later, or the easiest wire fencing to put up and the cheapest you can buy: poultry netting or "chicken wire."

CHICKEN-WIRE FENCING

Poultry netting is made from 20-gauge wire that's only 1/16-inch in diameter, wound together in a honeycomb pattern of interlocking hexagons. Each six-sided figure shares a side with six adjoining hexagons, as in the wax comb of bees. As with honeycomb, the hexagon fence pattern encloses the greatest area with the least material in a structure that has great inherent strength so long as the integrity of the design is maintained. Break one length of wire however, and a good-sized section of the intricate structure collapses.

To ensure that the net holds up, reinforcing wires are run through the top, bottom, and – in the larger sizes – the middle of the chicken-wire fabric. They absorb all the lateral tension of the fence, relieving the fabric itself of horizontal stress. Without the horizontals, the netting would stretch out into a rope if you tried too hard to pull it tight.

Poultry netting is lightweight and flimsy stuff. It's fine for containing feather-weight birds and keeping rabbits out of the peas, but it can be chewed open by dogs, cut with scissors by children, and bulled through by pigs or larger stock. It will begin to rust and become unsightly in perhaps four years and rust through in about seven – so it isn't really a permanent fence but rather a medium-term screen.

I've seen working poultry fences made from chicken mesh that was simply unrolled and wired to poles stuck in the ground or stapled to trees. Such fences are floppy-topped and unattractive, but they're effective if fastened well to the uprights and staked to the ground. Chickens will fly up and light atop any *rigid* fence but won't try landing on the top of floppy wire more than once; it doesn't give the wide, firm perch their awkward grasping claws need. They'll sway there briefly, flapping and screeching, then bail out.

Well-anchored chicken wire will keep the vegetable garden safe from rabbits and if floppy enough, it will deter raccoons and woodchucks. The looser the wire, the harder it is for the heavier animals to climb – but the more of it you must bury forever to keep them from burrowing under.

For a quick and easy poultry yard, you can staple one end of the netting to one side of the hen house, unroll it around uprights, and staple the other end to the other side of the house. For a garden fence, just unroll it around verticals placed at the corners of the garden plot. Making fence with chicken wire sound easy, and it is; but there are a few tricks to it.

Controlling Stretch

Unlike any other fence fabric, chicken wire will stretch readily in all dimensions. It will even form itself around compound curves (indeed, chicken wire is what is bent around a framework to supply the surface for large plaster or papier-maché sculptures). That stretchability can be an advantage; the netting will adapt itself to

NETTING SIZES

Poultry netting comes in 50-foot rolls of 20-gauge galvanized wire with reinforcing wires at top, bottom, and through the middle in larger sizes. The rolls come in pairs; that is, you can buy two rolls uncut for a 100-foot unbroken run of fence. Or the merchant will cut off a single roll for you.

Height (feet)	Mesh size (inches)	Weight/roll (pounds)	Cost/roll ($)
1	1	5	8
2	1	9	13
3	1	14	18
4	1	19	25
2	2	5	8
3	2	7	10
4	2	12	13
5	2	14	15
6	2	19	18

The heavier and more costly 1-inch mesh is stronger and more rigid than 2-inch, so is easier to put up. It will also keep tiny chicks in and chicken-feed-loving ground squirrels out.

The 1- to 3-foot heights aren't good for much but low rabbit fences around the garden. Unless the fence is fastened to sturdy stakes (5 feet high at minimum), even a flock of hungry ducks can charge the netting and bull it down. If you put wing-clipped poultry behind the low stuff, they may not be able to fly out, but dogs can jump in.

Four-foot netting is too tall for a rabbit fence and too short for poultry, but it's perfect for training tomatoes and cucumbers and green pea vines. Bury the lower few inches of 5-foot wire for a garden fence that woodchucks can't dig under. For poultry, I use 6-foot-high mesh and bury the lower 12 inches or so.

Reading the level line while sinking posts for a chicken run.

Unrolling the 6' poultry netting around the posts. Note trench to bury lower portion of the netting.

changes in ground elevation and curves in the fence line more quickly than any other metal fabric.

I like to bend the bottom several inches of a poultry fence out horizontally and staple it to the ground or bury it to deter digging predators. That would take a lot of cutting, crimping, and bending with most fencing, but with poultry netting I only have to cut where the fence rounds a sharp turn.

Layout

Chicken-wire fences are rarely very long; if you are going to the bother of stringing a long fence, it is better to invest in heavier and longer-lasting woven or welded wire. For a little backyard puppy-holding pen, a poultry run, or a one-season support for the pea vines, you don't even have to lay out a fence line except for the sake of looks and pride of workmanship. Set posts by eye or pick your trees as you unroll fence, and the fabric will hand-stretch to fit.

For anything more ambitious than the simplest enclosure or plant support, though, you will want a straight fence line, a straight and even fence top, and fair curves. Lay out posts and twine as with any fence.

If you'd like a perfectly level fence top on sloping ground, tap in your corner stakes and enough line stakes just deep enough to support a level line all along the fence. Be sure to put a stake in all dips. Start the level line at fence-top height above ground at one end and use your line level to string it level all around. Now go along and measure from string to ground. At the point where you find the string is the greatest distance from the ground, sink the stake so the top fence-fastener is just fence-height above the ground (or fence height less a foot if you plan to bury some fabric.) Wood posts should extend an inch or two higher than the fabric top will be above ground. Set steel posts so that the top hook is at fence height.

Re-level the line in both directions from the low point and sink stakes to the same level all along the line. Now, when you string the fence, it will have a level top that reaches ground at every point. Where it is too long, you can roll it up or cut in a dart if needed.

Use stout wood or heavy-duty steel posts at ends and corners of any real fence, chicken-wire included. Using 6-foot mesh with the bottom 12 inches buried, I buy 7-foot U or T posts at $5 apiece and place them every 5 feet or less. The fabric can't be tensioned much more than hand-tight horizontally, and it lacks much vertical strength. Posts must be close together to keep the mesh taut enough that a fat hen won't belly it out any time she takes a flying, squawking leap away from a competitor's peck.

Fastening the Fabric

The ends of any chicken-wire fence must be well fastened, both the reinforcing wires and each wire of the net. Otherwise you are begging for stretch as you tighten the fence. Make sure the fabric at the cut end isn't distorted when you start; have a 48-inch fence exactly 48 inches high and all the little hexagons in the mesh perfectly shaped.

Begin by fastening all the horizontal wires to the first post or poultry house if the fence runs over an even grade. On a down slope, fasten only the top wire, and fasten only the bottom wire on an upgrade; wait till you've unrolled a little fence to fasten the others. Unroll the netting snugly around the whole fence line, keeping the top wire taut so long as you are going down, the bottom wire taut while going up. At the post nearest every grade change, crimp in any tucks needed to continue on without leaving waves in the wire. Poultry netting crimps easily by hand. Don't pull the wire really tight between uprights – just snug.

Wrap the start and end of wires securely around steel posts, and twist them back and around themselves, but don't hammer the posts' hooks closed; you don't want to have to pry them all open when time comes to replace the fabric.

If you're fastening the fabric to wood, you can use a staple gun to tack down the mesh, but fasten the reinforcing wires with the smaller ¾-inch size of steel fence staples.

Fence Staples

Staples are tricky. The sharpened points on opposing ends of a staple's U shape are often different lengths and are cut in opposite directions, so they can swivel right out of the wood if you try hammering them in with a single, hard blow right on the top. They can pull out if you hammer them in so points are arranged vertically in line with the grain of the wood. Also, unless the staple's legs point down into the wood slightly, animals leaning on wire can pull them out. Holding the staple securely, and canting it at a 45-degree angle across the grain, with its top angled up and longest leg down, I tap the sides of its rounded top with the hammer – first at one side, then at

Putting in a fence staple.

the other. That sinks one side, then the other, till the ornery points are buried.

Once it is started, I sink the staple into the wood by hammering straight down with light blows. Staple steel is soft; if you whack a staple too hard it can mushroom or bend and fail to clamp the fence wire firmly to the wood when you want it to, or it can clamp too tight when you want it loose.

When fastening the start of a fence wire, sink the staple into the wood all the way. But when stapling line wires in mid-fence, leave the staple loose so the wire can be tightened. I bet you never thought there was so much to stapling, did you?

To fasten the hex-wrapped wires of the chicken-wire fabric, just wrap each loose end of fabric wire around a steel post. In wood, the reinforcing wires are fastened with staples. To fasten the mesh I use an Arrow T-50 stapler with ½-inch staples. For best holding, put staples over the wound sections of wire, bending the free end of the wire back on itself and over the staple. Tap the bent wire and this first staple flat with a hammer. Then staple both lengths of wire again and sink that staple with the hammer. I always tap staples in well; the gun doesn't bury them well enough to hold.

For ultimate holding power, fasten a length of board over the whole cut length of wire to clamp it to a poultry house or a fence post. I use furring strips and screw them on tight with dry-wall screws and a little high-torque electric drill.

Gates in poultry wire can be as elaborate as you like. I've used prefab gates as in the Max pen, and I have built wood-frame gates, covered them with netting, and hung them off wood posts with strap hinges. Easiest is a poor man's gate as described below under barbed wire.

A Buried No-Dig Skirt

Keep dogs and other pests from digging into a pen by burying the bottom foot or so of fence net – easily done with good-bending poultry netting. You can bend the bottom foot out as you string the net, or you can wire on a separate skirt.

If I'm feeling ambitious, I dig out the sod in a strip along the bottom of the fence before the fabric goes on. Then I bend the lower end of the fence out to form a horizontal skirt and peg it down with forked sticks or weight it so it lies flat in the shallow trench. I then replace the sod, which reroots, fixing the screen in place. Any creature trying to dig in will be scratching on steel once it excavates below sod level. I've never lost a chicken to digging predators in a well-buried chicken-wire run – though the wire rusts quickly.

Simpler is to cut the grass close to the ground along the fence line, lay the wire out, and weight it well or staple it to the soil with forked sticks. Grass will grow up through the mesh, fixing it to the ground. Open to the air, the wire will resist rust longer than if buried and constantly exposed to acid soil and water.

Added Reinforcement and a Covered Run

The horizontal braces or spreaders that I used at the gate of Max's pen can strengthen the top of a chicken-wire pen and make it appear more finished. I've never used furring that way, but we supported the netting around the run of an earlier poultry yard with maple poles.

I find that a 5-foot run of chicken wire is the maximum that should be hung without support in either the horizontal or vertical dimension. So, when covering a run using 6-foot wire, I set the side and end posts 5 feet or less apart. Then, when laying 6-foot-wide wire over the top, I can overlap it 6 inches or more on each side.

To support chicken wire roofing a poultry run, I string electric-fence wire across from upright to upright in an X pattern. Our current run is located in a lilac thicket,

which gives the chickens woody trunks to roost on and offers us lovely flowers to look at in the spring, but which sheds a lot of leaves in fall that can accumulate on the wire roof of the run and keep the winter snow from filtering through. To support that added weight, I ran a length of wire down the center of the run, wired it to the intersections of each X, and stapled it to trunks of the lilacs growing in the run. If you have the sense not to put your chickens in a lilac thicket, you may want to sink a stake in the center of their run to support canopy-wire net.

The top netting is simply laid over the wire support, snipped where needed to get around the lilac trunks, overlapped at the seams for strength, and tightened loosely. I twisted the cut ends around the top horizontal reinforcing wire of the side netting where needed to keep it in place. As with all poultry-netting fences, I attached the canopy with the minimum number of connections needed to keep it standing, but no more – knowing that it would rust and have to be replaced in a few years.

BARBED WIRE

After chicken wire, the next farm fence in order of expense and difficulty is barbed wire: two strands of 16- to 12-gauge steel wire twisted together, with two- or four-point barbs bound onto the strand every 4 or 5 inches. "Bob Wahr" is at once the stockman's friend and enemy. Bob W.'s a pal because he's cheap and goes up quickly; an 80-rod reel, containing 1,320 feet of 15½-gauge, two- or four-point "barb," costs less than $40 and in an hour's time will string into 330 feet of four-wire fence that would cost $120 and up if you bought welded-steel mesh fence fabric. Ol' Bob can be an enemy, too, though, because he'll for sure scar the cows (and you) as he gets his work done. Nevertheless, he does the job if you keep him in shape; once the early cattlemen exchanged open range and annual cattle roundups and drives for wire fence and railroad transportation, the Old West was a memory, and the cowboy on horseback became a full-time fence mender in a Jeep.

One personal note: I'm from New England, where most of the cattle are sweet-tempered Jerseys and Holsteins with names like Elsie who get milked twice a day, not half-wild Brahmas or even registered Hereford beef steers. I know that barb is still used extensively in real cattle country, and I've used it myself for hogs and beef steers. But I think it's inappropriate for homestead or hobby-farm livestock that are as much pets as food animals. The barbs can rip the hide of an animal deeply enough to draw blood. Hogs I've known ignored cuts, and a mud bath usually healed them. Cows and sheep and goats will try to keep a cut clean, but if the wound is located where the animal can't reach, it can become infected or infested with blow flies. At best you'll have a hefty vet bill and a scarred and undervalued hide to sell. At worst you'll have a dead animal.

Barb properly stapled so it runs loose to expand and contract.

With electric fence so convenient and cheap and easy to install (you don't need to stretch it) – and with solar fencers available to charge the wire in remote areas, the psychological persuasion of modern technology is replacing the brute force of Ol' Bob most everywhere. See chapter 9 on electric fence for details.

But if you run beef cows or replacement heifers or have a lot of back acreage to fence, barbed wire is the quickest way to get it done. I'll tell you how to set fence posts for any tensioned wire, single-strand or fabric, and I'll explain how to string barb. Just don't ever use the pointy stuff to fence horses. The things barbed wire can do to a horse's silky flank defy description.

Preliminaries

First, check out the local fences. Your neighboring farmers have worked out fencing techniques over generations of battling the local rains (that can soak soil and loosen fence posts) and snows (that can pack above fence level) – techniques to cope with wind, sun, shade, water- and grass supply, and all else that can influence livestock behavior and fence efficiency. Find out how the neighbors make fence, and plan to follow their lead if their fences work well.

Then, get a pair of thick horsehide gloves with gauntlets to protect tender wrist skin. Barbs that are long and pointed enough to send a message to thick-skinned range steers can make a lasting impression on you, too, unless you protect yourself. Thick trousers are in order; if you roll 40-plus-pound reels of barbed wire around long enough, one is sure to bounce hard off your skin. High boots are good too for the same reason. And, especially if you are working around horses, which can carry tetanus bacteria, keep your tetanus shots up to date. Barb can cause a puncture wound.

You'll need a supply of 1½-inch fence staples, at a cost of about $1 a pound, and you'll need a good combination fence tool or a hammer, a staple puller and a heavy-duty wire cutter. You'll also need a wire stretcher. Barbed wire must be stretched or it won't hold stock that really wants to escape; a sow in heat will root under or pry apart slack wires and squeeze through, gouges or no. You can get the slack out of the wire by heaving on a crowbar snagged on a barb and levering off a well-sunk post while someone else hammers in the staples. And, there are one-man stretchers – yard-long hardwood handles that you snag wire to and lever against the post. It takes considerable strength to hand-stretch fence wire properly, and it takes agility to stretch and staple at the

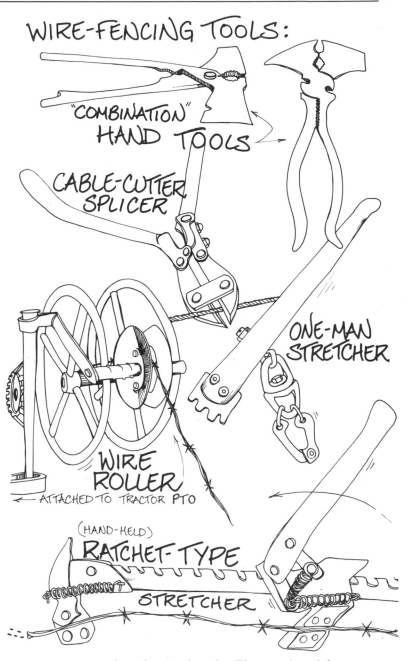

WIRE-FENCING TOOLS:

"COMBINATION" HAND TOOLS

CABLE-CUTTER SPLICER

ONE-MAN STRETCHER

WIRE ROLLER

← ATTACHED TO TRACTOR PTO

(HAND-HELD) RATCHET-TYPE STRETCHER

same time with only two hands. The weekend fencer is advised to invest in a proper fence stretcher.

Ranchers used to string barbed-wire fence with horse power – the genuine equine article. These days they use a power wire roller with its own electric motor or one that operates from the power take-off on Jeep, truck, or tractor. Usually barb is run off its spool onto the wire roller's large reel. On the fence, one end of the wire is attached to an end post, and the reel is allowed to freewheel while the vehicle is moved forward to run off a length of wire. Then the roller is used to take up slack, to tighten the wire and hold it till it is stapled to the posts. The catalogues listed in the equipment appendix contain level-winding wire rollers for about $170, as well as other wire-fencing tools.

Never stretch barbed wire with the vehicle itself by hooking the wire to your Jeep's tow hook or to a tractor tow bar and hauling on 15- or 12-gauge mild-steel fence wire with a ton or more of Detroit iron. I know it's been done by farmers for years, but more than a few of them have scars to show for it. A novice can easily overstretch a run of wire; it can snap and come flying back at bullet velocity as you are putting in staples. Unwinding a snarl of barbed wire from around your neck can be a real headache – if your head is still on and in operating condition, that is.

For small pastures I tension wire with a 20-year-old block and tackle. It consists of twin blocks containing two pulleys apiece connected by a single rope looped around and around the pulleys. Each block has a wire-grip at the end; you extend the ropes, hook up the wire, then pull the rope to draw it tight. The free end of the rope goes through a little hinged tube that acts as a brake. You may want to stretch fence with a come-along, a handle-operated ratchet-wheel that takes up a length of steel cable. You can't overstretch wire with either tool, and they also serve to hoist hogs for butchering, to pull trucks out of ditches, and for other farm chores. Cost is about $35 for either tool.

Both the block and tackle and the come-along require a tree or post to pull from. More specific to stringing barbed wire is a mechanical fence stretcher with a fixed hook or dog at one end and another dog on a traveler that is levered along a toothed steel rod much like the bumper jack in your car's trunk. That tool will stretch or splice two lengths of wire unassisted. You attach wire ends to L-shaped dogs at each end of the stretcher (or attach one dog to a fence post or tree and the other to a wire to be stretched), and ratchet the wire(s) up as tight as you like. The catalogues all sell fence stretchers, as well as a splicing kit with soft-metal splicing sleeves (you pull broken wire ends together, slip a sleeve over the broken ends, and crimp them together with a medium-sized cable-cutter.) A ratchet stretcher sells for less than $30 in some catalogues, and a complete splicing kit costs about the same.

Setting Posts

The straighter the fence the easier it is to stretch wire, so for the best pasture fence, do a careful layout with twine and stakes just as you would for a front-yard fence. Plan to set line posts no more than 15 feet apart; 12 feet is more conventional for calm-tempered animals, and 8 feet is the usual distance for hogs and rambunctious stock. End- and corner posts that contain the tension of the wire should be at least 6 inches thick, line posts 4 inches through at minimum. You'll need one 6- to 8-foot-long post and one or two braces for each end and three or five posts for each corner. If your fence runs more than 150 feet, you should put in a line stretcher – a set of posts with a brace between them – in mid-run. You'll also need stretchers anywhere the fence dips or crosses a rise; the downward tension can pull staples from an unbraced hilltop post, and the upward tension can pull a post in a dip clear out of the ground.

Most barbed-wire fencers cut and split their own posts. Naturally rot-resistant wood such as black locust, red or white cedar, cypress, mulberry, sassafras, or Osage orange is good if you have it. Lacking those aromatic woods, use a good hardwood and soak the lower 3 feet in the preservatives listed in the wood fence chapter. Lacking your own timber altogether, you can purchase pressure-treated posts, but the cost quickly gets beyond the range of cheap fencing. If you have to buy posts, you may as well go first class and put in a steel fabric or board fence. Most probably you'd be cash ahead with electric fence.

To set posts you'll need the tractor-mounted post-hole driver or auger or a clam-shell post-hole digger and tamping iron mentioned in the chapter on wood fences. Dig your post holes as you would for any fence – but since the wire can be unreeled to any length you care to cut it, you needn't observe careful distances between posts as with rail and board fence. Dig holes, and tamp soil well around them or pour a concrete footing as appropriate to your soil (and outlined elsewhere).

BRACING POSTS

Unless you brace each end- or corner post, any well-tensioned wire will pull it out of the soil. The simplest way to brace a post is to sink a deep stake at a point at least 1½ times as far down the fence line from the post as the top of the post is above ground, and install a diagonal brace that you cut on the spot to fit between stake and post. Notch the post just down from its top, notch the stake at ground level, and insert the brace. Cut your brace ½-inch longer than need be and ram it home with a sledgehammer. No need to nail the brace, as the fence wire will pull it tight.

A twin-post diagonal brace replaces the stake with a full-sized post. The diagonal is installed the same way, but you can run a loop of smooth wire around the tops of the two posts. Wrap both loose ends of the wire around one post and twist them together well. Then, put

BRACING SYSTEMS
FOR WIRE FENCES

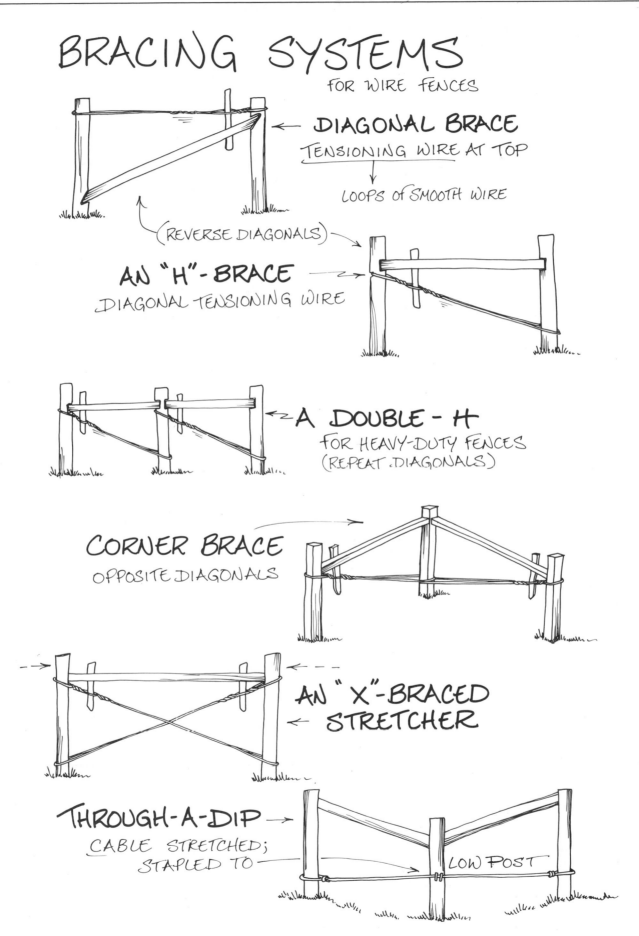

← **DIAGONAL BRACE**
TENSIONING WIRE AT TOP

LOOPS OF SMOOTH WIRE

(REVERSE DIAGONALS)

AN "H"-BRACE
DIAGONAL TENSIONING WIRE

A DOUBLE - H
FOR HEAVY-DUTY FENCES
(REPEAT DIAGONALS)

CORNER BRACE
OPPOSITE DIAGONALS

AN "X"-BRACED STRETCHER

THROUGH-A-DIP →
CABLE STRETCHED;
STAPLED TO

LOW POST

a stick through the loop at midpoint and twist to tighten the posts against the tension of the diagonal, which sets up a counter-counter-tension to resist the pull of the wire. Make the stick short enough that it will clear the diagonal when canted over sideways to revolve but will rest against the diagonal to hold tension in the wire when straightened. Revolve the stick from the bottom to the outside so that when it is lodged in place, it will be on the outside of the brace. If you revolve it from the top and out, nosy cows can nuzzle it loose and get a sharp crack on the snout for their curiosity.

The most effective brace is the H configuration. Sink a brace inside the fence line 1½ times as far from the end- or corner post as the posts are high (6 feet apart for a 4-foot fence). Then notch the corner and brace posts several inches down from the tops and insert another post as a horizontal brace. Rig a loop of smooth wire from the top of the down-line brace post to the bottom of the corner or end post. Insert a stick and tension. Note that this wire arrangement is the reverse of the diagonal post. The simple diagonal resists the tension of the fence wire directly. But the diagonal wire in an H brace acts as a lever on the vertical brace post, which stresses the horizontal brace against the corner post to create counter tension against the pull of the fence wire.

Tensioning Tension Wire

You do not have to tension the smooth-wire loops to the breaking point; it isn't the degree of tension that is important but the fact that significant tension exists. Twist the loop of wire enough that the twist-stick wants to revolve sharply – like the prop on a rubberband-powered model airplane. The wire will stretch in time, so check the tension monthly for the first season, then check two or three times a year.

For particularly long fences, or large herds of large stock, or for the high-tensile fences described in a later chapter, you should erect double-braced ends and corners. Simply add a second brace stake, a second horizontal, and another wire tensioner.

To build a corner where fence wire will pull at a post in two directions, sink your stoutest post and array paired braces away from it at a 90-degree angle.

Once ends and corners are in, sink line posts every 8 to 15 feet depending on stock being controlled and contours of the land. Make sure the posts are in a straight line, and place one at every dip and atop every rise along the fence. These must be well-anchored posts, but they serve only as battens – to keep the wire strands spaced so

Contented cows behind barbed run.

animals can't pry them apart. You may find that local fencers use metal stays – twisted nail-size 9-gauge wire – between line posts. On level land, and fencing large stock, you can space posts up to 100 feet apart and use stays between them. Suspension fences of four to six strands of 12-gauge barbed wire with twisted wire stays arranged each 15 to 20 feet serve as boundary fences in cattle country. They whip and sway when pushed, and beat well-fed and -watered cattle into line.

Every 100 to 150 feet along extended runs and at especially steep digs or rises, build a line stretcher: two posts with a horizontal brace between them, with tensioned wire loops in an X pattern.

To traverse a steep dip, sink a post or posts at the bottom, place posts at the top of each rim, and notch and place lateral braces between them. Heavy cable stretched between bottoms of the rim posts and stapled where it meets the posts down in the dip, can help hold the latter down. In loose or sandy soil you may have to set the in-dip posts in concrete.

In much of the arroyo country of the West, it's futile to try keeping posts in gullies that carry flash floods. Better to make a swinging flood gate of strap iron or stout wood bolted together. Be sure it is heavy enough that stock can't push it open. Hang the flood gate from the rim posts, and keep it clear of trash – lest it carry the whole fence downstream next gully washer. Here again, you are best advised to seek advice and follow local practice.

Stringing Wire

The number of wires you string and the distance apart you string them depend on the animals you are fencing in or out.

A single-strand barbed-wire fence isn't good for much at all unless you electrify it. Animals can jump over or slink under with minimal damage. A two-strand barb fence will retain placid cattle. Set one wire so that it is at lowered-nose level and the other at mid-chest-height of the animal being fenced. For adult cattle, that is about 18 inches and 3 feet for the respective wires; for calves, 1 foot and 2½ feet.

A three-wire fence is better than a two-wire, and a four-wire fence better yet. For a universal three-wire fence for small stock, set the bottom wire 6 inches off the ground, the second 1 foot above that, and the third 1 foot above the second. A four-wire fence for cattle has each wire a foot apart.

Fencing hogs in barbed wire is a challenge. A 3-foot fence with one wire at ground level and six more arranged 6 inches apart will work – but is getting expensive enough that you are better off with standard hog fabric. Most hog yards aren't very extensive. And you'll still have to ring their noses to keep them from rooting under.

Sheep in full fleece are impervious to barbs. You'll need a 45-inch-high, six- to nine-strand, drum-tight fence with the lower three strands 4 to 5 inches apart and with 9 inches between upper strands.

Goats will stand up and test a fence every way but sideways – and some young kids will try that as they leap about testing legs designed for bouncing over rocks. Goat hair isn't thick like sheep fleece, and a goat's skin is thin and easily torn – especially on a full udder. Don't fence dairy goats in barbed wire any more than you'd use it to fence a horse or your pet puppy.

To start a line of wire, wrap the free end once or twice around an end post so the run of wire will extend from in back of the post. Staple the wire at least twice where it overlaps itself at the back of the post. If you're hand stringing, poke a stick through the hole in the reel and unroll the wire to the next stretching post. It is good to have a helper. You'll find that reels get heavy if you work alone – backing up and holding 40-plus pounds far enough in front of you to keep the wire from snagging your britches.

Fasten the wire on the *outside* of ends and corners and any curves in the fence line so the wood, and not the staples, will bear the load. But run it along the *inside* of straight runs so animals will feel it before they scratch or lean on the line posts.

When you get to the next stretcher or the end or corner, run the wire in back of the post. Now, tension the wire. With a tractor and reel the job is *easy;* put the PTO in gear, tighten, and staple twice. Cut the wire at an end, but continue the fence on around a corner.

With a manual stretcher, you must adjust to the tool's limitations. With a lever-type one-man fence stretcher, set the wire loosely in a staple and cinch it up tight as you can in the sawtooth wire-grip at the base of the tool. Place the toothed end of the tool on the post and lever the handle down and back. When the wire is tight, hammer the staple home with a free hand if you can find one.

With a ratchet-type stretcher, fasten the wire to the forward dog so that with a good pull you can hook the other dog behind the post. Then ratchet the wire home and staple.

Using a come-along or block and tackle, you need a truck, a tree, or another post to fasten the tool to. Then, you can stretch the wire past the fence post and staple. I don't bother to take the truck into the pasture for wire stretching. I simply loop a length of logging chain around the nearest tree and fasten the block and tackle to that. My pastures are all in heavily-treed terrain, however. In the plains, you'd have to brace up dummy posts to pull against for stretching, and before I went to that bother, I'd find a truck or tractor to use as an anchor – renting if I couldn't borrow one.

Once the wire is tensioned between end posts, go along and staple it loosely to the line posts. You'll take the time to measure the space between wires at each end where you are tensioning. But it's easiest to make up a fence stick to set line wires. Mark off distances between wires on the stick and use the marks as a guide. Snug the staples down just hard enough that the wire is tight but can still slide if it needs retensioning.

You're done. If you fence an entire pasture with Ol' Bob Wahr and he doesn't rip the front of your shirt or the shins of your jeans, I'd like to hear about it.

Trees as Fence Posts

The maples and oaks surrounding pastures in our part of the world are boobytrapped with remnants of long-forgotten barbed-wire fences. The tree grows out to envelop the wire stapled to it, protecting the old steel from air, water, and rust. Often the tree completely conceals the wire, and old barb has dulled many a chainsaw. Posts are better, but with apologies to wood cutters of coming generations, you can still use trees to hold up a barbed-wire fence.

A few staples punched into live, slippery tree wood won't hold a well-tensioned fence. But don't be tempted to start a fence with a wire looped all around a tree trunk; it could girdle the bark and kill a young tree. Better is to start the fence at a solid post and use the trees only as line posts. As you string wire from tree to tree, chip off bark to sound wood and hammer a staple in part way, just to keep the wire in place. Continue stringing the wire till you reach a proper corner post. Tension wire between posts, and only then hammer in the staples.

If I use a tree as an end or corner post, I take the time to set an eye bolt (for ends) or screw-hook (for corners) into the tree for each wire. Those are dollar items in any hardware store – a closed or open loop at the end of a screw-threaded bolt. Get the largest size you can. You'll need a brace with a bit that's the same size as the shank of the screw. Drill a hole into solid wood and screw in the bolt with a length of steel rod through the hook or eye. To start a fence, run each wire through an eye bolt and crimp-fasten the end to the main run of wire with a crimp-fastener. Or run it through the eye twice, hitch the turns tight, and bind the end to the main run of wire with fence wire-binding.

At a corner, eye bolts would force you to cut and splice or run the entire length of wire through the closed eye. Better is to set screw hooks deep enough into the tree that you can just barely slip the wire between bark and hook end. Run the wire through and tension. In a few years the bark will have grown out to close the hook so that the wire couldn't come out if it wanted.

GATES

Any post that will hold a tensioned-steel wire fence will hold a gate. Sink a pair of stout end posts a gate-width apart. If you are planning a hinged, swinging gate, brace the hinge-side gate post (the one that will hold the weight of the gate) with a wood rail that slopes down from the top of the gate post at a 45-degree angle. Sink the brace rail at least 2 feet into the ground or into a concrete anchor. Or, make an H brace as described earlier in this chapter, by connecting the gate post to an adjoining down-line post with a rail set several inches below the post tops.

You can make a simple gate from a rectangle of poles or flat lumber nailed together or fastened with carriage bolts: see details of gate construction at the end of the chapter on wood fences. On a narrow walk-through gate add a single angled brace extending from top of the latch side to bottom of the hinge side, making a Z with the top rails. Two angled braces – making a giant M with the vertical side members – are better for a long, drive-through gate. Many occasional gates are made a few inches larger on each side than the gate opening, leaned against the posts and either tacked in place or attached with loops of fence wire. If the gate you need will be used often, however, you are better off making it fit the opening with an inch clearance at each side. Hang it from a pair of large black-iron or galvanized-steel strap/butt combination hinges (see chapter on wood fences). Each hinge of that type has one long narrow hinge plate that screws onto the horizontal top or bottom rail of the gate, and a rectangular plate that screws to the gate post.

An X-braced gate in a welded wire country fence.

Slip-rail

Primitive slip-rail gates have been used in farm fences for centuries. The simplest and most elegant have holes drilled through posts on each side of the gate. From one to four rails slip in and out to open or close the fence. Most such are made of a rot-proof wood, though I've seem some fine old slip-rail gate posts in Britain and northern New England, Quebec and the Maritimes made of hand-cut granite posts, laboriously drilled to admit the rails.

Brackets and Ladders

You can buy large steel brackets, screw them on opposite sides of a gate opening, and slip rails through. Or, make a set of primitive wooden ladders. Sink a parallel post just *inside* the fence line and about a foot away from each gate post. Connect those inner posts to the gate posts every 1 to 1½ feet with horizontal rungs. It is a good idea to bind the tops of the posts together with several loops of fence wire for added strength. The fence rails slip through the rungs, making a gate. Be sure to build the ladders on the inside of the fence, so that stock pushing against the gate will stress the main gate post, not the ladder.

Electric

The catalogues list electric and electronic gates. Some have an electric eye; when a cow breaks the beam a horn yowls, chasing the critter back into the pasture. Others raise or lower like a railroad-crossing gate. You must run house current to the fence for those, and you need code-approved underground cable, fittings, and junction boxes. The work is best left to a licensed electrician.

Cattle Guards

Some catalogues and your local farm-supply store will have cattle guards – pipe grids that you set into the soil or concrete anchors over a hole or ditch. Unless they are spooked, hooved animals won't step on them for fear of catching a foot in the space between the pipes.

Metal Gates

The easiest swinging gates to erect are prefabricated of sheet metal. You'll find them at prices from $30 to $75 at any farm-supply store and through some catalogues. Made of steel panels or tubing, those gates are inexpensive for their holding power. Hinge pins and latches are nothing but L bolts that screw into holes you bore in the gate posts. The gates hang on and stay put thanks to gravity and come right off any time you like. I've never been able to remove a well-set hinge pin, but replacements are cheap.

A Poor Man's Gate

For an opening that will be used infrequently, make a poor man's gate: nothing but a flap snipped in the gate fabric with a vertical board stapled on at the cut end. Sink two good end posts 3 to 6 feet apart anywhere along the fence you want a gate opening. Staple the wire securely to both of them. Where the wire meets one post, staple on a stout hardwood gate board. Even better, sandwich the wires between two boards and bolt them together. Cut the wire between gate board and post, and the flap of fabric will fold back to let you pass.

For a closure make two loops of stout smooth wire or lightweight cable to fit snugly around top and bottom of gate post and gate board. Staple one to the bottom of the gate post. Make the other loop to fit around the top of gate board and fence post – but staple that one to the gate board. You can pull the top loop up, angle the gate board to one side, and step over. If you have a load to haul through, pull the top loop up off the gate board, then pull the gate board up and out of the lower loop and bend the wire gate back.

MAINTENANCE

Patrol your wire fence several times a year to check staples and tensions. If a single strand of wire is sagging, use a crowbar to put a kink in it at a post. The catalogues also list patented wire tighteners that twist the wire on itself. If the sag persists, a visit with the fence stretcher is in order. Cut the wire at mid-sag, pull the ends together and splice. (And be glad that you didn't hammer staples in those line posts tight.)

If posts begin to sag, you can put in an extra brace post. Or, rig a *guy*. To guy an end, sink a stake 1½ times as far from an end post as the post is high off the ground and rig a wire loop and twist-stick. To guy a corner, rig a pair of loops back away from the fence at a 90-degree angle – a mirror image of the fence line.

In time any wire will rust – even the 12½-gauge four-point galvanized a neighbor uses to keep in his herd of buffalo. Chances are the barbed-wire fence will be replaced by something more modern. If you are replacing old barb – fence you strung yourself years ago or that an earlier generation put up on the place you just moved onto – may I make one sincere request? Please go out and reel in the old wire. It's a nasty job, I know, pulling all those rusty staples, or digging wire from overgrown tree bark, or just cutting all the wire strands, then reeling up the snaggy, brittle old stuff. If you can't cart the old wire away, at least roll it up and stack it against trees or rock piles. Please don't let the posts rot and fall over, to hold strands of wicked points a few inches above ground level and hidden in the weeds. More hikers' ankles have been skewered, horses' hocks slashed, snowmobile tracks ruined, ATV and motorcyle chains broken, and nice new sickle-bar teeth extracted by old barbed wire than by any other hazard of country living.

WIRE-FABRIC FENCE

If you have set up and tensioned end- and corner posts and planned gates for a barbed-wire fence, you have the frame for a welded-wire-fabric fence. It is more costly and harder to put up than barbed wire, but it has vertical stay wires in addition to the horizontal line wires so is a more effective fence. You can get welded-wire fence in graduated line-wire spacings – with wires close enough together at the bottom to contain even little chicks if you get it snug to the ground. Most such fence these days contains a crimp in each length of line wire between stays, and the crimp will spring under pressure, making for more evenly tensioned fence.

You can specify fence fabrics by a numerical code – the first one or two numbers indicating the number of line wires, and the last two giving the height of the fence in inches – but no one except a fence-industry specialist would understand you. Feed stores in our neighborhood sell fence fabric in different heights with four configurations: horse, cow, hog, and poultry. Styles, prices, and availability vary around the country. But sample fabrics include:

Poultry fence: 15½-gauge with 6-inch stays and twenty-five line wires arranged 1 to 4 inches apart bottom to top. 330 feet of 5- or 6-foot-high wire weighs 180 pounds, costs $130, and – in stouter wire and with an insurance run of charged electric wire at the top – is about the only thing I've found that will contain goats. (Also comes in 115-foot lengths at 68 pounds for $75).

Sheep fence: 12½-gauge with 12-inch stays and eight line wires spaced from 4½- to 9 inches apart bottom to top. 330 feet of 45-inch-high wire weighs 125 pounds and costs $150.

Cattle fence: 11-gauge with 9-inch stay spacing and nine line wires 6 inches apart. 330 feet of 48-inch fence weighs 220 pounds and costs $115.

And then there is *hoof-guard*, which is closely spaced at the bottom so horses' hooves can't get caught, and *bull corral*, which is made of ¼-inch, 4-gauge wire that's thicker than most nails and costs $190 per 150 feet FOB Colorado. The last needs 6-inch staples to hold it to railroad ties. There are dozens more kinds of welded-wire-fence fabric. Check the local feed store for available varieties. But check those weights closely, too. One person can easily horse around 65-pound rolls of welded-wire poultry fence. It will outlast hex netting twenty to one and goes up quickly. The 125-pound rolls of sheep fence take a strong back, but if well-tensioned, the fence will hold sheep better than barbed wire, and it won't snag away so much wool.

Installing It

To install welded-wire fence, cut out stays to get a good free foot of line wire and wrap ends around a post. Staple well, as with barb, and unroll it out to the nearest braced post – rolling it in the vertical position. That takes some doing: this fence is stiff.

To tension, you can pull one line wire at a time with your stretcher, starting with the center wires and working out – but that is liable to distort the fabric. Better is to invest in or make a *stretcher clamp*, which closes down over the whole width of fence. A 48-inch clamp costs about $50, or you can make one from two lengths of heavy-duty fence post with holes drilled through. Clamp the posts over the end of a run of fabric, cinching them tight together with bolts. Then attach chain in a Y pattern near the top and bottom of the clamp and hook to your fence stretcher. Or save the bother; the catalogues sell fabric stretchers complete for about $100. With really large wire, you may need two stretchers, one at top and the other at the bottom of the clamp.

Welded-wire fabric needn't be tensioned as thrumming tight as single-wire fence; no beast can wiggle through it. Stretch it tight enough that it springs back smartly and so that it looks good – with a straight top wire. Once the wire is tensioned between end posts, go along the line posts, snugging the bottom wire as close to the ground as the fence's purpose demands (right at ground level for dogs), and staple the line wires. You'll find that the new crimped fabric will adjust to ground contours more readily than you'd imagine, even after it is well tensioned. If the fabric resists being pulled down for stapling to a line post in a slight dip, persuade it with a crowbar; insert the crooked end over a lower wire and, pressing against the post, ratchet the whole fabric down a bit at a time.

Heavy-Gauge Fabric

The larger-gauge fabrics for range animals and breeding stock are heavy, stiff, and very hard to install without a crew of strong backs and/or power equipment. Even chain-link is easier to work with; its links are hinged together, and it is limber if creaky. A 200-pound roll of welded 8-gauge wire is hard to set upright, and the fabric is so stiff it is close to impossible to unroll by hand. You really need a fence reel for the back of the tractor to string the stuff. Get local advice, equipment, and assistance to install heavy-duty mesh fencing. Ditto for cable fencing, which is used in some parts for corrals and holding pens.

Panels, Hybrids, And Hog Fence

Heavy fabric does come in one form that is easy to manage: panels. These are 10- or 20-foot-long and 4-or 5-foot-high sections of rigid welded mesh with heavy-gauge line wires in graduated or even spacings. They come in hog, cattle and combination sizes, weighing from 45 to 55 pounds and costing from $14 to $20 apiece FOB the manufacturer. Meant to be hooked together around wood or heavy-duty steel posts to form temporary holding pens, sections can also be installed as permanent fencing for small areas. Many a pig has grown into contented ham in a 10-foot hog-panel pen with a feed trough and water spigot at one end and a shady lean-to at the other.

"Hog-tight" is more than a country expression. To contain any stock, fence must be kept well tensioned. Hogs are the orniest to keep in bounds; a hungry pig can squeeze through loose barbed wire or under loose fabric and will root its way under anything if it's bored or hungry. Many farmers make up a hybrid fence – stringing barbed wire at the bottom of hog fabric or hog panels to deter rooting.

Large animals enjoy leaning or rubbing against fence, in time pushing over posts or stretching fabric. A string or two of barbed wire at the top of a fabric fence will discourage that.

Probably the most effective fence you can raise is a hybrid of a stout steel fabric on large wooden posts with several strands of electrified barbed wire along the top for gnarly-hided grazing stock and a strand of bare electric wire along the bottom for moist-nosed rooters.

Speaking of electric fence: it is our next topic.

This hybrid fabric-barb farm fence has H-braces reinforced with twin turnbuckle-tightened rods in an X shape.

9

ELECTRIC
FENCE

The cheapest, easiest to install, and most humane stock containment or pest-deterrent you can use supplants the strength of a simple physical barrier with the product of human brain power: electronic technology.

An electric fence applies gentle persuasion rather than coercion, through one or more strands of bare steel or aluminum wire strung between posts and charged to deliver a convincing but short-lived – and thus harmless – electric shock when touched. You train domestic animals to respect the fence or place it so that wild marauders can't help but feel the effect where it counts most – on the moist nose. In theory, once shocked, the beasts will avoid the wire so long as their memory holds.

Electric fence can be rigged as anything from a one-strand rabbit barrier around the carrot patch to a Down Under-style, permanent, multistrand, spring-loaded "high-tensile" fence strung between braced end posts and carrying enough high voltage to keep a whole county full of winter-hungry deer from a young fruit orchard. Here's how to design, install, and maintain the electric fence that's best for your needs.

THE FENCER

The heart of electric fence is a fence charger, or *fencer*, which combines an electrical transformer with a timing mechanism to develop those brief but memorable shocks. The electricity may come from a battery's 6 or 12 volts of stored energy, from a small photovoltaic system, or from (greatly modified) house current. Fencers come in several styles, but all produce a high-powered jolt for brief periods of time. The most persuasive chargers are imported from Australia and New Zealand, where they are used to electrify sheep fence by the 100-mile leg. They turn 4 or 5 amps of 240-volt utility-line power into pulses of 3,000 volts at 30 amps – almost 100,000 watts of power – which could turn a whole herd of sheep to shish kebab were the charge not limited to a few *ten-thousandths* of a second's duration. Were this fencer to malfunction and hold the charge any longer, fuses would blow instantly, deactivating the fence. If they didn't blow, the fencer would self-destruct.

A typical North American brand of 110-volt house-current-powered charger can develop about 4,000 volts at half an amp – 2,000 watts. That is also a potentially

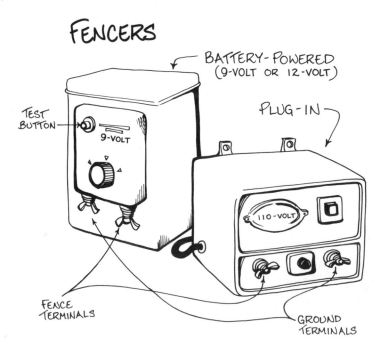

FENCERS

BATTERY-POWERED
(9-VOLT OR 12-VOLT)

TEST BUTTON

9-VOLT

PLUG-IN

110-VOLT

FENCE TERMINALS

GROUND TERMINALS

ELECTRICAL TERMS

The electricity that can be released as direct current (DC) by a storage battery, or the alternating current (AC) that comes into your home through the utility lines or via an underground cable is measured in amperes (amps), volts, and watts.

Amps is a measure of the current of electrons that passes through a copper wire or other electrical conductor. For what it's worth, you have one amp when 6,250,000,000,000,000,000 (that's 6.25 *quintillion*) electrons pass a single point in one second. Voltage is the pressure, the electro-motive force, that a battery or generator imparts to the current. And watts is a measure of work-producing power determined by multiplying volts times amps. A common 60-watt light bulb draws a little more than half an amp of your 117-volt house current (60w = .5a × 117v).

To affect an adventurous horse or a cabbage-seedling-prone cottontail without harming it, a fencer can arm your electric fence with most any combination of amps and volts, so long as the duration of the shock is appropriate to the power behind it. The more power, the briefer the shock must be to be harmless.

Every fencer has an overload preventer — like the electrical system in your home that blows a fuse or a circuit breaker if you keep too many appliances plugged into the same outlet for too long. *Any time* a malfunctioning fencer senses too much current going out for long enough to be even remotely dangerous to man, beast, or furry pet, its disconnects will blow. The fail-safe systems are designed to be as foolproof as humans can make them in any UL-approved fence charger.

dangerous charge, but the pulse lasts for less than a thousandth of a second and occurs no more than fifty to sixty times a minute. Better-grade battery-powered fencers have less oomph behind them, so release longer pulses (lasting about half a second each) at a fraction of the more powerful unit's voltage. Some low-priced battery units release a constant low charge, which is less effective and can drain the battery quickly if the fence is shorted out.

The jolt from my own house-current-powered fencer feels like you've been hit by a rapid-fire electric peashooter: *brrrrrrrrrrrrrrt*. You feel it, and you pull back instantly, but there is no real pain, and no burn: just a strong and unpleasant memory. I am told, however, that a fencer shock *can* interfere with cardiac pacemakers and other electrically-powered high-tech devices that are serving to make our lives longer and more productive. If she's so equipped, forewarn Great Aunt Emma to unplug the fencer any time she goes out to bust broncs in the electric-fenced pasture.

Fencers are effective and safe, but don't try to improvize as some new country arrivals have and wire a fence to a length of electric cord, then plug it directly into a wall socket. You'd be lucky to blow all the fuses in your main switch, and you *could* electrocute anything that brushed the wire, yourself included. House current straight out of the plug can be lethal. Don't try hooking fence to a welding transformer, a model-railroad speed controller, or any other home-brewed device either. Get a proper fencer, and be sure that it has the Underwriters Lab approval sticker. Though not UL-approved, old-style "weed-cutter" chargers with replaceable mechanical pulsers are still sold, and many farmers swear by them. Those chargers have been known to deliver harmful shocks, however. It's best for the novice or small landholder to stick with UL-approved fencers.

THE ELECTRIC CIRCUIT

You'll recall from junior-high science that *electricity* is the flow of free electrons from the positive to the negative terminal of a power source through a *conductor* such as metal, water — and water-based living things, animal or vegetable. Steel fence wire is good conducting material that's held away from any other conductors, such as moist soil, trees, or metal fence posts, by *insulators* made of a nonconducting or *resistive* material such as glass, ceramic, or plastic. The hot, or positive, post of the charger is connected to the fence. The negative post of the charger is attached to ground, literally, by being wired to a stake driven into the soil.

Any connection between the ground and fence wires creates an *electric circuit*, permitting electrons to flow. Normally, each time the charger pulses, trying to send a charge out over the wire, nothing much happens. Despite the push – the voltage – behind them, the electrons have nowhere to go, so there can be no flow of current, no *amperage*. The circuit is *open*, with no physical connection between the hot positive posts and the return negative post of the fencer. Only when your curious saddle pony brushes the wire with his velvety muzzle, and horseflesh becomes a conductor between the fence and ground, does the circuit *close*. Then, a brief shot of current flows at light speed from positive post of fencer to wire, through soft and lovely pony nose to moist and ground-contacting pony hoof, then back through the soil to the negative post of the charger. *Zap*. A shock is delivered. The pony, suddenly wiser, will pull away, breaking the contact and opening the circuit again.

If a tree limb, tall grass, or other conductor falls across the wire, connecting it to the ground, you have a short circuit. If the connection is a good one and the soil is moist, full fence current will flow at each pulse, draining power from the fence and reducing its effectiveness. If the fencer is battery-powered, a short can drain the battery in no time. Plan frequent patrols of electric fence to check for shorts. If that is impractical, be sure to get a fencer with a short-alert, a light that flashes each time the fencer pulses to ground.

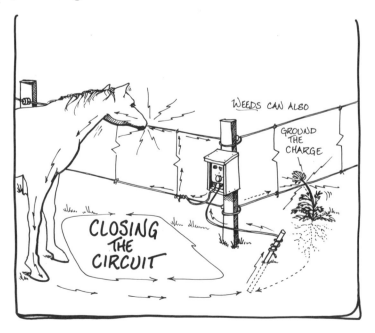

WEEDS CAN ALSO

GROUND THE CHARGE

CLOSING THE CIRCUIT

AN ELECTRIC GARDEN FENCE

You'll have to spend $25 to $35 for the smallest fencer available, but it will charge enough wire to surround several acres. A roll of conventional (nonelectrified) wire-fence fabric and enough stakes to encircle your vegetable patch alone would run twice that or more. Buy a bag of two dozen little slotted plastic insulators for a dollar and change, and nail them to yard-long tomato stakes hammered 6 inches deep for a perfectly satisfactory one- to three-strand electric fence. You can use more elaborate stakes, of course. At a dollar or two per stake, lightweight fiberglass T posts are nonconductive and thus require no insulators and come with clips to hold the wire. They push right into the soil and pull out as easily, so are quickly movable. Wire needn't be more than hand tight, but you can prevent sag by guying corner posts; attach a length of wire to the post top and run it to a wooden ground stake or a screw-type or duckbull anchor. String 19-gauge steel wire on the insulators; a 500-foot roll costs under $10, and a handy person will find a thousand uses for the leftover wire.

The simplest and best insulators for a quick fence are plastic, shaped like thread spools with a hole through the middle, and having grooves cut around the spool and sometimes little eye hooks molded in one end. You hammer them onto a tree, building, or fence stake and slip the wire into the self-cinching slot. Use regular flat-head nails for a permanent installation. If you think you might remove the insulators in future, use double-headed fence nails that give your claw hammer or nail-puller a purchase no matter how well the nail is inserted.

The least expensive small garden-plot-sized 110-volt fencers run a low-power continuous (nonpulsed) charge, others with more clout have pulsers, and I recommend the latter for better and longer service. Neither requires attention once turned on. Small battery-powered fencers use a 6-volt Eveready "hot-shot" or Ray-o-Vac charger battery that will cost $15 to $20, will last a growing season, and will power a big farm lantern or your doorbell over winter.

Those little garden fencers aren't waterproof or particularly sturdy, and most models must be kept under cover. Install yours in a dry spot in a shed or in the house. You can build a weather-tight box out at the garden for a battery-powered fencer. Have the charger readily visible (put a window in an outdoor box) so you can see the

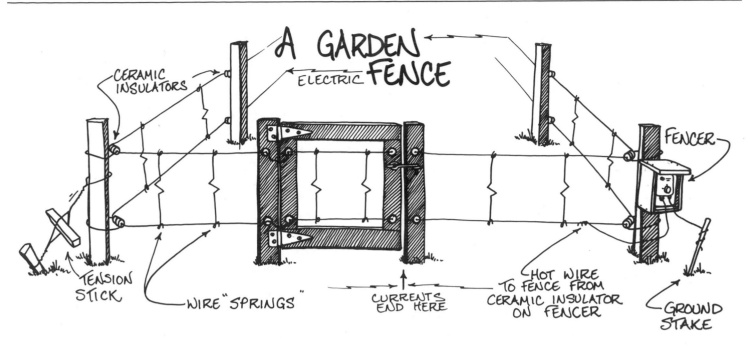

A GARDEN FENCE

CERAMIC INSULATORS · ELECTRIC · FENCER · TENSION STICK · WIRE "SPRINGS" · CURRENTS END HERE · HOT WIRE TO FENCE FROM CERAMIC INSULATOR ON FENCER · GROUND STAKE

red blinking indicator that tells you it is operating. Most chargers also have a test button or separate white blinker that indicates whether the fence circuit is open or grounded. On our mountain top, with most fence bordering woods, branches frequently fall on the wires or a wet leaf blows onto an insulator, making a connection between wire and fence post. In either case the result is to ground and deactivate the fence till the branch is moved or the leaf is cooked dry by the current. If the fence doesn't reactivate by the time animals begin moving, I make a quick tour.

My own house-current (as opposed to battery-powered) charger protects the big garden and a pair of 2-acre horse pastures. The charger lives in the house where I don't have to make a special effort to check it. I run a length of common, two-wire, plastic-coated lamp cord from charger to fence. You can string this or any other insulated wire out under a window sash and wrap it around nails in trees or posts with no worry about inadvertently grounding the charge. Even if the insulation does wear, the cord from charger to fence is as harmless as the fence itself. That does *not* apply to the power line running from the plug in the house to the charger. That wire contains potentially lethal 110-volt AC electricity, and any frays at all on that line demand immediate repair.

Installing the Fencer

Strip insulation from one end of the two-wire cord, attach to the fencer (turned off), and, keeping track of which of the two wires is which, run the line out to the fence. The wire from the charger's "Fence" lead (the one with the insulated ceramic post) should be connected securely to the fence wire. In a multiple-wire fence, connect the strands together with securely-wrapped wire where the fencer and ground-stake lines are attached so all wires will be uniformly charged.

Soldering will make the best connection in any electric circuit, but it isn't necessary with electric fence; the short little jolts of current fairly beg to flow. You needn't even wrap electric tape around the connections – just wind the wires together good and tight and be prepared to wire-brush off a little dusty corrosion that will crop up after a season.

The wire from the fencer's "Ground" post should be wrapped securely around bare metal on a painted or galvanized-steel stake hammered in as close to the fence and as deep as you can get it. Eight feet down is not too deep in some dry areas, and during especially dry weather you may have to water the stake to ensure a good circuit. If the length of fence is more than a few hundred feet, put in two grounds connected together. If your fence runs over a mile, three or four ground rods will make for a better circuit. Place them 5 to 6 feet apart and connect them to the fencer with the heaviest-gauge wire you have handy; weather-proof insulated wire is best. The wetter the soil the better it will conduct, so install the ground in a low spot or near a spring if your summer weather is dry.

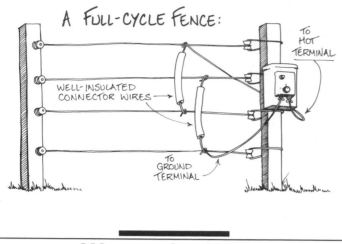

Wiring the Fence

A single-wire garden (or any other) electric fence should be arranged to make contact at mid-chest height on the body of the creature to be kept honest. That way it will catch the inquisitive nose of your would-be marauder, be low enough that the animal can't shrug under without zapping an eartip, and high enough that it can't slide over without shocking a soft underbelly. That's about 5 inches above the ground for rabbits, groundhogs, and raccoons. (I have seen a wise old 'chuck hunker down and slide under a wire placed the usually recommended 6 inches high.) Better yet is a wire just 4 inches high with another wire 5 inches above the first. A third wire up another 6 inches completes a really effective backyard garden fence. You can step over, but most pests won't think to; they assume they can walk through the spiderweblike wire, and quickly learn better.

Single strand electric fence.

Low as it is, that fence will deter dogs if they're not running hard and will restrain got-loose pigs and sheep for a while. It won't deter grown goats if there's cabbage to be gobbled (nothing much short of a moated castle wall will), or large stock which can step over or bull through, tangling the wire in dangerous snarls about their hocks. Don't expect any one- or two-wire electric fence to keep out your free-ranging poultry, even if their wings are trimmed so they can't fly. Fowl inspect things by eye, not by nose. Plus, feathers are perfect insulators, keeping chicken or duck warmth in and electric current out. If the birds do get zapped on the bill or foot, they'll squawk in panic and run straight ahead – and into the garden if that's where they're aimed and the fence permits. For chickens you need an 18-inch high three-wire fence with wires 6 inches apart and springs or thin stakes or battens every yard or so to hold the wires together and keep the birds from springing them apart as they run through. A better solution, however, if predation by poultry is your main garden problem, is to string poultry netting or chicken wire (covered elsewhere).

Trim grass under the wire or the fence will lose its zap after every heavy dew. Moist blades will drain off much of every charge, the fence will lack effectiveness, and a battery will lose power quickly. Once an animal has gotten through a shorted-out electric fence, it may ignore the shock when the juice is on. I pull the stakes, move the whole fence a couple of feet to one side, mow, and put it back.

Training Domestic Stock to Electric Fence

Our grazing stock pastures on next-door borrowed land where I'm not about to put up an expensive wood or wire-fabric fence. So the first question asked when daughter Martha and I went serious horse shopping was, "Has he been trained to electric fence?" We'd been taught about horses that weren't so trained by Midnight, a 20-year-old Welsh pony who learned about electric wire on his own after a youth misspent behind board fences. He'd roll in the dust to give his thick coat extra dry body (and electrical resistance), and squeeze through any electric fence known. Then he'd trot happily to the barn, where he'd clean out the dog and cat bowls, knock over the chicken feeder, and crown his day by biting open feed sacks and nearly foundering on grain.

Before you string that first wire, be prepared to train your stock. Start them as young as you can. String a length of charged wire between doughnut-shaped corner insulators 6 inches off the ground at one end of a pen. Don't make it part of the feeding routine, but let the beasts get good and hungry, then scatter a little feed under and just outside the wire. They will go after the feed – grab a little, and get zapped on the snout when they try to gobble it all. Keep it up till the animals avoid the wire consistently. While training, never leave the wire uncharged so your animals will find it can be harmless. And be careful: pigs squeal and whirl on their hocks when first shocked; cattle jump back, turn, and run a space; while a zapped horse can rear and bolt in its instinctive flight reaction. Don't try training large stock to electric fence in a barn stall or small building pen – or on a tether.

PLANNING A PASTURE FENCE

In designing a pasture fence, consider the strength and behavior of the animals to be restrained and their incentives to escape. A single wire will do for steers and milk cows, sheep or young goats, and feeder piglets that have plenty of food, water, and shade – tame animals who are as much pets as livestock and who won't wander far if they do get out. Some mares and gelding horses will stay inside a single strand and some won't. But *no* bull or stallion will be kept in by one wire or several if a female in heat passes upwind. The cow or mare won't stay put either, and they can injure themselves trying to get through the wire. Don't try to restrain large animals' stronger urges with a lightweight electric fence.

Consider what other attractions will lie beyond the fence in each season of the year. If your pasture will be grazed out and the animals eating hay come September while a neighbor's lush, watered lawn or irrigated corn crop lies just across the hot wires, many animals will hazard a shock for a good meal. Dogs run most actively in the spring and gather in semiferal packs. You may want to string wire to keep them away from the spring lambs as much as to keep the sheep in. In either case design in an extra hot wire or two and provide plenty of sturdy line posts.

Background is important. A physical boundary such as a tree line, stream, road, or standing cornfield offers a tangible backup to an electric fence. Herd animals running for fun or in a panic never head toward cover but aim for the open. Still, strands of fence wire are hard to see against most natural backgrounds. An animal can collide with the wire and break it or become dangerously entangled. Especially if you are placing new electric fence without a strong natural backup – such as stringing a wire across the pasture to initiate a strip-grazing program – plan to tie flags every few feet along the top wire. Strips of fluorescent plastic tape are nonconductive and best, but thick twine or strips of old cloth will do. Tape them on or tie them tight, or you'll have to adjust their location after every rain. Loosely tied flags will get wind-blown to downwind stakes. If you use conductive material for both flags and fence supports, wet flag material can flop onto the conductor and ground out the fence.

Laying Out a Pasture Fence

Wire for a pasture fence should be tensioned tight enough to stay off the ground and be strong enough that an animal will take it seriously if the charger goes out for a while. You'll need strong ends and corners – anything from a barn to a big tree to braced or guyed steel posts or the braced wood posts discussed under barbed wire. First step is planning the fence, on paper if the topography is complicated, and picking locations for the heavy supports. Put a strong post at the tops and bottoms of any hills or culverts so runs of wire will be straight and tight, needing little between but battens or lightweight line posts to keep the wire separated and off the ground. Before setting the fence, clear the fence line so stock can see the wire and no weed plants will short it out. Mow a pasture, cut brush in an overgrown field, or saw out saplings in the woods. If the fence crosses a traveled drive or private road, you can order a spring-hinged drive-through gate from the mail-order houses. These gadgets have weighted, charged wire dangling down off horizontal members to keep any animal in check, though your truck can pass through at will. The gate will swing open and will close automatically.

Well-braced corner of a 5-wire hi-tensile electric fence which protects a young apple orchard against deer.

The larger the stock, the heavier-gauge wire you will need. The taller the animals, the more strands are required, and the wilder and more stampede-prone the stock, the stronger will be posts needed to back the electric wire with true coercive strength. In choosing wire layout, follow the logic of the garden rabbit barrier; put the wires where they will make best contact on the beasts to be restrained. String a single wire at high, mid-body level so the target animal will be shocked going over or under. The top strand of a two-wire fence should hit at upper-mid-breast (the level of a horse or cow's lowered nose), the other midway between the top wire and the ground, so interwire spaces won't permit a careful crawl-through. Three wires or more presuppose some need for holding power; put the top wires just below breast-top, the second just above belly level, the third midway between the middle wire and the ground.

If you are fencing out pests or predators seeking entrance, consider their habits. A deer can jump 5 feet straight up from a flat-footed start. Still, 5-foot-high, five-wire fence will keep most of them out; they try to walk through the wire. Some deer are smart enough to slink under, so the bottom wire of a six-wire deer fence should be no more than 6 to 8 inches high, the other wires 10 inches apart. That's not what you read in fence-material sales literature based on Australian experience; but they don't have fence-smart white-tails like ours. Coyotes, dogs, or wolves need a running start to get very high at all, and with a good run may clear 4 feet or more. They are great at slinking under, too, and will seek out dips in the ground to make it easier; keep bottom wires no more than 6 inches off the ground. A five- or six-wire deer

fence will keep dogs honest. With serious potential for either problem, or with range stock needing a degree of physical restraint, charged barbed wire is an inexpensive possibility; simply string tensioned barbed wire on large ceramic insulators. I'd also suggest that you consider high-tensile fencing, described below.

Wire gauges get smaller as the wire gets larger. Twenty-gauge is the thin little stuff used for poultry netting – chicken wire. Nineteen- and 17-gauge are okay for garden fences. Sixteen- and 15-gauge are multipurpose electric fence wires for small stock and docile cattle. Three strands of "heavy-duty" 14-gauge wire on deep-driven steel posts will hold a horse or a beef steer. Four strands of 12½-gauge on large wooden posts will hold an angry buffalo long enough for it to feel the shock.

Fence Supports

You can fence dairy cows temporarily on good graze with a single strand of 17- or 15-gauge wire on insulators nailed into tree trunks and/or wood sticks hammered into the ground. (If you're new to livestock keeping, don't use posts of soft pine, cottonwood, aspen, white birch, or most other quick-growing trees. The posts will rot and collapse of their own weight in a year's time. Before it happens, the savvy local gentry will be chuckling and lining up to see them go. Use cypress, red cedar, locust, or other naturally rot-proof woods if you can find them on your place, and except in northernmost snow country, soak the underground lengths of posts in creosote over winter to delay termites.) Five-foot sticks sunk 18 inches into the pasture soil will hold a single strand just fine, though you'll want stouter wood or steel posts as ends or corners. With a double-headed (easily extracted) nail, hammer an insulator on each post where you can use the truck bed or a rock as an anvil – before you set the post. Then, chip a point on one end of the post with your hand ax and set it. Make fence when the ground is wet and easily penetrated. A quarrying-type 4-foot prybar is good to open a hole in the soil; then posts can go in deep enough to stay put without getting split from repeated hammer blows. When placing insulators on trees, chip off any thick bark so the nail gets a hold on live, good-holding wood, and be sure the run of wire stays clear of bark protuberances or drooping branches that could blow into it in a wind.

A more permanent fence with multiple wires should be supported by stout wood or steel corner and end posts with sturdy line posts every 20 to 50 feet and battens where needed in between. Six-inch pressure-treated or creosoted wooden fence posts are fine for electric fence but require a post-hole digger and proper setting. Easier to place are steel posts. Forged U-shaped posts with holes or hooks punched out of the midrib are strongest, most adaptable to various fence types, and as expensive as wooden posts – up to $5 each. The type with a broadened lance foot on the bottom stays put best of all steel posts – and you'll need a heavy post puller or specially rigged jack to get them out. Through-bored insulators are quickly installed through holes in steel posts with long bolts and wing nuts, or to wooden posts with screws or double-headed nails.

Forged T posts are about equal to U posts in cost and fence-carrying power. They have hooks for wire-fabric fence but no through-holes, so they require a special clip for mounting insulators. The clips and attached wires can slide up and down the post for easy adjustment, however. Some T posts come with an anchor plate riveted or welded near the bottom. When the post is installed so the anchor is well below ground level, the sod will grow over the plate, roots will bind in it, and the post will be there to stay. Self-insulating heavy-duty fiberglass posts (big brothers of the little T-post battens) are notched so wire can be clipped right on, are as sturdy as steel and much more flexible, and don't corrode. They cost about the same as steel, too: $4.50 for a 5-footer to about $6.50 for an 8-foot post.

L-angled sheet-steel posts come next in strength and cost, followed by rod-type steel posts in several sizes. Rod posts will accept insulators and wire fasteners on J hooks threaded for wing nuts at any point in their length. Choose your posts carefully for strength equal to the task,

ease of installation (and removal if need be), and ability to accept insulators and fasteners at the heights you need.

Mix and match as your pocketbook dictates. There's no reason a fence can't be strung between doughnut insulators hung off two big trees with an assortment of supports: big steel posts in the dips and hills, old cement reinforcing rod with J-hook-fastened insulators at key points, and little fiberglass T battens or simple wood sticks hold-

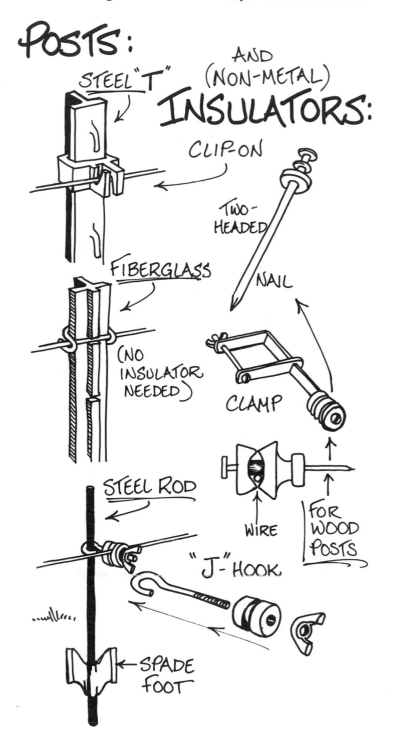

POSTS: AND (NON-METAL) INSULATORS:

STEEL "T"

CLIP-ON

TWO-HEADED NAIL

FIBERGLASS

(NO INSULATOR NEEDED)

CLAMP

WIRE

FOR WOOD POSTS

STEEL ROD

"J-" HOOK

SPADE FOOT

ing plastic crimp-insulators in between. Our own horse fence is a two-strand affair with double-guyed U posts at the ends, corners, and every 50 feet or so of fence. I have ⅜-inch steel-rod spade-foot battens placed every 15 feet between, spades sunk just to ground level with a boot-heel for easy removal. Corner posts are single guyed with fence wire to screw-in steel-rod earth anchors, and the guy wire is hand-tensioned whenever the fence threatens to sag perceptibly. Martha's horse, Doc, is a fence-wise jumper who stays in so long as the water is fresh and he's grained on time. Otherwise he hops the fence and goes visiting the neighbor's feedlot, which keeps us well trained. I figure it's better that he can get out if he needs to, as long as he doesn't do it often or wander far when he does.

Setting posts in most soils takes nothing but a sledge-hammer and a good arm, but the tops of steel posts fatigue with repeated blows, bell over much as a wood-splitting wedge does, and can bend. Fiberglass doesn't. If you have a great many posts to install, you may want to

Electric hi-tensile gate post.

invest in a post driver – a steel tube capped and weighted at one end. You just raise and lower it on the stake, and down it goes. The stake top doesn't get bruised as easily as with a sledgehammer. Some models have a spring built in to help lift the driver after every downstroke.

Pasture Fencers

The high-output fencers sold today are effective, safe, and come with a year warranty that should see you through any problems they may develop.

If your fence is in easy range of the house or a wired outbuilding, choose a house-current-powered fencer. Energy costs are less than with a battery-powered model, and all you need do is plug it in and keep the fence circuit clean. All fencers using 110-volt house current must be kept under weather-tight cover. A 110-volt AC charger rated to charge 15 miles of fence will cost around $45, a 25-mile unit, $75. Those mile ratings are optimistic, based on a single-wire fence with no weeds draining current and running in a good-conducting, moist soil. Get the most powerful charger you can justify; it won't develop significantly greater deterrent, but it will push the current out over greater distance and through more undergrowth. You will pay a bit extra for all solid-state circuits, where rectifiers that tame the house current are made of computer-chip-type silicon and the timer that turns the juice on and off every second or so is nonmechanical. There's nothing to wear out but the indicator lamp and the on-off switch, which should last for a generation or two.

For remote locations, you'll need a battery-powered fencer. Prices are about the same as for equivalent house-current-powered models. Waterproof fencers with an internal battery compartment are made of a heavy-gauge steel, are well sealed, and can be mounted on a fence post to withstand rain and weather. Periodically check the gaskets in the battery compartment, treat the outside with a hard auto wax, and apply a good silicon grease to the terminals, and the battery's life and appearance will be extended considerably. Fifteen-mile-rated fences use an $18, 6-volt dry-cell battery. You can get still more range with 12-volt fencers that operate off dry cells or – better – rechargeable automotive-type batteries that will last for years but will cost considerably more. You will also have to build a waterproof box to house the charger and separate battery. Get a "deep-cycle" marine or golf-cart battery that is made to hold power through the discharge cycle and stand up to repeated charges and discharges. You'll have to haul the battery home and give

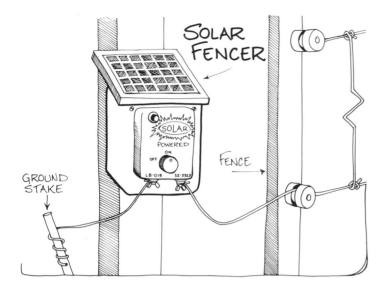

it a slow charge every three months at minimum; monthly charges are often needed during the growing season. That takes a $25 to $50 battery charger, which every country place ought to have anyway. The life of each charge depends on length and number of fence wires, moisture in the soil (the wetter it is, the easier current will flow) and frequency of actual contact by repelled critters, but mainly it depends on whether weeds touch the wire. I don't like the stuff myself, but many farmers spray herbicides along their fence lines to keep down weeds the animals don't trim from beneath the wire.

The most up-to-date fencers are not only fully solid-state in construction, but they have built-in gel-cell batteries that never need water, *and* they are solar-powered. They come in 6- or 12-volt models for a steep $150 to $250, though prices have begun drop now that the cost of photovoltaic cells has begun to fall. The battery will run down over three weeks of solid, leaden overcast but will perk up in only a day of full sun.

Lightning Protection

A lightning bolt can blow your fencer and possibly cause a fire if the charger is inside a building. I always put a lightning arrester between the fencer and the fence. You should also install one every few hundred yards along an extensive fence if you are in thunderstorm country. An arrester is nothing but a fuse having its own ground line to be connected to its own well-sunk steel post. (Don't rely on the 3-inch metal probe that comes at the end of the ground line on some arresters; ground the arrester well on a deep steel post.)

If the megavolts of a lightning bolt strike the fence, the current will melt the fuse and go to ground before the fencer fries, possibly taking your house or barn with it. I'd install a separate lightning protector even if the fencer has one built in. The internal fuse will work once, but you may never know that it has blown. If it has, you may need professional service technicians to open the box and replace it. Outside arresters are available in any feed store.

A lightning protector that did its job. Note the hole burned in the left-hand side by a lightning bolt which didn't even melt the fuse strip.

Gate hook, insulators and posts.

Stringing the Wire

With the posts laid out and hammered in and the fencer ready to go, stringing the fence itself is a cinch. Use the wire as a layout cord to get your stakes straight. Hammer stout posts at the corners and at any turns in the fence. Attach one end of the wire by a ceramic doughnut-shaped end insulator at a braced corner or a gate opening, and run it to the nearest turn. Pull it tight, then lay out the rest of your posts and line stakes, hammer them in, install insulators, and attach the wire. For stock-containment, have insulators facing into the pasture. For predator control, face them out.

Don't let loops stay in the out-going wire to tighten up and kink; revolve the reel so they work out. Keep just enough tension on the wire to make a taut fence. Don't worry about cutting wire if it makes installation easier or is needed to take up slack once the wire begins to sag. A simple wrap-around splice will reconnect it just fine. Install lightweight wood or fiberglass battens each 10 to 15 feet to keep wires separated and off the ground. Or, put in "springs" – lengths of wire looped on and crimped in a Z fashion between runs of wire.

Gates

You'll need openings along the fence. Electric gate fasteners can be installed anywhere you might need to get through; cut the wires near a post and hook them on.

Those simple electric-fence "gates" are nothing but a hook connected to an eye by a spring, all encased in an insulating plastic handle that lets you latch and unlatch the gate without getting shocked. Rig a loop in the wire at a post to hold the hook, and attach the eye end of the gate to the loose end of the wire, stretching so the spring maintains proper fence tension when hooked up. Just grasp and pull against the spring to open or close. When a gate is unhooked and dropped on the ground, the entire run of fence is deactivated, so be sure to train your younger folks to refasten gates every time they take the pony out of the pasture. Make it a habit with everyone using the fence.

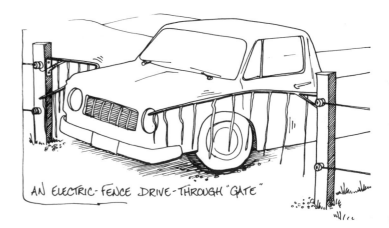

AN ELECTRIC-FENCE DRIVE-THROUGH "GATE"

TROUBLESHOOTING THE FENCE

Any time the "Fence" light on your charger quits blinking, you have a short. Something has created a path between hot wire and ground so the potential current is not returning to the charger. It can't deliver a shock to your livestock, either.

The problem can be a limb that's fallen across the wire, wet leaves blown down across an insulator connecting wire and a metal post, or nothing but a film of water over everything after a hard rain. Trained stock won't nose under or bull through an electric fence the second it goes dead – indeed, they won't bother to test it during the heavy weather that causes most shorts – but they will get through if the charge is weak for several days running.

If our fence doesn't reactivate by midmorning of the first dry day following a wet period, I patrol the wire with the little fence-checker, looking for the cause of a short. Usually the problem is a windfall limb that's easy to spot and remove. Often, it is nothing but a marking flag that's been wind-blown across an insulator. But sometimes the short is hard to spot. A hidden twig or dislodged wire keeper may have shorted the wire. To isolate the spot, I apply the checker to the wire between each pair of insulators. So long as the little neon light glows, I know the circuit is good. When it dims or goes out, I know which length of wire is the source of the problem.

Another way to spot a short is to listen. Shorting current seldom has a clear electrical path and must *arc* – that is, hop across small air gaps to reach ground. That creates a tiny lightning flash, and you can often hear it buzz or snap with each pulse of the fencer. You'll often hear a little buzz across each insulator when the fence is wet, too – a temporary mini-short that will disappear when the fence dries.

A faster and higher-tech method of short-location is to carry a little battery-powered transistor radio out to the pasture with you. Tune it to the upper end of the AM band where there is no station, turn the volume to high, and hold the antenna (in the back of the case, or in the handle) close to each insulator. An electrical arc generates radio waves across a broad spectrum, and the radio will pick up a burst of static with each pulse across a short in the fence, just as it crackles when lightning strikes close by or passes overhead during a thunderstorm.

A fence in tall grass or one which closely borders a tree line will often have several shorts after a heavy rain or snow storm. I don't stop after finding one short; I patrol the entire fence. Repairs are less shocking if you unhook gates or shut off the fencer. That makes it hard to spot the short and fix it on the same trip, however, so I carry a set of rubber-handled needle-nosed pliers for quick, shock-free repairs of easy shorts. If the repair is more involved, you can ground the fence just behind the short and bleed off most of the charge with a temporary shorting cable. Attach a length of wire with a hook on one end and a polished metal stake at the other. I use a copper rod (a length of old plumbing pipe with the end hammered closed and ground to a point), a 3-foot length of fence wire, and a small gate hook. All connections are soldered. To ground the fence, I hold the grounding cable in a nonconductor (the rubber-handled pliers, or my leather belt if I've neglected to bring the pliers), snag the hook on the wire, pull it tight, and shove the rod into the soil with the rubber sole of my boot. If the soil is wet, very little juice gets past the ground, and I don't get zapped when I remove the clip holding the wire to the insulator and remove the piece of leaf stem or old flag that is causing the short.

POLY WIRE FOR QUICK FENCE AND STRIP GRAZING

A great new innovation in electric fencing is *poly wire* made from ten or fifteen strands of brightly-colored plastic filament interwoven with half as many strands of thin stainless-steel wire. It conducts beautifully but is flexible as twine. Strong enough for temporary fence for mild-mannered stock, and more easily seen than bare steel, poly wire isn't wildly overpriced at $50 for about a third of a mile of wire and an equal sum for a reel to store it on.

Poly wire isn't intended as a permanent fence. It is best used for quick one-strand containments and for dividing your pasture into segments for controlled grazing. I use it to sic the horse onto what passes for a front lawn on our country place whenever tourists lost on our mountain begin to frown at the shaggy grass as they pass in their Saab Turbos. Permanent posts with corner insulators wired on are hidden in the bushes at the corners of the yard to support the ends, and plastic T-post battens every 10 feet keep the wire up off the ground while Doc is playing Lawnboy. I run the wire through slotted plastic insulators nailed into tree trunks up to the nearest length of hot-wire pasture fence and tie it on with a bow knot. You can cut poly wire anywhere and reconnect it for full electrical flow with nothing more than a square knot.

Strip grazing with movable electric fence has become a science in the sheep country of New Zealand and Australia. By rotating pasture segments between intensive graze and fallow time, and by eliminating shade and water so livestock have to eat grass to get fluid, the ranchers force weight on their sheep and cattle in minimal time with optimum utilization of the pasture nutrients. The critters don't go cherry picking like Doc – nibbling just the choicest green clover heads and grass tips – but will harvest everything edible, fertilizing as they go, of course. Once the graze is down far enough to encourage new growth, but before animals have pulled the plants out by the roots, an adjacent strip of lush browse is opened, the stock is moved, and the first strip is allowed to grow back.

If your field started out as nothing but a wild meadow like ours, dividing it up with temporary electric fences lets you work it into proper pasture a bit at a time. After a section has been grazed, you can go in with a scythe or lawn mower and cut the unpalatable goldenrod, ferns, and young woody-stemmed plants that haven't been grazed down. Fertilize or lime if needed and seed with a better variety of forage plant in the fall. It may take several mowings before the woody plants have been killed and meadow turned to pasture. But after that, your stock will keep it in condition for you.

TENSION FENCES

The ultimate electric fence provides the holding power of a wire fabric or post-and-plank fence at a half the cost by stringing high-tensile steel wire between braced end posts maintained under opposing tension. End and corner posts are essentially the same as you'd need for heavy, tensioned barb or steel-fabric fence.

The same Down-Under sheepmen who pioneered strip grazing use electrified tensile fence to keep sheep in and dingoes (wild dogs) out. High-tensile fencing has even proven effective in holding elephants. There aren't many elephants in our neighborhood, but a five-wire fence design keeps Eastern coyotes from the sheep and

Braced corners.

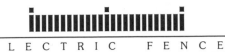
white-tailed deer from the young apple trees, even over our long, cold, and food-short winters.

High-tensile wire costs more than conventional electric fence wire. The high-powered fencers needed to charge many miles of it don't come cheap, either, and putting up the braced posts takes work. But you can fence 100 acres in a few days for 25 cents to $1 a running foot using high-tensile, and a well-made fence using 12½-gauge, Class-3 wire will last over sixty years, according to industry estimates. It is a high-tech alternative to post-and-board fence for horse farms, a replacement for barb or wire fabric for stockmen, and an economical way to avoid losing plantings for most any fruit or vegetable farmer bothered by deer or other unwelcome guests. High-tensile wire is elastic – with a tensile strength of up to 200,000 pounds per square inch and a breaking strength of up to 1,800 pounds. That's four times stronger than conventional galvanized fence wire. Cost is about the same as for equivalent-sized barbed wire: around $45 for an 1,800-foot roll of 12½-gauge. Line posts are needed every 15 to 50 feet between braced ends and, whether wood, steel or fiberglass, they cost about $5 apiece. Battens, needed each 10 to 25 feet, run $1 to $2, and the heavy insulators needed to hold tensioned wire on the end posts cost $1.

Each wire of a high-tensile fence must be tensioned properly at the end posts. A conventional fence stretcher can do the initial stretching, but an in-line line tensioner that will run you about $4 per wire per end is needed to fine-tune tension over time. You may also need to install $5-and-up springs in the wire to withstand heavy stock pressure or snow loads. An $80 spinning jenny is helpful to reel the wire out without break-inducing kinks. And, just as in setting wood posts for conventional fence, you'll need the use of a tractor with an auger attachment unless you are willing to put long hours in with a hand- or small-engine-powered post-hole digger.

A conventional fence charger will power high-tensile fence – but not very much of it. For a long fence, or a fence traversing grassy land that is seldom mowed, you'll need an "Energiser" imported from Down Under. A $350 model will fire up 130 miles of clean, single-strand fence; a $250 model will handle 75 miles of single-strand or 10 miles of five-strand fence in heaviest weeds. The charger, special tensioners, and steel wire are expensive and available only from a limited number of sources – who will offer the expert advice and assistance (including custom fence design) that you should have as you embark on high-tensile fencing.

A tensioner.

A QUALIFIED RECOMMENDATION

High-tensile fence is marvelous stuff. It's cheap for what it can do, quick to go up, as long lasting as any fence, and it needs a minimum of care. But it is high-tech equipment requiring more skills than we come equipped with intuitively. The high-powered fencers take expert installation and weather-proofing. Erecting the required braced corner and end posts in any number requires power equipment that can be dangerous. Tensioning any fence wire with anything but hand tools can be dangerous too. I can't recommend that you undertake any mechanized fencing without experienced guidance. If you're seriously interested in the new, high-tech electric fence, consult the nearest supplier from the list at the back of the book. Your cooperative-extension agent will probably know of locally-adapted designs and may be able to introduce you to a nearby stockman who is trying high-tensile on his own place and has the equipment and skill to help you erect your own.

10

OTHER FENCES:

CLASSIC HORSE FENCE,
VICTORIAN IRON,
CHAIN-LINK,
POST-AND-BRACKET

Some fences defy neat classification by their purpose, such as wooden livestock fences that serve an ornamental function, and metal ornamentals that would hold a regiment of Cossacks at bay. I've grouped some of the most popular and useful here.

CLASSIC HORSE FENCE

Nothing makes a country place look more substantial than a sleek horse or two knee-deep in breakfast on a lush pasture that is surrounded by split-rail or wide-board horse fence. Painted glistening white, the fence conjures up thoughts of Churchill Downs, mint juleps, and Thoroughbreds – even if the horse on your place is a stubby-legged little pony cross like Martha's blue-eyed strawberry roan, Doc.

Building a board horse fence takes no special skill, although to fence a large area practically demands a tractor and auger for digging post holes. You will need larger posts and rails than you use around the house, and to find them you may have to seek out a lumberyard that specializes in horse fence.

There is no fixed rule for size, arrangement, or number of boards in a horse fence, except that lower rails should be hoof-proof. That is, the distance between rails set in the bottom 3 feet of fence, and between the bottom rail and the ground, must be either smaller than the front of a horse's hoof or larger than a hoof, so a pawing or stepping horse can withdraw a foot poked through without hanging up a hock. In our paddock, hoof-proof fence has rails set less than 4 inches or greater than 14 inches apart.

Round Rails

A three- or four-rail white cedar horse fence is popular in our part of the country. Ten-foot peeled cedar rails are arranged on 7- or 10-foot posts set 30 to 48 inches into the ground. The round rails are 9 to 10 inches through, whittled into paddles at each end and inset into holes in the post. The fence costs $30 a section, or $3 per running foot. The same design in a lighter weight – 4- to 5-inch dowel-ended rails and 6- to 8-inch posts – costs $5.50 per rail and $5 for a 7-foot post, or $21.50 per section and $2.15 per running foot.

A properly made 3-rail horse fence.

Post-and-Board

Posts for a typical native wood flat-board fence are 4 × 4 × 8 or 6 × 6 × 8 pine and cost $4 to $5 apiece. Fences carry two to four flat rails made from 2-inch boards of native red oak from small or nobby trees that would otherwise go for firewood. Some of the boards are a bit knotty, but the cost for 2 × 6 × 10 sections is only a dollar and change. The fence costs about $2 a running foot – cheap for wood fence. Below-ground segments of the posts are soaked (not pressure treated) in preservative so the outer inch or so of wood is protected. They will last twenty-five years. If untreated the oak planking is good for about ten years. Labor aside, it's cheaper to replace the boards than soak or pressure treat them.

The 8-foot posts are sunk 3 feet into the ground and rise 5 feet above it. Boards are spaced evenly and butted together then fastened with 16d galvanized nails – on the inside of posts for best holding, on the outside for best appearance. Many horse keepers run a single electric wire along the top to keep the family steed from scratching or leaning on the top rail. The wire will also prevent the horse from top-rail cribbing (gnawing the wood) but won't protect bottom rails. The best anticribbing measure I know is to work your horses hard so they don't get bored stiff. Next best is to use red oak for rails; it has a sour smell and a bitter taste, is hard chewing, and in my experience will stand up to cribbing horses better than pine, cedar, or white oak – which some horses find positively tasty. The top rail of your fence should be higher than your biggest horse's shoulder – so the horse won't be tempted to arch its neck over to nibble grass, possibly working the top board off and picking up splinters in the process.

VICTORIAN IRON FENCES

Nothing sets off a brick town house or an ornate frame Victorian like a black iron fence with scrollwork and fluted post caps – either free standing or gracing spaces between wooden walls or brick columns. But unless you are a blacksmith or a trained welder you'll be hard pressed to make such a fence by hand.

About the only metal fences suitable for easy do-it-yourself installation are larger versions of the tubular sheet-metal (thin steel or aluminum) railings and porch columns that were popular some years ago. Measurements must be precise, and any cutting requires a good arm with a hacksaw or power metal-working tools. Installation of a metal fence requires precise measurements and full concrete footings for posts and it is really a job for a professional. Most building-supply firms will have catalogues showing prefab sections and raw stock, however, if you'd like to check styles.

Iron fence has always been costly and is traditionally restricted to protecting institutions and homes of the affluent. Since chain-link fence became available two or three generations ago, that flexible, easy-to-install, and much less expensive fencing has replaced iron. Today, iron fence is mainly appreciated for its ornamental rather than its practical value. It has a delicate yet firm "iron fist in a velvet glove" look.

A lovely filigreed iron fence.

If you share my affection for nineteenth century iron-work, you'll find that antique iron fence is available – at a price. An old-house recycler I know says that removing iron fence for reuse is so costly that it is done only to preserve genuine antiques or unique examples of ironmongery. Disassembling welded or rusted bolt-together fence sections is difficult, and each post must be dug up and chipped from its concrete anchor. If below-ground sections are badly rusted, replacements must be fabricated. Costs are in the same range as for antique wood- and coal-burning stoves – open-ended, but starting at $1 a pound. And iron fence is heavy stuff!

New Iron

Iron fence is not hard to make if you have the proper metal-working equipment and skills, but it is awfully expensive for an average homeowner's budget. Current estimates for a typical 48-inch-high residential fence range from $25 to $35 *a foot*, depending on size, length, number of gates, and ornamentation.

The simple palings of this iron fence blend well with the brick piers.

A typical 4-foot fence might consist of posts made from 2-inch iron tubing set 3 feet deep in 1-foot-wide concrete anchors and placed a minimum of 6 feet apart. Rails are cut from U-shaped channel iron; set into them are palings or pickets of square steel-bar stock in 1/2-inch or larger size. Sections are cut and welded together in the shop to be assembled on the site.

Most shops will do a limited amount of ornamental work: heating and twisting or scrolling bar stock. But the truly ornate cast-iron ornamentation and hammered-steel filigree is ordered from specialty manufacturers or importers of Taiwanese and other iron. The ornaments are welded on or attached with set-bolts.

Iron fence these days is made to order only, and only by a handful of metal fabricators. You must go to a supplier that specializes in selling recycled building materials, a building-restoration specialist, a firm serving municipal and residential construction, or a local welding shop and iron works. Look in the Yellow Pages under Blacksmiths or Iron.

CHAIN-LINK FENCE

Chain-link fence has assumed the institutional role that iron fence filled sixty years ago. Prisons, military installations, and industrial plants are ringed with the stuff, and it has an unfriendly look. But – especially with several strands of barbed wire on arms jutting out along the top – chain-link is an effective guarantor of privacy.

In these parlous times many townsfolk see fit to ring their properties with chain-link. It is an unbeatable protective barrier around a swimming pool; indeed, a pool fence may be legally required by your local ordinances before you add the first drop of water. Nothing else makes as sturdy a kennel or pet run, and chain-link is tough enough to hold any escape-prone animal. When posts are embedded in a concrete pad, this fence makes a permanent, corrosion- and contamination-free cage that can be hosed down for easy cleaning.

Structure

In the best grades of chain-link fence, a rigid framework is built of cement-anchored tubular-steel posts bolted to rigid-steel horizontal top rails. A cheaper version has square stamped sheet-steel posts linked by heavy-gauge wire that is looped around each post top.

Chain-link fabric comes in 50-foot rolls and in heights from 3 to 12 feet and up. It is made of 13- to 9-gauge aluminum-alloy wire or of green vinyl-coated or galvanized-steel wire. Each vertical length of wire is bent in zigzags to make 2- or 2⅛-inch diamond mesh (1¾-inch mesh for tennis courts, so balls won't lodge in the netting).

Adjoining vertical lengths of fence wire are intertwined at each zig and zag, and parallel wire pairs are twisted together at top and bottom. Untensioned, chain-link fabric is quite loose and will roll up for easy transport and unroll for quick attachment. The fabric is stretched between vertical *tension bars* that are woven into the cut ends and fastened to *terminal posts* at corners and gate posts with steel *tension bands* and to line posts and top rails by clips or *tie wires*.

Chain-link costs from $3 to $7 a running foot depending on height (top post and tensioners included), and end and corner posts cost from $10 to $25 apiece. Good gates run about $50 and a double driveway gate three times that. Figure on spending from $5 to $10 a running foot for high-quality fence between 3 and 6 feet in height.

Each post must be sunk a minimum of 2 feet deep in a concrete anchor. The weight of the most popular fabric for home use — 48-inch, 11½ gauge — is a little over 1½ pounds per foot. Fencing with chain-link isn't cheap, and it is heavy work best left to a crew with a tractor and earth auger. A $50-per-hour crew can fence your backyard in an afternoon.

Putting it Up Yourself

Don't plan on using chain-link on steep grades or sharply rolling terrain. The fabric will stretch to fit gentle

---

TOOLS FOR CHAIN-LINK FENCE

Layout tools
Post-hole digger
Concrete-mixing gear
Heavy-duty cable cutters
Fence stretcher and bar clamp
Socket wrench (ratchet-type)
Stout pliers

Gate hinge.

undulations in the ground, but it will go straight across a sharp dip and have to be dug into a sharp knoll. Besides, it looks out of place on a grade; chain-link is for flat ground.

Your first step if you're considering a chain-link fence is to visit a fencing or swimming-pool contractor or building-supply outlet for ordering information. You can buy rolled stock in 21-foot lengths and fittings in bulk if you have a large area to fence, but you will need heavy-duty steel cutting equipment to work it. Best for the amateur is to order materials precut to measure. You can usually rent the installation tools where you buy your fencing materials.

The manufacturer's sheets will give you price and quality differences between grades of fencing, sizes of posts, and (most important) size of gate openings. Typical gates are 3 feet, 3 inches wide or 4 feet plus 3¾–4 inches for hinge and latch.

A Plan

Draw a to-scale flat plan and a frontal elevation of the fence indicating locations of terminal posts (corners and gate posts), line posts, and gates. Put a line post at any change in elevation and at 7- to 10-foot intervals on the flat, spacing to depend on fence weight and quality. Around a pool you may want to space posts closer together for appearance's sake. Deliver the plan to your fence supplier, who will cut fabric, posts, and top rails to fit. Be sure to specify how deep you need to go so posts will be the correct length.

Put in conventional stakes and guide lines, dig 12-inch-wide post holes, and set terminal posts in concrete. End posts should be set 3 feet deep at least and tall enough to allow for fabric height plus distance the fabric bottom will run above ground – plus 1 inch. Mark ground level – the grade line – measuring from the top down on each post to be sure it is set at the correct depth. If the fence rises more than 5 feet, you must install angle braces or double-brace posts between each terminal and the adjoining line post. Run angle braces from below the top tension band at a 45-degree angle into a cement plug sunk as deep as the terminal posts themselves. Embed the lower 2 feet of the angle brace in concrete.

Chain-link is not simply run around the outside of terminal posts but is tensioned between round tension bands on each post. When tightened, it extends between center lines of terminal posts. Braces and line posts must be set just inside that fabric line. Stretch one mason's line along the outside of terminal posts, about 6 inches from the top, to get the layout for line posts. For easiest alignment, you may string another line near the bottom, though it will have to come off for hole digging. Hold a line post next to a terminal post and judge how far from the guide lines the line post must be located to be aligned with the center line along which fabric will run. Usually, the distance is only about ¼-inch.

Distribute line posts so they are evenly spaced at 7- to 10-foot intervals between terminals, dig post holes, and set posts in concrete. Use your spirit level to check plumb. Crown the tops of the concrete in a low aboveground cone to repel water from the metal. Let the concrete set up for at least 24 hours; two days is better.

Next step is to bolt on the horizontal brace rails. The butt of each rail slides (sometimes with difficulty; have a file handy) into a cast-metal *rail end*. The ends are bolted to vertical posts with *brace bands*. Ends of terminal posts are topped with a *post cap*. Line posts are topped with an *eye top*, a cap that has a rail-thickness eye cast in. The brace rail just slides through the *eye*.

Before erecting the frame, be sure to slide all fittings on posts and rails:

1. **On each terminal post slide on a tension band for each 10- to 12 inches of fabric width (use three for a yard-high fence, four for a 48-incher). On top of the tension bands slide the brace band, which will hold the rail end, which will hold the brace rail.**

2. **On each brace rail slide on the eye tops, which will slip over the ends of the line posts.**

Now fit rails' eye tops to the line posts, slide on rail ends, and bolt the rail to the brace bands already slipped over the terminal posts. Leave the round bolt end of all bolt-tightened fittings on the outside of the fence; nuts must be on the inside, where they can't be removed. Don't try tightening the bolts with pliers; an adjustable or box wrench will do the job slowly; a ratchet-type mechanic's wrench with the correct size socket for the nut is invaluable.

Loop cap on line post. Fabric fixed to top rail with wire ties.

Adding Fabric

Lightweight fabric can be bent around end posts, but for the best job, cut and tension separate lengths of fabric for each fence line. Fasten one end of a length to a terminal post with tension bands.

One margin of the fabric has exposed twists where wire pairs are attached, so is barbed. The other margin is knuckled over, so is smooth. Put the scratchy side up to deter fence-climbers, or put it down to deter crawl-unders. If the smooth side is up, you can lean on it to chat with neighbors. Arrange the fabric so that it is about ½-inch below the top of the terminal posts.

Thread a steel tension bar through the end of your fabric and fasten it to the post using the tension bands, already in place. Unroll the fabric to the next terminal post, affixing it every few feet with wire ties to keep it from flopping over. Pull as tight as you can by hand. *Do not cut* the fabric till it is stretched and ready to be bolted in place.

Now fasten your fence stretcher as near as you can get it to the far post and still have stretching room. Affix the fence clamp and pull the fabric tighter than it needs to be, but not so tight that it attenuates or seems to lose width, and not so tight that the post bends. To remove wire overlapping the post, use stout pliers to unwrap the twist connections at each end, and twist the wire out of its mate much as you remove a corkscrew. Run the tension bar through the new end, attach the tension bands, and release the stretcher. The fence should be tight. If it's not, and the wire is loose enough that it rattles against the line posts when you try to make waves in it, retighten and remove the next wire or two to make the fabric shorter, and reaffix.

Finally, tighten all the bolts and affix ties to fasten fabric to rails and line posts every 12–15 inches.

Gates

Gate hinges and latches bolt on the same way the little gate went on the metal fence discussed earlier. If you have a two-gate driveway, you'll need a *ground stake*, a vertical steel rod that bolts to the free, unhinged side of one or both gates. On a paved drive you can drill a pocket for the stake to slip into. On a dirt or gravel drive, it is good to pour your own paving stone with a stake pocket molded in (general directions in the mortar-work chapter). For the stake pocket, mold in any open-ended tube. Be sure that any stake pocket reaches from the surface to soil under the paving so water will drain away rather than pool in the cup, leaching or freeze-cracking the cement or rusting the ground stake.

Finishing Touches

If you have to splice chain-link fabric, put two ends next to each other. Remove one vertical length of fence wire – by untwisting top and bottom and revolving the wire to unscrew it from the fabric. Weave the two ends together by lacing this sawtooth-bent wire through them, turning the wire corkscrew fashion.

If you want to add privacy or a less sterile look to a chain-link fence, weave strips of bright plastic or natural fiber diagonally through the fabric. You'll find suitable decorative materials at most swimming-pool contractors' shops.

To add more deterrent to a chain-link fence, you can purchase steel arms that fit over post tops to hold three strands of barbed wire. Terminal-post arms cost about $10, and those for line posts run some $3 apiece. They angle away from the fence at 45 degrees and, when strung with well-stretched barbed wire, will keep most anything out (or in).

An even quicker way of attaching rails to posts, pointed out to me by my publisher, Jack Williamson, is a sheet-metal bracket newly patented as the Shire Horse Fence Clip (see address in appendix). The clip slips over heavy-duty T-type forged-steel fence posts and will hold the ends of two 1 × 4 or 2 × 6 rough-wood fence rails. Fence posts can be faced with a vertical length of rail to give the appearance of a post-and-board fence, but the posts are indestructible steel and go in quickly with a post driver. The clip offers a quick way to put up an attractive board fence in a fraction of the time needed to dig wood posts. A length of electric wire along the top board discourages horses from leaning onto the fence.

POST-AND-BRACKET FENCE

Every so often an enterprising inventor comes up with a simplified way of affixing fence rails to posts with special brackets of one kind or another that lets you avoid the work and expense of nailing or cutting joints to put rails on posts. The sheet-metal joist hangers that are increasingly used to attach wood framing and flooring members in mass-produced housing will get a wood fence together in short order. I use a battery-powered, low-speed, high-torque screwdriver to fasten hangers to wood posts and rails using dry-wall screws. Those screws will rust and so are good only for farm fence unless the screws are counter-sunk and the holes plugged.

RETAINING WALLS

I had a little to say about retaining walls in chapter 3 on building with stone. Much of that goes as well for retaining walls made of other materials. Whatever its fabric, a retaining wall is a fence with a solid bank of soil on one side of it. Retaining walls put a vertical face on a hill, telescoping rise into a minimum of lateral distance. They break precipitous land into relatively level terraces, permitting mountain farmers to cultivate fields and letting you and me turn sharply sloping yards into flat and cuttable lawns.

A low retaining wall need be nothing but a conventional stone or mortared-brick wall with a good footing. But when a retaining wall rises much over 3 feet, it needs special construction methods. A cubic yard of water-soaked soil and rock can weigh a half-ton, and the wall must have a combination of footing, weight, and purchase to hold the load.

Wood

Creosoted railroad ties or 4, 6- or 8-foot PT landscape timbers can be simply laid atop one another in walls 4 to 5 feet high, and soil can be piled behind them. Set the ties one-over-two, two-over-one, just as you lay brick or stone. Between each joint lay a timber on end as a back-tie that will reach from the wall into the soil bank. Tamp soil well after each layer of timbers is laid, so the back-ties will hold fast.

For a higher wall you can set each successive layer of timbers back a few inches to make a slightly stair-stepped, sloping wall. Use back-ties here, as well, and toenail timbers together every foot or so with galvanized 6-inch spikes.

A normal amount of water will drain through timber walls, but if ground-water flow or periodic rainfall is considerable, put a foot-thick gravel or crushed-rock layer between wall and soil fill. Leave 2- or 3-inch spaces between ends of timbers, and fill them with gravel.

Stone, Brick, and Block

A contractor can get you big concrete castings molded in a low H shape which build together in a wall like kids' Lincoln Logs. They are too big to handle without a crane, but they hold entire mountain sides in some locales and should be considered if you have a lot of soil to retain.

On a smaller scale, you can build a retaining wall up to 6 or 10 feet high of brick, block, or stone. Follow the fence-building directions given in earlier chapters, but build according to the specifications in the accompanying illustration.

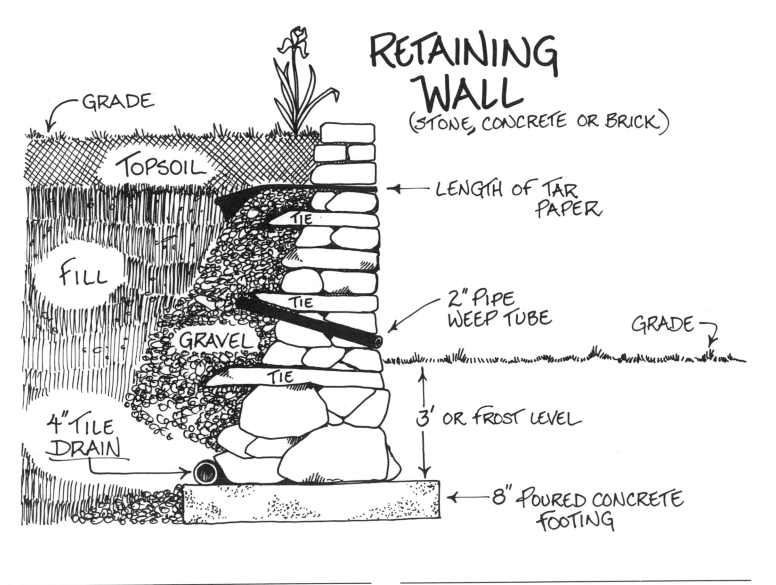

RETAINING WALL
(STONE, CONCRETE OR BRICK)

GRADE

TOPSOIL

FILL

GRAVEL

4" TILE DRAIN

LENGTH OF TAR PAPER

TIE

TIE

TIE

2" PIPE WEEP TUBE

GRADE

3' OR FROST LEVEL

8" POURED CONCRETE FOOTING

BASE

The wall base should be below frost and on an 8-inch poured-concrete footing if at all possible. Build the footing according to specifications given in chapter 4 on masonry fences, and calculate size by the height-to-width formula that is illustrated in chapter 3.

DRAINAGE

Place a run of 4-inch drain tile all along the back of the footing to drain off water and relieve pressure on the base of the retaining wall. Behind the wall lay a 1- to 2-foot band of gravel or crushed rock, and every 10 feet along the face of wall at ground level install an up-sloping weep tube of 2-inch plastic pipe running into the gravel bank. The tube will relieve water pressure from the higher portions of wall.

TIES

As you build the wall, it is good practice to install ties into the bank. Building with rock, aim long stones back into the compacted soil. With block or brick, mortar in 6-foot lengths of concrete reinforcement rod with one end hammered into a sharp hook to snag a hole in perforated brick or a cell wall in block, or to provide a good purchase inside a mortar bond.

A retaining wall can rise above grade at the top or not as you wish. Don't carry the gravel layer to soil level, but put in a good 6 inches of loam for grass or flowers. Keep soil from leaching down into the gravel by laying tarpaper along the top of the gravel and into the wall just before you add the top layer of soil.

To build soil pockets in a retaining wall, leave gaps in rock or brick structure and fill them with soil. For greatest stability, at each side of each pocket lay in a tie stone or retaining rod.

"MENDING WALL"
From the poetry of Robert Frost.

Something there is that doesn't love a wall,
That sends the frozen-ground-swell under it,
And spills the upper boulders in the sun;
And makes gaps even two can pass abreast.
The work of hunters is another thing:
I have come after them and made repair
Where they have left not one stone on a stone,
But they would have the rabbit out of hiding,
To please the yelping dogs. The gaps I mean,
No one has seen them made or heard them made,
But at spring mending-time we find them there.
I let my neighbor know beyond the hill;
And on a day we meet to walk the line
And set the wall between us once again.
We keep the wall between us as we go.
To each the boulders that have fallen to each.
And some are loaves and so nearly balls
We have to use a spell to make them balance:
"Stay where you are until our backs are turned!"
We wear our fingers rough with handling them.
Oh, just another kind of outdoor game,
One on a side. It comes to little more:
There where it is we do not need the wall:
He is all pine and I am apple orchard.
My apple trees will never get across
And eat the cones under his pines, I tell him
He only says, "Good fences make good neighbors,"
Spring is the mischief in me, and I wonder
If I could put a notion in his head:
"Why do they make good neighbors? Isn't it
Where there are cows? But here there are no cows.
Before I built a wall I'd ask to know
What I was walling in or walling out,
And to whom I was like to give offense.
Something there is that doesn't love a wall,
That wants it down." I could say "Elves" to him,
But it's not elves exactly, and I'd rather
He said if for himself. I see him there
Bringing a stone grasped firmly by the top
In each hand, like an old-stone savage armed.
He moves in darkness as it seems to me,
Not of woods only and the shade of trees
He will not go behind his father's saying,
And he likes having thought of it so well
He says again, "Good fences make good neighbors."

ENDWORD

I mustn't close without acknowledging Robert Frost's justly famous poem "Mending Wall." Every other modern fence book I've seen quotes it, and the fencing industry has made a slogan of Frost's refrain, "Good fences make good neighbors." Of course Frost didn't necessarily agree with that sentiment. The poem isn't about walls or fences at all, but about the barriers to communication that we erect between ourselves.

The poet's view is better reflected in his first line: "Something there is that doesn't love a wall." I hope you don't make your fence unlikable. Build it well and solidly, but make it as low and as open as possible. Design the neighbors' side to be at least as attractive as your own. Keep the fence in fresh paint, good repair, and fine humor – much as one of my favorite people does. She is a bit retiring and has an 8-foot iron fence and a solid hedge around her house. But she is well liked even by people she's never met, because of her practice of hanging a wicker basket of fresh-cut flowers on her gate post on pretty spring mornings. A little sign on the basket reads: *Have One, Please.* Frequently my well-fenced friend finds more flowers in the basket at day's end than she put out to begin with.

As in that case, a fence can be less a barricade than a friendly border that draws people together. At its best, it will summon people to lean and talk at leisure, making a *good jawin' fence*, as the old-timers say in my part of the country. A fence can be a comfortable place for people to exchange views with a directness that is hard to achieve without that thin but supportive screen that separates yours from mine but doesn't separate you from me.

When you think of, and build, your fence in that spirit, those two lines of Robert Frost's needn't be as contradictory as they appear.

APPENDIX

Selected Books and Booklets

GENERAL

A Book of Country Things
by Walter Needham and Barrows Mussey

The Stephen Greene Press
Lexington, MA
(Distributed by Viking Penguin, Inc.,
40 W. 23rd St., New York, NY 10010)
A treasury of preindustrial country ways, farm fencing lore included.

The Complete Book of Fences
by Dan Ramsey

TAB BOOKS, Inc.
Blue Ridge Summit, PA 17214
A 240-page soft-cover book that covers choice and installation of all types of fencing. Much fence-industry data. By mail from TAB.

Fences Gates & Bridges
by George A. Martin

The Stephen Greene Press
Lexington, MA
Reprint of a marvelous 1887 book that comprises a complete manual of country fencing wisdom from an earlier age. Assumes a familiarity with basic woodworking skills but worth checking out from the library.

LIVING FENCE

Plants & Gardens

Brooklyn Botanic Garden
1000 Washington Avenue
Brooklyn, NY 11225
Many among the Botanic Garden's fifty or so $2.25 booklets on trees, shrubs, vines, and all aspects of plant culture and propagation offer invaluable help in planting and nurturing a living fence. Send for the free ordering and membership brochure.

MASONRY FENCE

Concrete, Masonry and Brickwork

(Technical Manual No. 5-742
by the U.S. Department of the Army)
Reprinted by Dover Publications,
180 Varick Street, New York, NY 11501;
in Canada by General Publishing Company, Ltd.,
30 Lesmill Road, Don Mills, Toronto ONT.
A well-illustrated, large-format paperback. Easier reading than the technical trowel-trade and construction manuals, but with reliable detail lacking in the chatty garden-path-and-gazebo-type home-masonry books. Send for Dover's free mail-order book catalogue.

STONE FENCE

Building Stone Walls
by John Vivian

Storey Communications
Pownal, VT 05261
Nicely illustrated, and the writing may seem familiar. At bookstores.

The Forgotten Art of Building a Stone Wall
by Curtis Fields

Yankee, Inc.
Dublin, NH 03444
A charming little book by a fellow who rebuilt the stone walls on his farm to be better than they were when new. Unique insights into hand quarrying rock.

WOOD FENCE

How to Build a Fence

Wolmanized Residential Lumber
Koppers Company, Inc.
436 Seventh Avenue
Pittsburgh, PA 15219
As comprehensive a booklet on wood-fence construction as you can get into 20 pages. By the makers of the most popular brand of pressure-treated lumber. For $1 by mail.

How to Design & Build Fences & Gates

Ortho Books
Chevron Chemical Company
742 Bancroft Way
Berkeley, CA 95701
Full-color magazine-format book on planning and building wood fences, with lively writing and fine photographs and color illustrations of both fence designs and installation procedures. In racks in book and garden-supply stores.

How to Plan & Build Fences & Gates

Lane Publishing Co.
Menlo Park, CA 94025
Sunset Books' workmanlike contribution to residential wood-fence design and installation. Marvelous color photos of conventional and unique fences. Found on racks in book and building-supply stores.

SPECIALTY ITEMS

FOX VALLEY DRAFT HORSE FARMS

10014 South Grant Highway
Marengo, IL 60152
Makes the Shire Horse Fence Clip that attaches wood fence boards to steel posts without fasteners.

MAIL-ORDER CATALOGUES OFFERING FENCING SUPPLIES

The following mail-order firms offer free catalogues containing good fencing supplies.

CENTRAL TRACTOR FARM & FAMILY CENTER

1515 East Euclid
Box 3330
Des Moines, IA 50316

C. H. DANA COMPANY, INC.

Hyde Park, VT 05655

FARNAM FARM EQUIPMENT CATALOG

P.O. Box 12068
Omaha, NE 68112

MODERN FARM

1825 Big Horn Avenue
Cody, WY 82414

NASCO (Farm & Ranch Catalog)

901 Janesville Ave.
Fort Atkinson, WI 53538
and:
1534 Princeton Ave.
Modesto, CA 98352

SPRINGTIGHT POWER FENCE

Brookside Industries, Inc.
Tunbridge, VT 05007

TECHFENCE

P.O. Box A
Marlboro, NJ 24951

WEST VIRGINIA FENCE CORP.

U.S. Rt. 219
Lindside, WV 24951

Sears, Roebuck and Co. carries all types of metal fence and supplies. If there's no Sears outlet near you, send for the *Farm and Ranch "Specialog"* from Sears, Roebuck and Co., 9245 Homan Avenue, Chicago, IL 60607. In the United States use their free phone: 800-323-3274. Sears also rents fencing tools and supplies a free booklet on building metal fence.

INDEX

More Good Books from

W WILLIAMSON PUBLISHING

RAISING RABBITS SUCCESSFULLY
by Bob Bennett

"Here is one of the better books on raising rabbits."—**Booklist**

Written by one of the foremost rabbit authorities, this book is ideal for the beginning rabbit raiser, raising for food, fun, shows and profit.

192 pages, 6×9, illustrations and photos.
Quality paperback, $9.95.

RAISING POULTRY SUCCESSFULLY
by Will Graves

"An easy-to-understand beginner's guide to raising chickens, ducks, and geese. A good choice . . ."—**Library Journal**

Complete how-to for raising meat only, eggs only or a dual purpose flock. Warmly and expertly written.

196 pages, 6×9, illustrations, photos, tables.
Quality paperback, $9.95.

RAISING PIGS SUCCESSFULLY
by Kathy and Bob Kellogg

Everything you need to know for the perfect low-cost, low work pig raising operation. Choosing piglets, to housing, feeds, care, breeking, slaughtering, packaging, and even cooking your home grown pork.

224 pages, 6×9, illustrations, photos, tables.
Quality paperback, $9.95.

RAISING MILK GOATS SUCCESSFULLY
by Gail Luttmann

Complete coverage of everything involved in raising milk goats from selecting, feeds, housing, care, breeding, diagnosis by symptom, dairy goat business. Excellent.

192 pages, 6×9, photos.
Quality paperback, $9.95.

THE COMPLETE AND EASY GUIDE
TO SOCIAL SECURITY & MEDICARE
by Faustin F. Jehle

A lifesaver of a book for every senior citizen you know. Do someone a special favor, and give this book as a gift – written in "plain English" here's all that red tape unravelled.

"A goldmine of information about the most complicated system."
—Milicent Fenwick

175 pages, 8½×11½.
Quality paperback, $10.95.

HOME TANNING & LEATHERCRAFT SIMPLIFIED
by Kathy Kellog

"An exceptionally thorough and readable do-it-yourself book."
—Library Journal

192 pages, 6×9, step-by-step illustrations, photos, tanning recipes.
Quality paperback, $9.95.

SIMPLY ELEGANT COUNTRY FOODS: Downhome Goes Uptown
by Carol Lowe-Clay

An outrageously good cook brings country cooking to its pinnacle. A cookbook that's not fussy, not trendy – simply elegant. Everything from country fresh Pizza Rustica to Crumbed Chicken In Wine Sauce, Country Pork Supper, Sweet Cream Scones with Honey Butter to Whipped Cream Cake with Almond Custard Filling. Over 100 recipes capturing the freshness of the moment!

160 pages, 8×10, beautifully illustrated.
Quality paperback, $9.95.

DINING ON DECK: Fine Foods for Sailing & Boating
by Linda Vail

For Linda Vail a perfect day's sail includes fine food – quickly and easily prepared. She offers here 225 outstanding recipes (casual yet elegant food) with over 90 menus for everything from elegant weekends to hearty breakfasts and suppers for cool weather sailing. Her recipes are so good and so varied you'll use her cookbook year-round for sure!

160 pages, 8×10, illustrated.
Quality paperback, $10.95.

THE KIDS' NATURE BOOK
365 Indoor/Outdoor Activities and Experiences
by Susan Milford

Winner of the Parents' Choice Gold Award for learning and doing books, *The Kids' Nature Book* is loved by children, grandparents, and friends alike. Simple projects and activities emphasize fun while quietly reinforcing the wonder of the world we all share. Packed with facts and fun!

160 pages, 11×8½, 425 illustrations
Quality paperback, $12.95.

KIDS COOK!
Fabulous Food For The Whole Family
by Sarah Williamson and Zachary Williamson

Kids Cook! is filled with over 150 recipes for great tasting foods that kids ages 8 and up can cook for themselves and for their families and friends, too. Recipes from sections like "It's the Berries!" "Pasta Perfect," "Home Alone," "Side Orders," "Babysitters Bonanza," and "Best Bets for Brunch" include real foods that are fun to eat. Plus Nutri Notes, Safety First, and plenty of special menus for Father's Day, Grandma's Teatime, picnics, and parties. One terrific book!

160 pages, 11 × 8½, Over 150 recipes, illustrations
Quality paperback, $12.95.

KIDS LEARN AMERICA!
Bringing Geography to Life With People, Places, and History
by Patricia Gordon and Reed C. Snow

Over 44 million Americans can't find the Pacific Ocean on a map. Let Gordon and Snow challenge your kids to know where they are and where they're going with this all-new approach encompassing the human-earth connection. This book breathes life into geography with experiential, hands-on learning. Kids of all ages will enjoy the 52 state challenges, games, memory techniques, trivia, and most of all, knowing where they fit into this great expansive country.

176 pages, 11 × 8½, over 500 maps and illustrations.
Quality paperback, $12.95

TO ORDER:
At your bookstore or order directly from Williamson Publishing. We accept Visa or MasterCard (please include number, expiration date and signature), or send check to:

**Williamson Publishing Co.,
Church Hill Road, P.O. Box 185,
Charlotte, Vermont 05445.**

(Toll-free phone orders: 800-234-8791.) Please add $2.50 for postage and handling. Satisfaction guaranteed or full refund without questions or quibbles.